CLASSIC CYCLE
ROUTES OF EUROPE

CLASSIC CYCLE
ROUTES OF EUROPE
THE 25 GREATEST ROAD RACES AND HOW TO RIDE THEM

WERNER MÜLLER-SCHELL

B L O O M S B U R Y

LONDON · BERLIN · NEW YORK · SYDNEY

Dedication:
For Werner Sr.

Note
While every effort has been made to ensure that the content of this book is as technically accurate and as sound as possible, neither the author nor the publishers can accept responsibility for any injury or loss sustained as a result of the use of this material.

Published in 2012 by A&C Black an imprint of Bloomsbury Publishing Plc
50 Bedford Square
London WC1B 3DP
www.bloomsbury.com

First published in Germany in 2011 by Bruckmann Verlag GmbH, Munich under the title
Radklassiker in Europa.

Copyright © 2011 Bruckmann Verlag GmbH, Munich, Germany.
This translation copyright © A&C Black 2012

ISBN 978 1 4081 5752 7

Acknowledgements
Front cover photographs and author photograph © Hennes Roth; back cover photograph © Ernst Lorenzi/Ötztal-Tourismus/www.oetzal.com
Inside photographs © All photographs come from photographer Hennes Roth, apart from Sport Communications: pp. vi, 7, 117; Martin Appel: pp. viii, 160; gmsport.it: pp. 3, 86 left, 89, 90, 91; maratona.it: pp. 13, 98, 99, 100, 101; Wernermüller-Schell: pp. 22, 94; novecolli.it: p. 96; Alexander Zelger: p. 102; Martina Nachlinger: pp. 104, 106, 107; Ernst Lorenzi/Ötztal–Tourismus/www.oetztal.com: pp. 142, 144, 145; André Walter: p. 146; EKZ Zürimetzgete: pp. 148, 151 below; Micke Fransson/Vätternrundan: p. 177.
Designed by James Watson
Translated into English by Rosemary Dear

This book is produced using paper that is made from wood grown in managed, sustainable forests. It is natural, renewable and recyclable. The logging and manufacturing processes conform to the environmental regulations of the country of origin.

Typeset in 9.5pt on 11.5pt Eurostile and Myriad by Saxon Graphics Ltd, Derby

Printed and bound in China by C&C Offset Printing Co.

CONTENTS

Contents

Contents

PREFACE

Once you've been bitten by the cycling bug it's very difficult to get rid of it. There's no remedy – and I hope there never will be one! A sport in which you get to know and appreciate the countryside and also meet all kinds of interesting people is too good to be true. There's a feeling of freedom that accompanies every tour. You set off and let yourself be carried along – by the roads, the wind, the sun and, of course, by the power of your own legs. Then it's up to you whether you just want to crank it out on the flat or climb steep slopes.

It's this very variety that actually makes cycling such a wonderful sport. There's also a variety of reasons for cycling: some do it as an antidote to stress after work, others like to do weekend rides, while others again take on the challenge of cycle sportives and share their passion with kindred spirits, and others still try to satisfy their sporting ambition in competition – either in cycling marathons or in hard amateur races.

As a member of this last group I have gained a completely new perspective from working on this book: that of sportive riders, who follow the routes of the classic races. Where previously my rides were mostly approached from the point of view of training plans, now the route was suddenly at the forefront of my mind: I had to be able to understand the routes of the big classics right down to the very last detail and to experience their history through the experiences of others.

And the experiences I have collected here are incredible. As if the sweat forced from the pores were not enough, there's also the real feeling of goosebumps when you find yourself at the crucial 'hotspots' of a particular race: climbing up to La Redoute on the Liège–Bastogne–Liège and imagining the freezing Bernard Hinault and his victory in 1980; conquering the Paterberg just like the heroes of the Tour of Flanders and remembering pictures of enthusiastic spectators on television; conquering the passes in the Dolomites on the trail of the Giro d'Italia …

Of course there are sobering moments during the research into these classic races. One such moment was a Fleming in his home town who led over kilometre after kilometre of cobblestones and was then left trailing by about a minute over a 5km stretch. And though the *kasseien* –the Flemish word for cobbles – are not exactly pleasant to cycle on, you can still get to like them since, in spite of this, there's also something romantic about them. These memories are a permanent feature of cycle sports. You know what I mean: once you've been bitten by the bug you just can't get rid of it – not even on cobblestones.

With this in mind I wish you all the fun in the world following the classic cycle routes of Europe!

Werner Müller-Schell

Left: L'Eroica is a very special event because of its vintage atmosphere.

Classic cycle routes of Europe

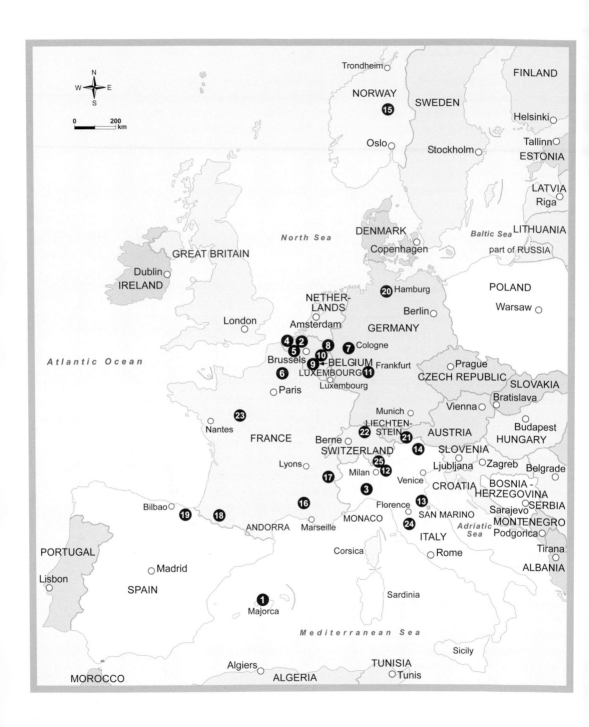

TOUR OVERVIEW
25 European cycle classics at a glance

Spring sorties

1 Trofeo Deià: On the trail of the Majorcan coastal classic (143km/1800m)
2 Omloop Het Nieuwsblad: The little sister of the Ronde (204km/1050m)
3 Milan–San Remo : The 'ride into spring' (295km/1780m)
4 Ghent–Wevelgem: A semi-classic for wind and sprint specialists (219km/1400m)
5 Tour of Flanders: Following in the footsteps of the professionals through the Flemish Ardennes (262km/1660m)
6 Paris–Roubaix: On the cobblestones through the 'Hell of the North' (258km/850m)
7 Rund um Köln: The cycling festival on the Rhine (201km/1900m)
8 Amstel Gold Race: On the zigzag course through Limburg (257km/3200m)
9 La Flèche Wallonne: The 'Walloon Arrow' (198km/3200m)
10 Liège–Bastogne–Liège: The 'Old Lady' of the classics (258km/3600m)
11 Eschborn–Frankfurt City Loop: Through Eschborn, Frankfurt and the Taunus (202km/1700m)

Summer specials

12 Gran Fondo Felice Gimondi: In the footsteps of the 'Phoenix' round Bergamo (165km/2950m)
13 Nove Colli: The classic in Emilia-Romagna (205km/3840m)

14 Maratona dles Dolomites: On the road in the heart of the Dolomites (138km/4190m)
15 Trondheim–Oslo: 'Den Store Styrkepøven' – the big trial of strength (540km/3400m)
16 La Ventoux: Rendezvous on the 'Giant of Provence' (170km/3500m)
17 La Marmotte: The Alpine classic of the Tour de France (174km/5180m)
18 Pau–Tourmalet: A unique Pyrenean stage of the Tour (181km/4400m)

Autumn adventures

19 Clásica San Sebastián: The race for the 'Txapela'(234km/2480m)
20 Vattenfall Cyclassics: On the trail of the professionals: an experience for everyone (157km/680m)
21 Ötztaler Radmarathon: The classic in the Tyrol (238km/5500m)
22 Züri Metzgete. From a professional classic to a classic for everyone (49km/500m)
23 Paris–Tours: The 'Autumn Grand Prix' (233km/450m)
24 L'Eroica: Cult tourism for connoisseurs and enthusiasts (209km/3350m)
25 Tour of Lombardy: The race of the falling leaves (260km/3200m)

Note
Since not even the Monuments of cycling are written in stone and the routes have often been changed slightly for various reasons, the following tour descriptions use the 2010 routes.

THE RIGHT PREPARATION

THE RIGHT PREPARATION

Things you must be sure to do

Classic cycle races aren't just the best-known, most steeped in history and most beautiful cycle routes, they're usually also the most difficult. With distances often well over 200km, hours at a time of climbing over alpine passes, short stretches of uphill slopes with a gradient of over 20 per cent in places, apparently endless plateaus with strong headwinds or crosswinds blowing over them, steep descents over narrow roads with many hairpin bends and, last but not least, bumpy stretches of cobblestones, every one of these tours pushes you to the limits of your ability. So you need to be well prepared to be able to handle the conditions confidently and overcome all the obstacles.

Fit through the winter

Of course, this starts with personal fitness. Most of the routes in this book are very long, so you'll have to start working on appropriate endurance training during the winter – that way when you're riding you won't experience any nasty sudden surprises in the form of an agonising slump in performance which leaves you sitting at the side of the road, exhausted. It's also a good idea to work on your fitness during the cold months – as far as family, friends and work will allow.

Cycling's never a problem when it's warm enough outside. But when there's snow on the ground or the weather leaves something to be desired, you have to switch to other kinds of sport instead. But you should see this as positive, a welcome change from everyday training, which can otherwise often seem monotonous: cross-country skiing, running, swimming, spinning, mountain climbing or ski touring are just as enjoyable, and will maintain last year's fitness and provide a good level of basic endurance for the next season.

You could also consider a training camp in the spring. A week or two spent just concentrating on cycling and living like a professional can work wonders and bring about a real boost to your form. With classic cycle races in mind this should improve your endurance in particular. Long sessions of 2–7 hours at an easy tempo will ensure that your body becomes thoroughly accustomed to the enormous distances.

The right training

It's a good idea to invest in the guidance of a coach for this. They will determine your personal strengths and weaknesses using a series of tests and then design an appropriate personal training plan. Even though it'll cost you money, you'll often get more from a personal training plan than from state-of-the-art equipment. Even sports enthusiasts who have little time to spare for their hobby can make the time they do spend training highly efficient this way.

You should also tailor your rides to your personal targets. A cyclist who wants to achieve the best possible result in the Ötztaler Radmarathon should train quite differently from someone who just wants to get round the course – in exactly the same way that preparations for a long but flat course such as the Paris–Tours differ from those for a short mountain time trial. A coach can help here too. But above all, for the tours in this book, the best thing possible is to stick it out in the saddle for a long time – endurance is needed too! You should also work on your strength for mountain routes.

Correct nutrition is also part of training. The evening before a long ride you should stock up on the right food: noodles, potatoes, rice or a lean piece of white meat should be on your plate so that you have enough reserves for the next day. And you shouldn't hold back at breakfast either; however, for preference you should choose light food such as muesli, bananas or bread and jam – but not so much that you can hardly sit on the bike for the first few km because you're so full and your body's concentrating all its efforts on your stomach, which is busy digesting …

A dense throng at the beginning of the Gran Fondo Felice Gimondi.

Cycling technique – often underestimated

Once you've chosen your own personal goal for the season – or even several of them – it's not just a question of developing the appropriate fitness, you also have to refine your cycling technique. Under no circumstances should you leave that out of your training. When you're standing at the start of the Paris–Roubaix race, the best endurance in the world won't help you if you've never cycled over cobblestones before. And when cycling a long route over several Alpine passes you should be just as well practised at cycling downhill as uphill. These technical subtleties are not difficult to learn – you just have to practise them a little so that you can cope with the corresponding terrain.

The right way to deal with stretches of cobblestones

Sections with rough pavés (stretches of cobblestones), which you often find in the Benelux countries or in northern France, take the most skill. This starts at a physical level: a lighter cyclist, for example, will have a worse time of it on the rough cobblestones than a muscular athlete who can move powerfully over these bone-shaking stretches. But there are a couple of tricks that can help you cope with bouncing about on your bike.

The Spanish climbing specialist Alberto Contador, for example, consulted the Belgian king of the cobbles, Peter van Petegem, training with him before the 2010 Tour de France, one section of which is referred to as the 'Hell of the North'. The result was that although favourites such as Lance Armstrong and Ivan Basso, for example, lost a lot of time on the way to Arenberg, Contador lost relatively little time and so laid the foundation (cobble) stone for his overall win.

Basically, you have to remember the following things when riding over cobblestones: first choose the right line – each pavé section has its 'sweet spot'. In most cases it's much better to ride over the middle part, which is a little higher, otherwise you should try to ride at the side. You often find a narrow strip of sand next to the stones where you can even avoid the juddering completely. At least this strip can come to your rescue when it's dry – but of course even here you have to observe the rules of the road.

When you reach the cobblestones you shouldn't under any circumstances grip the handlebars too tightly. That might work over short sections, but on other routes where the cobblestones stretch for over a kilometre you can't hold the handlebars tightly for that long. The best solution is to see yourself as a spring; that is, you don't hold on to the bike too hard but allow the handlebars room to 'jump' a little bit. At the same time you should bend your elbows slightly like a shock absorber, which minimises the strength of the vibrations even further. But you shouldn't take this to the extreme – too much of this technique is also problematic.

You should avoid riding out of the saddle on the pavés and instead engage a higher gear to shoot over these sections at a higher speed – for one thing you won't bounce as much if you do this, and for another it gives you a real boost to feel like Fabian Cancellara for a short time. In a nutshell: the faster, the better. If you're too slow the vibrations will build up so strongly that it really is no fun at all bumping over the stones. The 'critical speed' depends on the type of cobblestones, but it's approximately just over 30km/hr.

Wet and slippery conditions on cobblestones present a specific challenge: in this case you would be better off riding slowly and not risking any unnecessary falls. On bends in particular either the front or back wheel can slip very quickly and you are at risk of going down.

It's not just you who should be 'cobblestone fit', your bike should be too: a little less tyre pressure than normal (7–7.5 bar) and twice as much handlebar tape will reduce the vibrations and help to make them more bearable on long stretches.

A special feature – 'hellings'

Cobbles on flat sections aren't easy to deal with, but there's a special kind of cobblestone section in Flanders in particular that can almost drive you mad: the short, extremely steep inclines that the locals call 'hellings'. Even though these mountain climbs are often not much longer than 1km, lactic acid really hits your thighs.

In principle you should approach hellings in the same way as the level cobblestone sections. But you should be particularly careful when riding out of the saddle – even though it's tempting on a road with a gradient of 20 per cent, this is risky: one little slip of the back wheel and you can forget about climbing, because when you're hardly going any faster than someone on foot you'll just come to a dead stop and topple over. Cycling's no longer possible after that: you have to shoulder your bike like a cyclo-cross rider and carry it up to the end of the helling.

Cycling in the mountains

Cycling over long passes – whether they're in the Alps or the Pyrenees – is also something to be learned and planned for. Before you start off on the tour you need to get information about whether the mountain road is even passable. In the transitional months of May and September it's quite possible that the mountain won't be passable because of a spell of wintry weather. You can get this information from the local highway officials, and you should be able to get it in advance on the internet.

The best way to ride in the mountains? The magic formula for long ascents is to 'pace yourself': if you're faced with a mountain climb of 10km or more, too fast a start will ensure that eventually you'll be 'standing' in the real sense of the word, in a miserable state of collapse, losing both time and your nerve. To avoid this you should listen to your body, choose the steadiest possible pace and not let yourself be drawn into any battles for position with other cyclists, particularly during the first half of the route. You must always keep this in mind: if you're in a position to be able to overtake these cyclists, you'll be able to catch them up later just the same. You should only 'respond' in the last third of the competition.

You should also make sure that you engage the lowest gear possible – cyclists like Andy Schleck from Luxembourg are a good example – then you can keep your muscles loose with a high cadence and stay like that even on long climbs. Too high a gear can cause cramp and lead to knee problems in the long run. Regularly alternating between a sitting and a standing position can also help to ward off fatigue.

Powerful cyclists can experiment by moving the saddle back a centimetre or two so they can work more from the thighs. Slightly wider handlebars can also help with 'the long haul'. But these modifications are a matter of personal preference and not nearly as necessary as, for example, modifications when riding over cobblestones.

Safe, fast descents

If you ride up a mountain, then you also have to ride down it – a fact that is undeniable. But going down is even more important when it comes to cycling in high mountain regions, so you should also learn how to descend well. It is possible for a cyclist to lose the time he has worked so hard to gain on the climb as soon as he descends.

The first consideration when descending is, of course, safety. Rough road surfaces, potholes, road surfaces sticky with the heat (who could forget the terrible fall the Spaniard Joseba Beloki had in the 2003 Tour de France?), missing guard-rails on the route, animals or their droppings on the road, wet road markings, wet leaves in autumn – any of these things could potentially cause a fall when you're on the way down to the valley. Nor should you forget about normal traffic either, which can be especially dangerous in the narrow hairpin bends. You'd also do better to slow down by a kilometre or two per hour so that you don't unnecessarily endanger your life – and going downhill at high speed on 23mm tyres does exactly that!

It's important to keep both hands on the brakes so you can react in good time to any hazards. In principle you should brake on the outside edge of bends until you reach your intended cornering speed. That way your weight will be transferred backwards to avoid your back wheel locking. Let go of the brakes as you come round, bring the inside pedal up, straighten the inside knee and try to push your weight against the outside pedal. That way you'll come round as smoothly as possible. Try to keep as still as possible. As you come out of the bend you should stand up out of the saddle and pick up speed again. Of course there are also descents that are tiring just because they're so long. In this instance you must try to shake out your hands on the straight bits so that you're ready to brake correctly in the next bends.

You should also become proficient at riding in a group. In races that are open to everyone, like the Vattenfall Cyclassics, you cycle shoulder to shoulder with many thousands of other cyclists. If you get claustrophobia in a crowd like this or make a false move, it can quickly end in a fall. As a general rule just stick to your own cycling line and indicate changes by shouting, hand signals or gentle contact. It's particularly important that everyone keeps to the same line on bends.

The right clothing

The right clothing also plays a big part – especially in the mountains. A windcheater is part of the standard outfit. Something like this is easy to stow and you can even find room for it in your jersey pocket. The same goes for arm and/or leg warmers. In uncertain conditions you should also pack a waterproof jacket. If the weather is still cool, neoprene overshoes and gloves are a good idea, and a balaclava or scarf. In this case the onion principle is useful: wear as many layers as possible so that with changes in temperature you can adjust the layers according to the actual conditions.

It's also extremely important to wear a helmet. It's compulsory at almost every cycling event anyway, but protective headgear should also be worn on ordinary cycling tours. Helmets are made of such technically advanced material now that you hardly notice you're wearing one. And if you do fall on your head a helmet not only protects you from serious injury but could even save your life.

A well-maintained bike

Of course the most important piece of equipment is the bike itself. A cyclist is only as good as his tools. Whereas the professionals have their mechanics standing by and can just get on their bikes and set off, those for whom cycling

A participant in 'La Ventoux' fights his way up the mountain.

therefore more relaxed, manner past the scenery.

But maintaining your bike is also extremely important if you want to feel good on it. What's the use of being a fast cyclist when continual breakdowns get in the way of achieving a good placing? Nor is it much good discovering, just before you set off on a long trip in the Alps, that the brake linings are worn out. Or just imagine one of the screws on the handlebars working loose while cycling over a stretch of cobblestones – a horrible prospect, and one you shouldn't even think about on a mountain descent!

So that you're not troubled by such negative and depressing thoughts while cycling, make sure before every start that your bike is in good working order. A regular check at a bike shop you trust also helps to make you feel safer. They'll also tell you when you have to replace worn parts.

The final planning

If your training's in full swing and the equipment is doing its duty, you can put the finishing touches to your planning – and that depends on your particular goals.

The first step in a cycling marathon is of course registration. You shouldn't wait too long to do this since many events – for example, the Maratona dles Dolomites or the Ötztaler Radmarathon – are already fully booked long before the cut-off date. And even when you send off your registration in good time you may also need a little bit of luck to be able to take part because for some events lots have to be drawn for a place on the starting line.

Once you've finally received confirmation of your registration the next thing to do is make arrangements for accommodation. Individual cyclists

is only a hobby have to look after their bikes themselves. The weight and appearance of your bike shouldn't be the most important thing; feeling at home on it should. You can always take care of the other details later.

Correct position in the saddle is critical for feeling good. Many bike shops and institutes offer professional measuring and adjustment services, so you can find the ideal set-up for you. Good position in the saddle has several advantages: for one thing it increases your efficiency so you can generate more power, and for another you can stay in the saddle longer, particularly over long distances. Your position in the saddle also depends on your personal goals: an ultra-fit amateur racing cyclist essentially adopts a more stretched out position, whereas a tourist can cycle in a more upright, and

Jan Ullrich attacks on the Rund um die Hainleite.

who simply want to follow just one of the routes suggested in this book will also have to do this. Most cycling regions offer an extensive network of B&Bs, hotels and other places to spend the night. But there are still some corners where it's not so easy to find accommodation. Even looking for just one bed for the night in Sölden a day before the Ötztaler race can prove to be very difficult. So book in plenty of time!

Cycle tourists in particular, who want to split a long classic in two halves, should be aware of this. You could easily finish up, tired out, somewhere in the middle of the Belgian Ardennes after completing half of the Liège–Bastogne–Liège, and find that you have to search around for accommodation. You can avoid that by planning in advance of such a big tour and reserving the accommodation you need in good time.

It's also a good idea to get the equipment you'll need ready for the tour. You'll find a detailed kit list at the end of this chapter. Many events, such as the Trondheim–Oslo race, require lights to be fitted, and specific conditions must be met. When taking part in L'Eroica, for example, you're only allowed to compete on a 'period' racing cycle. Likewise, cycling the Paris–Roubaix course with a 250gm high-end carbon fork makes relatively little sense for an athletic amateur.

In the saddle
Once the waiting's finally over and the moment of truth has arrived, it's time to pack, ready for the tour. For a cycle sportive you can only take food rations and a small saddlebag containing tools for running repairs. For a tour you have to take much more. For example, if you have to stay the night somewhere, you shouldn't hesitate to take either a bike rucksack or a pannier – after all, you want to get away from the saddle and clean

your teeth at night. You should also take your passport and European Health Insurance Card (EHIC) with you. Neither of these is heavy, and if there's a problem you can use them to prove your identity. You should also take a mobile phone.

Eating and drinking on the road is also an important survival issue, which requires proper planning. For a sportive you can usually rely on the feeding stations. However, competitive cyclists often don't stop there, just taking new drinking bottles from the attendants and satisfying their energy needs during the race with gels or bars, which fit easily in the pockets of their jerseys. An 'emergency gel' is always important, and if you have a bad day for some reason it can be a life-saver. The golden rule is to try them out during your preparation period to see which foodstuff works best while you're on your bike. Never try out new things during a tour or a race, since if a product doesn't agree with your stomach things could quickly end in disaster!

The same is true for drinks. Some cyclists prefer energy drinks, others water mixed with powders and others still just take tap water with them. But the latter isn't a good idea because it contains hardly any carbohydrate or minerals and can easily lead to extreme loss of strength on a long route. In any case it's important to make sure you have a sufficient supply of fluid. On a hot day in the mountains you should drink up to a litre an hour to replace the fluid lost by your body. On cold and wet tours you don't need as much, but you should drink at least a small bottle (500ml) every hour.

If you've taken all these tips into consideration there's probably nothing left that can go wrong, and thus reassured you can now set off towards your goal of 'conquering' a well-known classic cycle race.

Kit list for a classic cycle ride

Basic kit
- Bike (well maintained: *see* pages 6–7)
- Floor pump
- Tools
- Light
- Helmet and buff
- Goggles
- Cycling shoes, socks and overshoes
- Long and short trousers
- Long and short jerseys, cycling vest
- Arm and leg warmers
- Wind and rain jackets
- Long and short gloves
- Heart rate monitor with chest strap

Before and after
- Ordinary clothing (tracksuit recommended)
- Trainers
- Plastic bags for dirty washing
- Washing things, personal hygiene items (suncream!), towel and hand wash

On tour
- Hand pump (possibly CO_2 cartridge)
- Two tyre levers
- Two spare inner tubes
- Repair kit
- Multi-tool for bikes
- Energy bars and gels
- Two big drinking bottles (700ml each)
- Money, mobile phone, passport and EHIC

Extras for cycle sportives
- Spare wheel
- Spare tyre
- Safety pins
- Racing licence/club certificate
- Registration confirmation/proof of payment
- Sports invitation and route description

THE CLASSIC
CYCLE RACES

THE CLASSIC CYCLE RACES

Before we move on to the classics it would be a good idea to begin by clarifying just what is understood by a 'cycling classic'. There is no really clear definition of the term. Essentially, the word 'classic' describes all those cycling events that enjoy a high level of importance with riders and fans because of their degree of familiarity, their course, their tradition or as a result of stories about their heroes. It's a blend of all these factors that makes up a classic.

So it will come as no surprise that the five 'Monuments' stand head and

The Côte de Saint-Nicolas is one of the decisive points of the Liège–Bastogne–Liège.

shoulders above all the other one-day races in professional cycling: these are Milan–San Remo, the Tour of Flanders, Paris–Roubaix, Liège–Bastogne–Liège and the Tour of Lombardy. These classics are the five one-day races that are generally the richest in tradition and the most prestigious, and occupy a special place in the calendar every year. All of them look back over more than 100 years of history, apart from the Tour of Flanders. Many a story has been played out on their streets; hard duels have been fought and heroes born. To date, these five races have been an enormous spectacle – the greatest celebration of the sport of cycling.

After the big five a whole range of events described as 'semi-classics' has been established over the years: races that can also look back on a long tradition, but will need a little time to catch up with the Monuments in importance (if this is even possible). These are events such as the Omloop Het Nieuwsblad, which is considered a compulsory date for all top Belgian cyclists, for example, but doesn't have the same international recognition and prominence. The same goes for the Ghent–Wevelgem, which perhaps lacks difficulty in its course profile, as does Paris–Tours.

Cycling's world governing body, the UCI, have been trying for years to raise other big events to the status of the major classics through the creation of series like the Road World Cup, the UCI ProTour and the WorldTour Calendar. Certainly races like the Clásica San Sebastián and the Vattenfalls Cyclassics are putting forward top-rank line-ups thanks to their good organisation, but they can't yet look back on the long history necessary for a classic. On the other hand the Züri Metzgete, a Swiss race with a 100-year-long tradition, isn't a race for professionals any more, but just for amateurs.

There has been a real boom in such competitions for hobby and amateur cyclists in the last few years. A massive 22,000 ordinary cyclists set off on the Cyclassics course from Hamburg – and so the ProTour race is incidentally also a real amateur classic. Also in this category (just as in the cycling sportives), a few classic events that have crystallised over time should definitely go on your to-do list: the best known of their type are surely the Ötztaler Radmarathon, the Nove Colli and the Maratona dles Dolomites. Just like the professional

classics they offer tradition, a first-class line-up and an impressive route.

A beautiful route, idyllic and demanding in equal measure, can also mark out a classic: the challenging but romantic atmosphere of the short ascent in the Ardennes on the Flèche Wallonne, the bumpy cobblestone section of the Paris–Roubaix, the endless white gravel roads of L'Eroica or the long climbs of La Marmotte and La Ventoux, familiar as part of the Tour de France, are all examples of this. The Majorcan coastal classic also belongs in this category, although unfortunately there is no official race or tour version yet.

These classics and their routes are described in the following section. As I said: the distinctions are fluid and also depend upon the opinions and claims of individual sportsmen. See which are your own personal 'classics' as you're reading!

The field for the Maratona dles Dolomites snakes its way up the Campolongo pass.

Race categories <<

Within the fluid boundaries of the definition, the races can be classified as follows.

Professional cycling

Monuments
The five one-day races that are richest in tradition and most prestigious are called the Monuments of cycling. They are the Milan–San Remo (Italy), the Tour of Flanders (Ronde), Paris–Roubaix (France), Liège–Bastogne–Liège (Belgium) and the Tour of Lombardy (Italy). Because of their long history and the numerous anecdotes and heroes that they've created, they attract tens of thousands of spectators out onto the side of the road every year.

The classics
Just like the five Monuments, the classic cycle races have achieved a high degree of importance with riders and spectators because of their particular characteristics, traditions, and so on. One such example is the Clásica San Sebastián, which not only boasts a world-class line-up and an impressive route, but also has a history going back 30 years.

Semi-classics
Semi-classics often lack either a world-class line-up or tradition. A semi-classic is a one-day race with less importance than a classic. One such example is the Omloop Het Nieuwsblad. In Belgium this race is very important, but from an international point of view it doesn't have the status of, say, the Ronde.

One-day races
Even though every race could technically be described as a classic or semi-classic, there are still events that have yet to earn this status. For example, the Trofeo Deià in this book has only existed in the form described since 2010, and so has no tradition to look back on.

Popular cycling

Amateur races
The name says it all: the next category after professional cycling. Here too there are classic races, such as the Vienna–Lassnitzhöhe or the Tour of the Odenwald. However, the line-up here is limited to a relatively small target group, so this race unfortunately hasn't found a place in this book. For amateur races you need a race licence.

Cycle sportives
There has been a boom in these since the beginning of the millennium. These events are very often closely modelled on the professional races (e.g. the Vattenfall Cyclassics) and thus usually take place on these tradition-rich courses. Varying route lengths guarantee – as the name suggests – that absolutely everyone can take part in them.

Marathon cycle sportives/gran fondos
A specific class that, from the perspective of the routes, may include the most beautiful races of all, such as the Maratona dles Dolomites. In principle, cycling marathons are very similar to all-comers' races, but they're typically routes that can frequently be well in excess of 200km. Most of them also include long climbs, which isn't necessarily the case in all-comers' races. Generally speaking, anyone can turn up at the start – however, when abroad you should have a licence for insurance purposes. In Italy this is often obligatory.

Tourist sportives
These tours are, as the name suggests, not races, and don't usually have timekeeping or ranking lists. These are about enjoying the route and simply coping well with the distance. An example of this is L'Eroica, in which totally different aspects, such as the idyllic atmosphere, count for as much as the fastest time.

Randonnées/Brevets
A special form of cycling tourism. Here the distances are often more than 200km and it's not the time that's important but managing to complete the course at an average speed. The longest rides of this kind, such as the Paris–Brest–Paris, measure over 1000km!

Left: The Spaniard Constantino Zaballa celebrates his victory in the Clásica San Sebastián.

SPRING SORTIES

1 TROFEO DEIÀ
On the trail of the Majorcan coastal classic

TOUR PROFILE <<

Race date: Early February

Type: Professional race

Start/finish: Deià (Spain)

Distance: 143km

Total vertical climb: 1800m

Riding time: 6 hours

URL: www.vueltamallorca.com

Route: You start off inland, then come onto the famous coast road after the halfway point passing through Alcúdia. The difficult part of the Trofeo Deià is the vertical climb rather than the distance. If you can manage it you should also take a good look at the landscape. There are some real highlights – particularly in the vicinity of the Puig Major.

Fitness: You should have a good level of fitness to begin with in order to cope with the Trofeo Deià and its numerous climbs. It's a good idea in particular to have cycled up a big mountain in the run-up to the long climbs of the Puig Major.

Equipment: The mountain profile practically shouts 27-tooth sprocket. A compact chainset is also a good idea for cadence-oriented cycling. Depending on the time of year it can also be very hot – two large water bottles are essential in any case!

There is no better place to start the cycling season than Majorca. This Balearic island isn't just one of the most popular holiday destinations in summer – in winter it's a sought-after place to escape the cold weather with a training camp. This is equally true for both professional and amateur cyclists.

Although the latter are there in early February to further develop their basic endurance, the professionals are there for a particular reason: the Majorca Challenge, a five-day series of one-day races, is one of the first events each year in the cycling calendar on European soil (*see* 'Background', page 23). One particular course here is the Trofeo Deià. Although this one-day race was held for the first time in 2010 and so doesn't have a long history, extensive sections of it lead over the famous coastal classic – a course that shouldn't be missed on any cycling holiday on this Spanish island. The circular course is 143km long, and includes the Puig Major, which among other things is the highest elevation pass in Majorca. In particular you should be prepared for a tour of the mountains in the second half.

Setting off from the Serra de Tramuntana

You start – as the name of the Trofeo would suggest – in Deià. The little community with barely 800 inhabitants lies on a hill on the flank of the Serra de Tramuntana, a mountain range situated in the north-west of Majorca, which give the island its typical rugged character. You start from the La Residencia Hotel, an idyllic and luxurious place to stay, where the restaurant is an inviting place to stop for a meal at the end of the tour – particularly as it's generally

Once you've conquered the Can Costa a well-earned descent to S'Esglaieta follows.

Over the next few kilometres the bridges are the only 'hills' worth mentioning.

18

acknowledged that food tastes at least twice as good after a long training run.

But there's not much time for cyclists to just bowl along early in the morning round a couple of bends heading towards Valdemossa after leaving Deià – which is incidentally the birthplace and home town of the Spanish professionals Joan Horrach and Vicente Reynès. After a short descent things start to get really tough: the reason being the Coll de Can Costa, 420m above sea level, which has to be tackled. The ascent, with its vertical climb of 300m with no hairpin bends and an accompanying average gradient of 5 per cent, is difficult to manage – but it does serve to get the engine going for the other tasks on the tour.

If you want, you can stop off in Santa Maria and have a look in and around the parish church, built c. 1216, the best of the places of interest in the village.

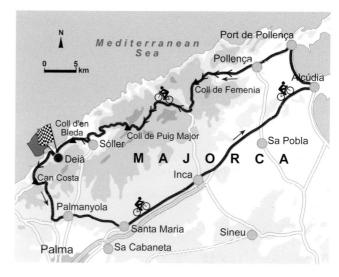

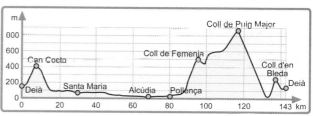

Shortly after the top of the pass the route takes a slightly downhill course to the left towards Valdemossa. After passing through the mountain village it then goes straight down past holm (holly) oak trees, typical of the island, to the lowlands towards S'Esglaieta. Here you turn left and the route remains relatively flat until you get to Palmanyola. At the roundabout at the end of the village take the second exit in the direction of Santa Maria. The next three kilometres take you gently downhill again through a deserted and at times wooded region, before you take the second exit once more at the next roundabout. Another five kilometres further on you come to Santa Maria del Camí, a town with about 5000 inhabitants. The clock now shows almost exactly 30km from the start. If

you want, you can stop off in Santa Maria and have a look in and around the parish church, built c. 1216, the best of the places of interest in the village.

Further on, turn left onto the MA-13A, which you follow for the next 35km. You'll pass through Consell, well known for its winegrowing, and Binissalem. If you do the tour on a Friday you shouldn't miss the weekly market here under any circumstances. The next important location is Inca – for many tours of Majorca this centrally situated town with more than 25,000 inhabitants is an important junction.

Alternative route via Moscari: after Inca the original route goes on along the MA-13, but if you want to avoid the traffic and see more of the scenery you should turn left towards Selva and then take the road to the right to Moscari and

After Pollença the favourites take up their positions.

Campanet. Those taking the short cut can also go straight on and take the beautiful ascent with its many hairpin bends up to the monastery at Lluc, and thus save themselves a good 45km.

However, the original route of the Trofeo Deià leads over the wide Palma–Sa Pobla motorway and along the MA-13A straight on to Alcúdia. This coastal town is one of the tourist hotspots on the island and often a favourite place to stay for those attending the training camps. This isn't surprising since the bay there offers a good 25km of sandy beach, and the mountains are not far away either. From there you can see the road to Port de Pollença, which follows the shoreline closely. But watch out: quite often the wind here isn't kind to cyclists! The Port

de Pollença promenade cries out for a coffee stop – with 82km on the clock you've really earned your cappuccino!

It's noticeably more wooded as you enter the mountain world of Majorca through the Vall de Son March.

It's a good idea to recharge your batteries, because now the mountains – and the coastal classic – finally begin. After you've left Port de Pollença in the direction of Pollença you then immediately head for the monastery at Lluc. It's noticeably more wooded as you enter the mountain world of Majorca through the Vall de Son March.

The climb up the Coll de Femenies is the first really long mountain stage of the day It begins with a bend to the right, and then a gradient of 5–10 per cent continues for the next 8km. The road winds upwards over several hairpin bends from 90 to 515m above sea level, mostly through woods. There's only a short downhill slope to give you some respite before you have to overcome another 1km climb up to the monastery at Lluc. You leave the monastery church, built in about 1250, on your right to fight your way on up to the next junction in the direction of Puig Major. Exactly 100km now lie behind the cyclists. If you need a rest there's a petrol station that can be recommended barely 300m from the junction. Although the original route branches off to the right, you should just make a short detour to the left.

Jens Voigt battles his way through the Trofeo last season.

The steeply rising rock face on the right and the dark green waters on the left, together with the sparse vegetation up here, combine to make a beautiful picture.

Now comes the highlight of the Trofeo Deià: the Coll de Puig Major. At 1445m above sea level it's the highest mountain in Majorca. The top of the pass is at 'just' 871m above sea level, but that's quite high enough – especially this early in the season. And the hardest part is right at the beginning: the road climbs at 12 per cent, and on hot days you're grateful for the trees lining the side of the road, which provide a little shade.

The route doesn't start to level out until you reach kilometre 110. Through a 250m long tunnel through the rock face you reach the Blue Gorge Dam, a reservoir that, among other things, supplies the drinking water for the capital, Palma. Even though many people will have struggled with the long

A Portuguese rider celebrates in Spain: Rui Costa wins in 2010.

ascent, they should definitely take a look to both sides: the steeply rising rock face on the right and the dark green waters on the left, together with the sparse vegetation up here, make a beautiful picture. A little further on you pass another lake, the Cúber reservoir, before giving everything you've got once more to get to the end of the climb. After 118km you've finally reached the top of the pass. Another 400m-long tunnel is waiting for you, then comes an incredibly fast descent!

The final stage begins in Sóller

You can enjoy this for a long time: the road winds its way down for a whole 15km, first of all over straight stretches with long wide bends, which later become real hairpin bends. The surroundings change from barren mountains to typical wooded island scenery. The further down you go, the denser the vegetation. At kilometre 133 you finally arrive in Sóller. From 871m above sea level at the top of the Puig pass down to only 30m above sea level – the longest descent on the Balearic island is over!

The rocky scenery of the Serra de Tramuntana is a constant companion in the second half of the Trofeo Deià.

In Sóller you have to keep a close eye on the route. First you turn left onto the MA-11, then right again immediately onto the MA-10. The final stage of the Trofeo can begin! If you're a tourist you should visit the botanical gardens here, which contain more than 400 plant species. But for cyclists things get really tough from here.

For now the last mountain of the day awaits – the Coll d'en Bleda: although you only have to cope with a vertical climb of 250m, the hard work you've already done makes it definitely something to be reckoned with. But in the final stage it's worth giving it all you've got. Numerous hairpin bends make the gradient of a good 8 per cent seem easier – and after another 4km it's all over. After that you've more or less done it. A short descent and then you find yourself in Deià again – you've reached the end of the Trofeo!

2011 results <<

1 Jose Joaquin Rojas (Spain), 3 hours 18' 59"
2 Gorka Izagirre (Spain), same time
3 Juan Jose Cobo (Spain), same time

Cyclists, check this out!

Although the Trofeo Deià is a professional event, amateurs can still come to the Balearic island to fulfil their dream: since 2010 the Majorca Classic by Max Hürzeler has taken place as a one-day sportive open to all. The 153km-long route includes parts of the Trofeo Deià, and begins and ends in Playa de Palma. However, the highlight is still the crossing of the Puig Major. Find more information at www.vueltamallorca.com.

Cycling and sightseeing

Quite close to the route of the Trofeo Deià you can find one of the wildest and most beautiful roads for cycling: Sa Calobra. Just before the ascent of Puig Major begins, turn right and you'll be rewarded with one of the most beautiful descents on the

Balearic island. Both the precipitous rocky landscape with its sparse vegetation and the route are particularly impressive. The highlight is surely the 'knotted tie' on the Nus de sa Corbata, a 270° bend which runs round and under itself.

Background

The Trofeo Deià is part of the Mallorca Challenge, a series of five one-day races that has taken place on the Balearic island every year in early February since 1992. It's organised like a stage race, and also gives an unofficial overall placing – however, riders are not under any obligation to take part in all the races and so can opt in or out at any time. Therefore the competition is not always the same. However, the Trofeo Mallorca, a race in Palma that usually starts it off, is a fixed size. Further well-known one-day Mallorca Challenge events are the Trofeo Alcúdia and the Trofeo Calvia. Since many professionals hold their training camps on Majorca, the event is often very well patronised.

Drafting helps to get through the flat sections.

TOUR PROFILE <<

Race date: Late February/early March

Type: Professional race (semi-classic)

Start/finish: Ghent (Belgium)

Distance: 204km

Total vertical climb: 1050m

Riding time: 8 hours

URL: http://omloop.nieuwsblad.be

Route: A beautiful tour through the Flemish Ardennes. You have stretches of cobblestones to deal with – but to some extent that's just what cycling in Flanders is all about!

Fitness: At only 204km the route is relatively short for a classic, so you can get through it in a day. Wind and cold weather are the toughest opponents – snow isn't exactly a rarity this early in the year! You should also have practised riding on cobblestones before the race – otherwise you're in for a nasty surprise!

Equipment: As is usual in this region, on the short, steep uphill slopes you should go for a lower gear. And since 13km of cobblestones are waiting for you, you should also kit yourself out with the appropriate spare parts.

You have to adjust to the rough cobblestones on the Het Nieuwsblad.

Omloop Het Nieuwsblad traditionally starts off the season of one-day races in Europe. The race is known to many by its earlier name, Omloop Het Volk, because it's only been called by its new name since 2009. This came about because the daily newspaper *Het Volk*, which until then had given its name to the race, was then taken over by *Het Nieuwsblad*. This newspaper was prepared to carry on with the sponsorship – but only under the new name.

This semi-classic is often seen as the 'little sister' of the Tour of Flanders (Ronde). And for good reason, since large parts of the course follow the route of the Ronde. But the founders of the race wouldn't be too happy to hear this since the Het Volk, when it was first held in 1945, was planned as a rival to the well-known classic.

The event is traditionally dominated by Belgians, who seem to cope best with the harsh weather conditions this early in the year – at the end of February other riders are still in the warm south. The race has been cancelled several times due to snow (*see* 'Background', page 29). Philippe Gilbert, Johan Museeuw, Peter van Petegem and the great Eddy Merckx are just some of the names on the list of winners.

> *At times as you're riding along the bumpy cycle tracks you'll have to expend extra energy trying not to ride into a pothole.*

Setting off from Ghent

Both the start and finish lines are in Ghent – so the competition has been known as the 'Ghent–Ghent'. You leave the capital of East Flanders from Sint-Pietersplein in a southerly direction through the district of Ledeberg (where the starting pistol for the official start of the professional race is fired) towards Merelbeke. Not long after this you come to a more level stretch and typical Flemish scenery: cornfields, meadows, the occasional solitary tree and the classic houses with their red tiles.

Heusden and Desdelbergen are the next places before you reach Beervelde. You go straight over the crossroads to the N449 and carry on further eastwards. In Lokeren (19km) – incidentally, this was the finish line from 1996–2007 – you turn southwards onto the N407. You stay on this road for 5km. In Overmere you go right again onto the N445. Three kilometres further on you reach Laarne (30km), where you branch off to the left – again to the south – in the direction of Wetteren (32km).

It has been flat so far, but now the route starts undulating. But these gentle rises are so slight that you're hardly aware of them. Quite the opposite: at times as you're riding along the bumpy cycle tracks you'll have to expend extra energy trying not to ride into a pothole. As you go through the idyllic town of Wetteren, remember

Etienne De Wilde, a well-known son of this town, who was one of the best road racers in the world in his day in the 1990s, and has two World Championship titles and 38 wins in six-day races in his palmarès.

In Wetteren you cross the railway line and then keep going in the direction of Zottegem (60km), which is also a stage town in the Drei Tage von de Panne, the most important stage race in the preparations for the Tour of Flanders.

In the Flemish Ardennes

You continue on, though for the time being not straight to Zottegem, but to the south to Oosterzele, Balegem and Oombergen instead. Once again it's more rural, the roads are rougher and the hills you could see almost 20km ago begin to loom up too. You notice that the initial stage is coming to an end. Enjoy this while you can, as from now on the Het Nieuwsblad really gets going!

After Sint-Blasius-Boekel (68km) you approach the first cobblestone section. A good 16km of the race is over bumpy terrain. So hold on tight when you get to the first section, Haaghoek near Horebeke (75km). And if there are cobblestones, then the first 'helling' – the Flemish name for the typical short but extremely steep climbs in the region – can't be far away. And it isn't: the Leberg's right there (77km). At 700m in length and with a vertical climb of 40m to be overcome it's a good opportunity to practise for the climbs to come. But be careful: this so-and-so also has a gradient of up to 16 per cent at the summit!

After the Leberg, the Berendries is an even tougher nut to crack.

After a short recovery phase through Elst and Michelbeke the next helling follows

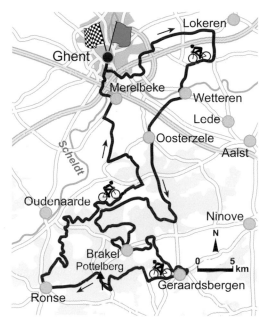

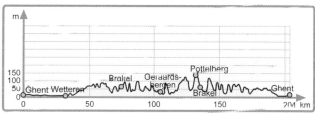

immediately with the Berendries (82km). Incidentally, both are part of the famous Tour of Flanders. After the Leberg, the Berendries is an even tougher nut to crack. Although it's not as steep, with a top value of 13 per cent, it's a good bit harder at 900m long with a vertical climb of 70m!

Once you've passed the summit you go right and on towards Brakel (85km), the home town of two ex-professionals, Peter van Petegem and Serge Baguet. While the former was ranked among the most successful in the chase for classics titles at the turn of the millennium, Baguet managed to win a stage of the Tour. Nowadays the Fleming runs a travel firm that provides, among other things,

In the last few years Tom Boonen has always been one of the favourites in the race.

to recharge your batteries because from now on things are going to be happening fast.

You leave the town over the Tenbosse (93km), a somewhat easier prospect with a climb of just under 12 per cent and smooth tarmac. But you can still get a good idea here of how the closely packed crowds of spectators for the Het Nieuwsblad constrict the streets. Go further on in the direction of Lierde (incidentally, the place where the World Press Cycling Championships was held in 2010), where you have to tackle the next climb, the Eikenmole (99km) – a shorter, harder mountain surrounded by trees, but which shouldn't cause too much of a problem. Beyond Deftinge (102.4km) you finally arrive at Geraardsbergen.

On the famous 'Muur'

This small, typically Flemish town, with its 31,000 inhabitants, is the venue for the best-known climb in the Flemish Ardennes: the Geraardsbergen 'wall'. The Muur, as this narrow roughly paved street is known for short, is the high spot of the annual Tour of Flanders. Since it has to be tackled just before the finish of the Ronde, this is where most of the deciding breakaways occur. You need to concentrate really hard here: straight after the first, still-tarmacked stretch has demanded everything of you, with its gradient well into double figures, crossing the rough cobbles – after a right-hand bend called the 'Kappelmuur' – will make it even harder. Hold on tight to your handlebars and stay sitting down, otherwise your narrow racing tyres will soon lose their grip on the slippery surface, with gradient peaks of 20 per cent.

Then comes a narrow descent. Although the Tour of Flanders would

the opportunity to get to know the classic routes (more information at www.baguetveloevents.be).

At kilometre 87 the Valkenberg finally waits for its conqueror. You bowl up to it through the houses until it towers above you with its 15 per cent incline. If you're going to tackle it you might consider putting in a short stop for coffee in the beautiful town of Brakel. It's a good idea

now turn in the direction of Bosberg, the Het Niuewsblad goes down again to the centre of Geraardsbergen, on to Everbeek (117km) and back to Lierde. A short 200m cobblestone section is easily done, so you can quickly turn your concentration to the remaining tasks. There are another good 90km to the finish.

The Pottelberg isn't any more difficult, but it's the biggest mountain in the race because of the vertical climb.

The route now leads further over winding romantic little roads – which on a beautiful day really show Flanders at its best – until you reach the next climb, the Pottelberg, at kilometre 132. This isn't

any more difficult, but it's the biggest hill in the race because of the vertical climb. It lies in the middle of a wood, with three bends that lead up a vertical climb of 100m to the summit. But in comparison with the Muur, which you've just done, the gradient remains really quite moderate. Once you've reached the top you leave the traffic-free section for the time being and turn left in the direction of Ronse. When you reach the town centre you'll have done 140km of the day's route so far – an ideal time to stop for a second coffee.

The next climb, the Kruisberg (142km), is waiting for you as soon as you leave the town. Although you have to tackle a vertical climb of a good 80m, the greatest difficulty isn't the gradient (which always remains in single figures),

You can feel the enthusiasm of the Belgians right from the start.

The Molenberg plays a decisive role in races.

but the cobblestones. Past Etikhove and Nukerke and over a good kilometre of a relatively flat but bone-shaking stretch of cobblestones you arrive 10km later at the next helling: with gradients of up to 15 per cent and smooth pavés the Taaienberg is one for the experts. There are just 50km left until the finish – you're on the final stretch!

Breakaway attempt at Eikenberg

You'll find you're on those picture-book little winding roads again, and you can now appreciate why only the strongest cyclists win a race like this. The wind's blowing, and the winding nature of the

roads makes it possible for a group to break away – for example, as they're approaching the Eikenberg with another gradient in double figures and its stretches of cobblestones – and disappear quickly from the competitors' field of vision. On the Eikenberg in particular you can manage to get an advantage over your opponents by cycling on the smooth shoulders at the side of the road. But by now you're really feeling your legs. None of the mountains you've tackled so far have been long, but they have been energy-sapping.

At kilometre 160 there's the tarmacked but very steep Wolvenberg before you finally reach, by way of Holleweg, a further stretch of cobblestones – the last and also very decisive helling of the Het Nieuwsblad: the Molenberg. The decisive attack often comes here – not surprising since the gradient is just under 15 per cent and paved once again.

The Paddestraat is often called the 'Hell of Zottegem'.

The rest of the route may be flat, but riders have to contend with numerous short sections of cobblestones, such as the Paddestraat (175km), just 4km after the Molenberg, which has often been called the 'Hell of Zottegem' – a bumpy 2.5km stretch that I guarantee will leave your hands numb and your legs like jelly. Immediately after that comes another cobbled section, the Lippenhovestraat in Zottegem, and as if there hadn't already been enough cobblestones, this one lasts for a whole kilometre and a half.

If you think that's it now, you're very much mistaken: you still have to zigzag through Baregem (180km) and Merelbeke (189km) towards the finish line. There are two more stretches of cobblestones – the 2500m-long Munte (183km) and the 700m-long Steenakker ('stony fields') 3km before the finish – which, as the name suggests, is a real slog of a rocky road.

But then you really have finished: with the route, with your strength and with your jelly-like arms. The houses of Ghent are a sign that it's not far now, and after 204km you finally reach the finish line at the point that also marked the start: the Sint-Pietersplein.

2011 results

1 Sebastian Langeveld (Netherlands), 5 hours 18' 03"
2 Juan Antonio Flecha (Spain), same time
3 Mathew Hayman (Australia), + 1' 01"
...
18 Russell Downing (Great Britain), + 0' 05"

Cyclists, check this out!

The Omloop Fitness Passage takes place in late May and is open to all. The event, at which you can choose from three different routes (60, 110 and 150km), largely follows the course of the Omloop Het Nieuwsblad and also includes some of the infamous cobblestone hellings, such as the Eikenberg and the Molenberg. Find more information at http://sport.be.msn.com/cyclingtour/omlooppassagefitness/2010/nl/.

Cycling and sightseeing

Cyclo-cross is still hugely popular, and in Belgium it's attracting more people than ever before onto its muddy courses. Huge numbers of people are crowding around the narrow muddy circuits there. Such is the enthusiasm for it that the best riders, such as Sven Nys, are often better known than professional road-racing cyclists. If you want to experience a carnival atmosphere you really should follow up on this tip. More information on international race dates at www.uci.ch.

Background

The arrangements for this semi-classic have often been threatened by weather conditions. Several times in its history, the weather the night before the race has been wintry and the riders have had to battle to victory through snow-covered fields in some places. The snowfalls in 1986 and 2004 were so heavy that the race organisers eventually had to cancel the race altogether.

3 MILAN–SAN REMO
The 'ride into spring'

TOUR PROFILE <<

Race date: Mid-March

Type: Professional race (Monument)/marathon sportive

Start: Milan (Italy)

Finish: San Remo (Italy)

Distance: 295km (professional race 298km)

Total vertical climb: 1780m

Riding time: 11 hours

URL: www.gazzetta.it

Route: An incredible course along the Italian coast, which is very attractive, particularly in the second half, both for its scenery and for cycling. One disadvantage: high logistical costs are inevitable when taking part because the finish line is 300km away from the start.

Fitness: The route doesn't present any difficulties from the point of view of gradients; the steepest climbs are between 6 and 8 per cent and are short. But because of the enormous length of the course a very high level of endurance is required. It's a good idea to ride in a group, to conserve strength by drafting.

Equipment: Since there are no particular obstacles in the form of hard cobblestones or steep mountains, standard 39/23 or 39/25 gearing is quite sufficient.

You can't really get lost on the Milan–San Remo – the route is very well signposted.

The Milan–San Remo is respectfully referred to as 'La classicissima', the 'most classic of the classics'. The race along the Ligurian coast is by far the most important and best-known Italian one-day classic and, as one of the five Monuments, also one of the most prestigious classics in the whole world. Because of its early start date at the end of March it has another nickname: 'the ride into spring'.

Milan–San Remo is a course for sprinters in particular, with almost exclusively fast finishers in the list of winners: Filippo Pozzato, Alessandro Petacchi, Paolo Bettini, Mario Cipollini, Marc Cavendish and Oscar Freire have all triumphed in recent years at the finishing line in San Remo.

A plain stretching as far as the eye can see

The cathedral square in Milan marks the start of the spring race for the professionals. But it's a little bit more scenic if you start at the cycling stadium in Rozzano, a southern suburb of Milan, as they do for the cycle marathon of the same name (*see* 'Cyclists, check this out!', page 35). You'll save yourself the worst of the traffic and also a couple of the 295km, which is an unusually long distance, even for a classic. Although it's not all that difficult it does demand good preparation to be able to stay in the saddle and pedal for so long. The logistics will also take some planning: you'll need accommodation in San Remo so that you can go back later by train.

It's still early in the day: the peloton on its way to the sea.

If this is your first time on this tour you can approach it in a more relaxed way at the beginning. The first 100km will fly by – a leisurely prelude. At worst a crosswind in the Po valley may blow a little unpleasantly in your face and slow you down. Binasco (10km) is the first destination, which you'll ride through early in the morning. Then comes Pavia (29km), very interesting culturally on account of its medieval buildings, then Casteggio (49km) and Tortona (76km), the home town of Luigi Malabrocca, the legendary winner of the black jersey, which used to be given to the cyclist in last place on the Giro d'Italia.

After 94km you finally reach Novi Ligure. This place is also closely connected with a famous cycling name: Costante Girardengo won the San Remo six times between 1918 and 1928 and has only been beaten in the ranking list of the most victories by the 'Cannibal' himself – Eddy Merckx has claimed seven victories. Giradengo's story is told in the Museo dei Campioissimi located there (see 'Cycling and sightseeing', page 35).

The course now leads on to Basaluzzo (101km) and Ovada (117km). It's still level there, but up ahead a chain of hills is slowly emerging. You're approaching the foothills of the Ligurian Alps which separate the Lombardy lowlands from the Mediterranean Sea. The scenery is also changing, with agricultural land gradually becoming bushy mixed woodland. Beyond Ovada the road starts to go uphill for the first time today.

The road is dead straight up to Turchino, with gradients of 4 per cent alternating with long, flat and in places smooth sections.

You ride under the motorway into a wooded valley where the climb to the

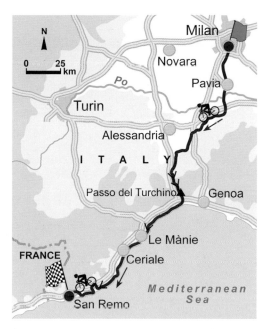

Turchino Pass begins. The vertical climb to the pass is barely 350m, which over a 25km stretch is equal to an average gradient of 1.8 per cent. There are not likely to be any great problems here. The road is dead straight up to Turchino, with gradients of 4 per cent alternating with long, flat and in places smooth sections. It's a bit more difficult once you've passed through the village of Campo Ligure (129km) halfway up to the pass. Even so, an incline of a good 6 per cent is still quite easy. Rather less pleasant is going through the pass itself (142km) through a gloomy tunnel some 150m long.

Once you've left this behind there's a winding descent, punctuated by a few

Once you've dealt with the Turchino you reach the coast west of Genoa.

hairpin bends, ending after 10km or so on the outskirts of Genoa. You've reached the sea! The Via Aurelia, the SP1, which you follow from now on, runs just a few metres away from the sea. You breathe the pleasant salt sea air along the whole length of the Riviera di Ponente, as this narrow densely populated stretch of coast is known. Rocky coastline alternates with sandy beaches. It's great fun cycling here – in spite of having already covered 160km.

The road runs along on the flat, with a short easy climb of no more than 5 per cent here and there along the way. In most cases just standing up out of the saddle is enough to get over these undulations. The only disruption to bowling along this coastal section is that you're now almost continually pedalling through villages, both big and small, and in some places bustling with activity; the traffic that shares the road with cyclists has also increased noticeably. So 'concentrate on your cycling' is the order of the day.

The mountains make their presence known

The next place you have to ride through is called Varazze (173km). It's already been a stage town on the Giro d'Italia five times; the last time this happened was in 2005. A monument to the unforgettable Fausto Coppi makes this an interesting coastal town for cyclists. After that comes Savona (184km), then you reach Spotorno after 197km. Although two-thirds of the course is behind you, the famous climbs of the race are still to come: the Cipressa and the Poggio. Despite the mild climate – the sea close by and the Mediterranean surroundings with palms and agaves at the side of the road have a positive influence on your personal motivation – you gradually start to feel the kilometres you've already completed.

You'll be even more aware of this once the road turns away from the sea in a sharp right-hand bend and starts an 8 per cent climb for a little over 4km. This climb is called 'Le Mànie', and you reach the top after 204km. The hardest climb of the whole race also signals the hardest stage of the Milan–San Remo.

For the next few kilometres the coast road is the peloton's almost constant companion ...

The 9km-long descent back to the coast, level at first but somewhat steeper later, makes up a little for all your efforts. The profile of the route also remains easy and level through Ceriale (227km) and Albenga (233km), but only briefly. After Alassio (239km) it's definitely more uneven. Once again the route climbs noticeably and doesn't settle back down straight away. First you find yourself climbing up to Capo Mele (246km), a 2km-long stretch with a good 100m vertical climb on a gradient of up to 8 per cent. Not long after this comes the next climb to Capo Cervo (251km), a stretch more or less the same length with another good 100m vertical climb on a gradient of about 5 per cent.

... but the precipitous rocks hint at the imminence of climbs, which will be steep and demanding in places.

In the professional race it's probably the heaviest sprinters who find these hills hard going.

The last hill in the Capo trio is the Capo Berta (259km), which rises straight up after a short downhill slope in between. At 3km long and with a vertical climb of just under 150m it's the longest and highest of the three hills. In the professional race it's probably the heaviest sprinters who find these hills hard going and so they switch to a slightly higher gear here – whereas normal cyclists are just happy that they don't have to tackle these hills at race tempo and they can use the small chainring.

You can find out about the history of the Milan–San Remo in the Museo dei Campionissimi.

After this the route runs on the level again, but there's not much time to recover because after about 11km the famous ascent to Cipressa begins. Those who desperately wanted to keep up with the faster riders on the previous mountains will now be feeling the effects! In San Lorenzo al Mare a street signposted 'Cipressa' branches off to the right and leads up a mountain slope in a loop a good 5.5km long. Meanwhile a gradient of 7 per cent and a vertical climb of 230m really hurts – after all, you've been in the saddle for a good 9 hours now.

But for professionals this isn't where the killer challenge happens and decisive attacks are ridden to get away from the field – this climb is too short for mountain specialists and, even if it were possible for someone to attack, in all

probability the peloton would catch up with them on the next level section. For after that there's still that last and decisive climb waiting: the Poggio.

But first you bowl along on the flat again. When you get to Riva Ligure (283km) you've almost reached the outskirts of San Remo and all that's left is one more climb – little do you know … An insignificant little turn-off to the right and a little sign with the name 'Poggio' snatches you back to reality. You've reached the foot of the Classicissima's famous killer climb!

Last attack on the Poggio

The gradient is now 6 per cent. It's an idyllic climb, if you don't have to beat your way up it at race speed: farmsteads lie on the slope, little vineyards, greenhouses, stone walls and little tiled water tanks. After about 2.5km the route levels out a little as you reach the Hotel Belvedere, only to rise once more for a short distance at 6 per cent on the last kilometre up to the village of Poggio, the highest point of the climb (292km). As easy as the Poggio is, after 290km it's a real killer! Among the professionals it's difficult for the climbers to get away from the field – by now the difference in performance between them is too small.

Concentration on your steering is required once again on the narrow bends of the descent that follows, and you also have to be careful when you join the main road nearby and finally go along the Via Cavallotti between the poplars onto the coast road, Lungomare Italo Calvino. You really don't need to do

The race is usually decided on the famous Poggio.

a final spurt on this tour. But you shouldn't under any circumstances play down your achievement – there are now almost 300km on the clock! It was a long day in the saddle, but the 'Ride into spring' was well worth the effort.

2011 results

1 Matthew Goss (Australia), 6 hours 51' 10"
2 Fabian Cancellara (Switzerland), same time
3 Philippe Gilbert (Belgium), same time
...
52 Mark Cavendish (Great Britain), + 5' 23"

Cyclists, check this out!

The Gran Fondo Milano–San Remo, a marathon sportive which is run on almost the same course as the professional race, is extremely popular with amateur racers. The Gran Fondo is a little shorter at 295km, but it includes the Milan–San Remo highlights: the Turchino, the Cipressa and the Poggio. Information on the race can be found from early June at www.milano-sanremo.org.

Cycling and sightseeing

About a third of the way round the Milan–San Remo course you come to the Museo dei Campionissimi in Novi Ligure, where the exhibits mainly concern the history of cycling – and of course the 'Primavera' plays a big part in this. The museum is on the Viale dei Campionissimi, and is so big you

can't miss it. Find more information at www.museodeicampionissimi.it.

Background

Even though the Milan–San Remo is known as the 'Ride into spring', the race can turn out quite differently: in the 1910 edition 63 cyclists lined up in the rain for the 'Classicissima'. The weather got worse and worse, and finally at Turchino wintry conditions prevailed – it began to snow. Although most of the cyclists gave up, the race was a turning point for Eugène Christophe. Do you know that name? Of course you do – he was the man who in 1913 became famous for repairing his bike in a blacksmith's at the bottom of the Tourmalet during the Tour de France. Christophe continued in spite of the snow, but he was soon so exhausted that he had to take refuge in a warm roadside café. After about half an hour, when he saw other competitors riding past, he resumed the race, caught up with them and finally won this epic. But the price he paid for his 12-hour struggle was high: he had to be taken to hospital immediately after he crossed the finish line with severe hypothermia.

TOUR PROFILE <<

Race date: Early March to mid-April

Type: Professional race (semi-classic)

Start: Deinze (Belgium)

Finish: Wevelgem (Belgium)

Distance: 219km (suggested route 178km)

Total vertical climb: 1400m (900m)

Riding time: 9 hours (7 hours)

URL: www.gent-wevelgem.be

Route: Unfortunately the first half of the race towards the coast isn't much to shout about: a lot of traffic and a lack of sporting highlights make the battle against the wind very difficult. But the second half, with its numerous hellings, is great fun. Although there's a circuit there, you can shorten it to 178km instead of the original distance of 219km.

Points to watch: The start and the finishing line are 40km apart!

Fitness: Ghent–Wevelgem is one of the easier classics. The only difficulty is the headwind or the crosswind, one of which will, in all probability, accompany you throughout the tour. Because it's possible to shorten it, you can manage the route in one day with no problem.

Equipment: Because of the steep climbs a compact chainset or an appropriate easily changed 27-tooth sprocket is a good idea. And don't forget your repair kit either – the cobblestones can be treacherous.

The beginning of the Ghent–Wevelgem takes place on wide main roads.

If there's a classic race early in the spring in Belgium that sprinters really look forward to, it's the Ghent–Wevelgem. The reason for this is that the 219km-long race across Flanders is mostly flat. That means that, although specialists often dominate the list of winners in the other big classics, cyclists with a good turn of speed are included in the roll of honour here: the Italian showman Mario Cipollini, the Belgian Tom Steels and, last but not least, the 'Tashkent Terror', Djamolidine Abdoujaparov, the Uzbek known for his daredevil sprints, are just some of the cyclists who have dominated in the last 20 years of the race.

Ghent–Wevelgem can certainly look back on a very long history: famous names such as Rik van Looy, Jacques Anquetil, Eddy Merckx, Walter Godefroot and Sean Kelly testify to the long tradition of races fought out since 1934. Its long history is what makes the race one of the most important in cycling: since 2005 it has been part of the UCI ProTour calendar, and since 2009 it has been part of the UCI World Ranking calendar.

Wind resistance required

Contrary to what you might expect from the name, the Ghent–Wevelgem traditionally begins not in Ghent, but in the market square in Deinze, a city a good 15km to the west of the capital of the province of East Flanders. Before setting off you should stuff the pockets of your jersey full – with protective clothing. If you want to follow in the footsteps of the professionals when doing this tour and choose a date early in the year, you also shouldn't forget your waterproofs or your windcheater – the Flemish classic has gained a reputation for unpleasant weather for very good reasons!

Once you have packed everything, start off from Deinze in the direction of Aarsele and Tielt. It's a good idea to use the cycle path that runs parallel to the main road, since the road is extremely hard to ride on. As you leave Deinze you'll come to a roundabout with a pretty fountain – the cycle path is well signposted here.

The road to Tielt is a relatively unspectacular one. It can be a good thing to have to battle here early on with a strong headwind which usually blows inland from the coast. You'll have to get used to this, or you won't be able to cope later with the strong wind on your way to the sea. In the professional race this first section is usually marked by numerous attacks. The small Belgian teams in particular try to form a successful breakaway group here, and so get themselves on TV.

Once you've skirted Tielt (9km) the road goes on towards Pittem (15km) and Koolskamp (21km). This little village is the venue every year for the Kampioenschap van Vlaanderen, a little one-day professional race, which in 2008 was won by the German sprinter André Greipel.

You don't have much time to look around – fighting the strong headwind demands all your attention.

The road goes straight towards the coast and then to Lichtervelde (25km). Apart from the many cows grazing in the meadows next to the road you won't find much in the way of things to look at. You don't have much time to look around anyway – fighting the strong headwind demands all your attention. And most of the course is still to come.

Falls are the order of the day for the professionals.

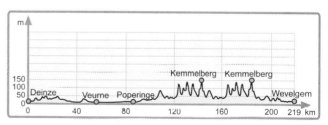

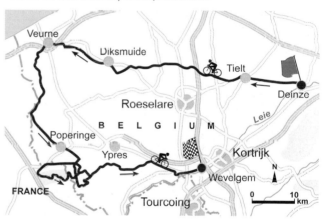

The road goes on to St Henricus (31km) and then to Kortemark (33km) with its village square of a design typical of this region, with a red-brick church towering above it.

The Kemmelberg is one of the killer climbs of the race.

The next destination now is Zarren (40km). You need to take care here: shortly after leaving the village you also leave the N35 and turn left onto the Steenstraat ('stone street') – as its name suggests, this is the first of the cobbled sections. The shaking on the rough cobblestones lasts for 2.5km. Hold on tight to the handlebars so that you arrive safely at Diksmuide, the next village on the route! There are now just under 50km on the clock.

As you leave the village you cross the Yser, the scene of a Second World War battle, and head for Kaaskerke. A kilometre or so further on you must be careful when you reach Vanhove. There you turn left off the N35 and on to the Rousdammestraat. Immediately after that the route goes to the right onto the Avekapellestraat before you turn left onto the N35 again. As soon as you've crossed the A18 autobahn through an underpass, you reach Veurne.

The Ardennes are waiting to the south

However, you don't go right into the town. After the first industrial buildings as you enter the town you turn left into Albert-I.-Laan and then you're in Bulskamp (68km). However, if you have time you should stop off in Veurne, perhaps for a coffee in the big market square. This is a particularly attractive place culturally as it's framed by a collection of historical buildings. It's only a couple of kilometres to the sea from here now. Previously the Ghent–Wevelgem took you all the way to the sea – but after several changes to the route in the last few years you now turn directly southwards.

When you reach Bulskamp you'll immediately notice that there's less traffic and it's more rural. After Wulveringem (71km), go on towards Izenberge. However, the quality of the roads also worsens noticeably with the decrease in traffic, and at Izenberge (75km) the next short section of cobblestones is waiting for you. You now continue in a southerly direction on quiet roads. Just before you get to Beveren (80km) you finally come on to the N364, a somewhat wider road with rather more traffic. You follow it to Roesbrugge (86km) and then Properinge (93km) – incidentally the birthplace of Jef Planckaert, a Flemish professional cyclist who was very successful, particularly in the 1960s. If you look ahead of you over the handlebars – and the road gives you a really good view – you can easily see that the scenery is slowly becoming more hilly.

The next big target is Reningelst, at kilometre 100. You get there by way of a good main road where cyclists can feel safe thanks to a cycle path on the right-hand side. Now it's a bit tricky: past De Ouderdom you turn right into the Vlamertingseweg, then left onto the Clyttesteenwen. Through De Klijte and along the Rozenhillestraat and the Kasteelmolenstraat and you eventually

come to the Zandbergstraat, where you have to tackle the first climb of the day, the Scherpenberg. However, the vertical climb of 50m doesn't hurt much. You should save your strength for the remaining hellings instead – depending on which route you take there are altogether eight or sixteen lovely mountains to be tackled.

You don't really have time to rest after the Mont des Cats – from now on the climbs come one after the other.

After the Scherpenberg you turn right immediately at the next junction towards Westouter (113km). Now you go towards France – yes, the next part of the course of the Ghent–Wevelgem takes place in the blue, white and red neighbour. Along the Poperingestraat you turn left onto Casselstraat and immediately cross the border. You arrive in Meteren (119km) and then the village

of Berthen where the next climb, the Mont des Cats (125km), is already waiting for you. For the professionals, who incidentally also ride through these streets during the Circuit Franco-Belge stage race in the autumn, this part of the race now belongs to the specialists. At the Mont des Cats a steep vertical climb of 100m has to be tackled. And you don't really have time to rest after that, because from now on the climbs come one after the other – six of them in a stretch of only 16km: Berthen, Mont Noir, Baneberg, Rodeberg, Monteberg and – last but not least – the Kemmelberg.

The Berthen takes its name from the commune of the same name and comes immediately after the descent from the Mont des Cats. But it's an insignificant difficulty, with a mere 40m vertical climb to contend with. Once you've dealt with this, the starting pistol fires for the next helling a little further on: the Mont Noir. At just under 150m above sea level it's the biggest hill of the race, but not one

Windmills and isolated farms – Belgium's charm continually strikes you on the route.

4 Ghent–Wevelgem

Standing up out of the saddle on the steep pavés is only advisable in dry conditions.

next hills are the Baneberg and the Rodeberg. And the Rodeberg is a much harder nut to crack: the gradient for the 138m vertical climb is in double figures. However, there's a nice little café near the summit where you can take a break. But you should be careful on the descent: with an incline of more than 12 per cent it's very steep, and because the road's straight you can reach a very high speed.

At the end of the descent you turn right onto Dikkebusstraat, ride through Loker and turn left in front of the next church – and here the Monteberg (141km) is waiting for you. This well-tarmacked climb is relatively benign to start with, but it'll be a real strain at the end: once again a good 12 per cent incline make the last 200m torture – especially as there's no chance of a breather. The road turns left onto the Kemmelbergweg: 400m of cobblestones here signal the decisive mountain of the race. If the sprinters are somewhere near the front at the Kemmel, they'll win – but if the specialists have enough of a lead they will be in front at the finish. And there's a reason why the Kemmel is famous: this climb has a gradient of up to 19 per cent, added to which the pavés are pure torture.

But once you've survived the Kemmel the worst is over. In fact, the professionals have to turn off here towards De Klijte to start a second circuit over the eight climbs that you've just done, but as a cycle tourist you can miss this out and make straight for the road to the finish line in Wevelgem – and so save yourself a whole 41km. You

that you should be afraid of since the gradient remains relatively benign, as hellings go.

High speed to the Rodeberg

After you've crossed the border back into Belgium again after the Mont Noir, the

Left: Marcus Burghardt battles his way up the Kemmel in 2009. He had won the race two years before. Right: In 2010 the Austrian Bernhard Eisel had the strongest legs and was able to sprint to victory.

reach Voormezele (191km), where the final section begins, over typical winding Flemish roads. With a bit of luck you'll have the wind behind you for the last 30 or so kilometres, blowing you towards Zandvoorde (201km).

The next important town is Wervik, incidentally one of the oldest settlements in Belgium. Past Geluwe, you head down the N8 to reach Menen, the last town before Wevelgem (219km) and the finish line, located in Vanackerestraat. You don't have to sprint like Cipollini and co. – but you can at least pretend to and use the drop handlebars!

2010 results

1 Tom Boonen (Belgium), 4 hours 35'
2 Daniele Bennati (Italy), same time
3 Tyler Farrar (USA), same time
...
35 Ian Stannard (Great Britain), same time

Cyclists, check this out!

The Ghent–Wevelgem is one of the few classic professional races that doesn't have an amateur, age-group or other cycle-tourism variant. In 2009 it was a sportive, but not in 2010. But that's not a problem: there are so many cycling events on the calendar in Flanders that you can always find something. An alternative would be, for example, the E3-Prijs, which also takes place on the roads of Flanders. In 2011 three distances were offered, all of them oriented towards professional racers: 60, 83 and 133km. For details see www.velo-tours.net.

Cycling and sightseeing

A good 20km north of the finish town of Wevelgem lies Roeselare. This little town is the home of, among other things, the Nationaal Wielermuseum, which is primarily dedicated to cycling and its history, and was opened in 1998 in a listed fire station. For more information visit www.wielermuseum.be.

Background

In 2010 Austria had reason to celebrate: Bernhard Eisler was the first red-white-red cyclist ever to win in the history of the race. Eisler beat the Belgian Sep Vanmarcke in the sprint by the leading group – it was the best result to date in the 30-year-old's career.

TOUR PROFILE <<

Race date: Early/mid-April

Type: Professional race (Monument)

Start: Bruges (Belgium)

Finish: Ninove (Belgium)

Distance: 262km

Total vertical climb: 1660m

Riding time: 11 hours

URL: www.rvv.be

Route: First of all you go from Bruges to the North Sea and then head south through the Flemish Ardennes. The second half in particular has continual climbs and descents, an apparently endless string of steep hellings and a bumpy section of pavés. The highlight is riding up the Muur from Geraardsbergen, the race's steep 20 per cent killer climb. The finish line is in Ninove.

Fitness: Several years of intensive cycle training doing at least 6000km a year are probably essential to ride such a long tour. If you want to divide the tour into two sections you could consider spending the night in Oudenaarde (139km).

Equipment: A really well-trained hobby cyclist can push on up the steepest climbs like the Muur with a gearing ratio of 39/26, but a gearing ratio of at least 39/27 or 39/29 is a good idea – or a compact chainset. Because of the many sections of cobblestones, you should ride with good tyres, which shouldn't be pumped up to full pressure. Weather-proof clothing is a must at this time of year!

Just before the summit of the famous Muur.

'Hellings' – what exactly are these short, steep climbs, described in cycling circles as vicious, which lead up the mountains in the Flemish Ardennes over narrow, bumpy roads and gain the respect of seasoned professionals? If you want to find the answer to this question you have to go to Belgium: to be exact, to the northern region, Flanders.

A cycle race that has been taking place there since 1912 is considered to be the most famous one-day race in Belgium, and along with the Milan–San Remo (Italy), Paris–Roubaix (France), Liège–Bastogne–Liège (Belgium) and the Tour of Lombardy (Italy) is counted as one of the five Monuments of cycling. It's also known as the Flandernrundfahrt, the Ronde van Vlaanderen or, by the locals, Vlaanderens Mooiste ('Flanders' finest').

As a result, it's no wonder they're proud of the race that along its 262km between Bruges and Ninove showcases all the advantages of the Belgian region: large towns, isolated villages, idyllic farmsteads, roads paved with cobblestones, little woods and wide plains alternating with hilly landscapes. But first and foremost there are the hellings, which play the leading role in the mountainous part of East Flanders.

All the big names have come here

The great importance of the race lies not just in the route but also in the incredible enthusiasm of the Flemish for their cycling. Ever since it was first held the Tour of Flanders has been a big event. This is also true for the sport internationally, as shown by the names of the cyclists who have given the race their stamp of approval: most significantly Johan Museeuw, who, like Achiel Buysse and the Italian Fiorenzo Magni, won the tour three times. Peter van Petegem, Michele Bartoli, Moreno Argentin, Jan Raas, Eddy Merckx, Roger de Vlaeminck, Walter Godefroot and Rik van Steenbergen are other big names who have also crossed the winning line first. The winding course is fully signposted so that mishaps are avoided.

You have to set off early – the 262km need to be done all in one day.

You start in the Grote Markt in Bruges. You won't be back among the beauties of this square, where the gothic town hall and ranks of baroque facades make it one of the most amazing squares in Europe, until evening at the very earliest. You have to start off extremely early – the 262km need to be done all in one day. To begin with you go south-west through heavily populated western Flanders.

In Wenduine (11km) you reach the coast and go for some time along the North Sea coast in the direction of Ostend (28km). It's mostly flat here. Next you head south again. After 38km you'll pass Gistel, incidentally the home town of Sylvère Maes, who was very successful in the 1930s and twice winner of the Tour, and then after 54km you'll reach the little town of Torhout. The next places on the way are Hooglede (64km) and Roeselare (70km), which is a particularly interesting place for cyclists. The Nationaal Wielermuseum (see 'Cycling and sightseeing', page 41) is there, and the town is also the birthplace of the most successful six-day racer of all time, Patrick Sercu.

In Ledegem (89km) the course finally turns east, and 10km later the professionals are given their first refreshments – just at the right time, as the long opening stage is finally approaching its end.

The first kasseien

Before you know it you're in Waregem (114km). This little town is well known, among other things, as the starting point for the Dwars door Vlaanderen, a Belgian one-day race that usually takes place a week before the Tour. And it also occupies a key position in the Tour of Flanders, because this is where the first section of cobblestones of the course is situated. This section is only some 400m long, but that's quite enough to give the concept of 'cycling' quite a different meaning. You'll be sorry if you don't keep your hands tight on the handlebars so you can at least try to force your bike to go in a more or less straight line …

The thumps and bumps that you get from the road surface beneath you reach the body almost unchecked, and you automatically try to escape these attacks by getting out of the saddle – but by doing so the pressure on the pedals is taken away and forward movement becomes almost impossible. Occasionally some bikes say goodbye to their pump and water bottle here.

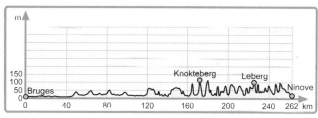

Only those who have done it before know how can you drag yourself over these 400m. But this is only a taster of what is to come, because the ensuing pavé sections are on the whole longer, and later on reach a length of as much as 2400m! Bouncing on cobblestones doesn't take just strength and fitness, it also leaves its mark behind on your morale.

You shift to the biggest sprocket, get up out of the saddle, bend low over the handlebars again – the next minute you've reached the summit and you're cruising back down the other side.

Suddenly you reach the first helling in the locality of Horebeke, after a good 130km of the course. Its name: Den Ast. A row of houses leaves just enough

Fabian Cancellara had no difficulty leaving his rivals behind in 2010.

room for a narrow cobbled road, which gradually gets steeper until it reaches a gradient of 14 per cent. You shift to the biggest sprocket, get up out of the saddle, bend low over the handlebars again – the next minute you've reached the summit and you're cruising back down the other side. 'That wasn't so bad', some think. But you shouldn't celebrate too soon: there are 17 more mountains to come.

After 139km you reach Oudenaarde. Cyclists who are not quite so fit can stay here overnight. That way you can split the tour into two and the following day, feeling fresh and rested, you can cope with the next lot of difficulties. You can also take a look at the Centrum Ronde van Vlaanderen, a museum dedicated to the Tour of Flanders (*see* 'Cycling and sightseeing', page 47).

Stay in the saddle and push on

Once you've left the town the climbs to the hellings become longer and more frequent. After 164km comes the Kluisberg, where the road is narrower and, at the beginning, very steep. Eight kilometres further on there's the Knokteberg, a local farm track that also has an incline in double figures. The first highlight is crossing the well-known Kwaremont (180km). This monster is 2200m long and almost completely paved with cobblestones. A maximum incline of 12 per cent leaves the muscles producing lactic acid – and you'll get a second dose of that a few kilometres further on at Paterberg.

Going gently uphill to begin with, you bowl along around a bend after which the road suddenly appears to climb like a wall in front of you. The gradient increases to a massive 21 per cent and stays there along a 100m stretch. If your strength gives out here or you lose your balance, your only hope is managing to clip out of one of your pedals so that you can prop yourself up! You can forget all about riding any further, and you'll have to push your bike up the remaining metres. Even if it's a struggle, keep sitting for as long as you can and push on upwards!

Now you're in the middle of the Ardennes and wide, level stretches are in short supply. It's constantly uphill and downhill, and you're mostly riding over narrow, armour-plated paths – which in good weather is really quite idyllic. Incidentally, you don't have any problems with traffic here – for one thing, because there are very few vehicles on the road, and for another because the Flemings are very considerate towards cyclists.

Once again on the Koppenberg you have to deal with pavés, just as you do 4km later on the Mariaborrestraat.

Once again on the Koppenberg (189km) you have to deal with pavés: it's one of the best-known climbs of the race, with almost mythical status. Though it's only a 70m vertical climb, you still have to deal with inclines of over 20 per cent – on bumpy cobblestones. It quite often happens that riders have to push their bikes up. Even the great Eddy Merckx once shouldered his bike here. In earlier years the hill was so bumpy that Bernard Hinault refused to take part in the Tour of Flanders so long as this climb was part of the route. After a serious accident in 1987 when a race official inadvertently ran over the Dane Jesper Skibby after he'd fallen off, this helling was finally removed from the route, and in the period that followed it was renovated and had the cobbles

Even at the start in Bruges you're rewarded with a fantastic scene. On race days a carnival atmosphere reigns.

The Paterberg climb, with its bumpy pavés, is one of the hardest climbs in the Tour of Flanders.

renewed at great expense. Since 2004 it's been a part of the tour again. The course goes on over the Mariaborrestraat 4km further on, a 2km-long bumpy section, and then the Steenbeekdries (195km), which isn't nearly as steep, but the hands on the handlebars suffer further torture – which you'll also feel just as much in your wobbly legs.

The Taaienberg (198km) (very steep, particularly in the middle section where the gradient is 15 per cent) and the somewhat easier Eikenberg (202km) are the next two torments. They're also cobbled. Anyone needing a rest will be disappointed because they come in quick succession. Over the cobbled Holleweg (205km) and Kerkgate (209km), you draw nearer to the final stage. In the professional race the riders who are favourite now try to secure a good position in the leading group, to weather the Molenberg, Leberg, Berendries and Tenbosse climbs as safely as possible.

Final section on the Muur

This is the decisive climb on the Tour – and also very typical of these short steep hills in East Flanders. You already have 217km in your legs when you get to the bottom of the Molenberg climb. Although it's not long, at 500m, 14 per cent and cobblestones are the key words that describe exactly why this helling really takes it out of you.

The other three, which follow within the next 17km, are somewhat easier. At least you're riding on asphalt here, so you can give your tired fingers a break. But the key point of the course is waiting for you: the famous Muur. And you know you're almost there when you're riding through the slightly undulating countryside and you see the sign marking Geraardsbergen after 243km. The climb to the Kapelmuur chapel at the top of the hill is perhaps not as hard as, for example, the Paterberg climb. But here, right at the end of the race, the wheat is separated from the chaff.

This section has very little to do with cycling. Your thighs are aching, your lungs are on fire, and even though the easiest gear is engaged, you can't pedal any more.

In Geraardsbergen you cross the river Dender, and immediately the white signs for the Muur point the way up the street. With an incline of 12 per cent the road goes between brick-built houses, then turns off to the right into a side street, and a narrow cobbled path leads the way up. But the hardest part is still to come: a 500m-long climb with an incline of almost 20 per cent at its steepest. Now it's all down to what reserves of strength you have, and to giving everything you've got. This section has very little to do with cycling. Your thighs are aching, your lungs are on fire, and even though the easiest gear is engaged, you can't pedal up the bumpy road any more. In 2010 the Swiss Fabian Cancellara launched an unbelievable attack, and so shook off his Flemish fellow campaigner Tom Boonen. But as an amateur cyclist you won't think of this episode while you're cycling – never before will you have longed so fervently for the end of a climb! Once you've reached the final left-hand bend you'll almost be up at the chapel (245km) and can collect your strength again on the downhill slope that follows.

Now it's not much further to the finish line in Ninove, just some 16km or so, which – how could it be otherwise – takes you through narrow, winding streets. There's just one more helling to go: the Bosberg climb near Moerbeke (260km). This is where the professionals attack again to take victory ahead of the others if they can. This section is almost a kilometre long and has an incline of 11 per cent, but you can tackle it slowly. Reserves of strength are easily used up.

Go straight through Denderwindecke (257km) towards Ninove, where you can finally park your bike in the district of Meerbeke. And even if you haven't flown over the pavés as gracefully as the professionals, you now know what's behind the Flemish word *hellingen*.

2011 results <<

1 Nick Nuyens (Belgium), 6 hours 01' 20"
2 Sylvain Chavanel (France), same time
3 Fabian Cancellara (Switzerland), same time
...
10 Geraint Thomas (Great Britain), + 0' 05"

Cyclists, check this out!

A day before the professional race, cycle tourists are offered a unique opportunity to get to know the course of the tour under official conditions; mountain bikers are also eligible to enter the Ronde voor Wielertoeristen. In addition to the long route of over 260km there are also 75km and 150km routes on offer. Find information on the organisers' website at www.rvv.be.

Cycling and sightseeing

Near the centre of Oudenaarde, which the Tour passes through, is the Centrum Ronde van Vlaanderen, another museum dedicated to the Tour of Flanders. This houses a lavish presentation of the history of this Monument and the sport of cycling in Belgium. Find more information at www.rvv.be/nl/crvv.

Background

The 2004 Tour of Flanders was Steffen Wesemann's finest hour: the German set off up the famous Geraardsbergen Wall with the Belgians Leif Hoste and Dave Bruylandts, and finally beat both of them in a sprint in the last few metres. This was how 'Wese' fulfilled his dream of victory in the biggest race over cobblestones in the world. This was only the second black-red-gold victory in the Tour since Rudi Altig won in 1964.

6 PARIS-ROUBAIX
On the cobblestones through the 'Hell of the North'

TOUR PROFILE <<

Race date: Mid-April

Type: Professional race (Monument)

Start: Compiègne (France)

Finish: Roubaix (France)

Distance: 258km

Total vertical climb: 850m

Riding time: 11 hours

URL: www.letour.fr/indexPRX_fr.html

Route: From Compiègne you go immediately north towards Roubaix. There aren't any really substantial climbs, just pavés as far as the eye can see. This bumpy ground stretches for a whole 53km, which is pure torture – even if you're not riding it under race conditions you still frequently think about giving it up. The start and finish are so far away from each other that you have to make appropriate logistical arrangements.

Fitness: You should have a good level of endurance to be able to cope with this route. You should also be used to riding on pavés – otherwise you'll have a nasty surprise and possibly won't see the finish line.

Equipment: You need a robust bike if you want to take on this course. The tyres should be puncture-proof and pumped up to a lower pressure than usual – this is more comfortable. Well-padded gloves also lessen the effects of the juddering. Some professionals even wind a second layer of handlebar tape round their handlebars, to help them get through the race.

You have to have a very special attitude to cycling if you're thinking of cycling the Paris–Roubaix. There are a good reasons why this race is also called L'Enfer du Nord, 'the Hell of the North'. This isn't meant at all negatively, but anyone who wants to make the strains of riding on normal roads worse with a good 50km of the toughest, often wet, slippery and dangerous cobblestones, must be really passionate about this sport.

In the majority of cases this is fed by TV broadcasts and reports on this professional race, which from its first edition in 1896 right down to the present day has survived as a cycling anachronism. To be honest, if the Paris–Roubaix didn't exist, it wouldn't ever occur to anyone to go looking for stretches of cobblestones to ride over. Nevertheless, these sections are a unique experience that enriches the sportive rider's 'career' – even if it's only to really get to know all the facets of our fascinating sport.

A split peloton

The majority of cyclists who've taken part in this race during its long history hated it the first time they took part. Your hands feel numb because of the vibration, you're covered in mud from head to toe and the mostly lousy weather doesn't make the Paris–Roubaix a pleasant experience either – and the same goes for the ones who win here too. But their relationship with riding the cobblestones is in fact a love–hate one.

In the whole history of the race, the one who coped best with the bone-shaking sections was the Belgian Roger De Vlaeminck (*see* 'Background', page 53): between 1972 and 1977 he won a total of four of the famous pavés – the cobblestone trophy for all winners

Take good care of your equipment – 53km of cobblestones will really put it to the test.

in the 'Hell of the North'. De Vlaeminck was ranked in the list of winners above Octave Lapize (who won three times at the beginning of the last century), as well as above the Belgians Gaston Rebry and Rik van Looy, who also won three times in the 1930s and 1960s, respectively. The Italian Francesco Moser and the insatiable Eddy Merckx have also notched up three successes. In recent times the Belgians Johan Museeuw and Tom Boonen have also left their mark on the race: they've both won three times. Boonen could even take over the lead in the rankings – he's still racing.

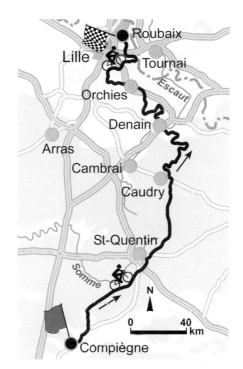

The route through some wooded sections is flat and proves to be ideal for cruising along.

Those who aren't put off by the difficulties and come onto the course start their cobblestone experience in Compiègne in the Place du Palais. The town is situated 80km north of Paris and is also worth a visit out of the saddle, offering a medieval castle, a town hall and more as tourist highlights. Once you've given your bike one last check and verified both the tyre pressure and the tightness of the screws, you can set off: you leave Compiègne in the early morning dawn and head north. The route through some wooded sections is flat and proves to be ideal for cruising along.

The less than spectacular road leads cyclists to the little town of Noyon (18km), and then to Guiscard (28km) and Roupy, which you reach after 50km and a good 2 hours of riding. There are no cobbled sections yet and the only difficulty is the wind, which is blowing against you. You can't see any hills either.

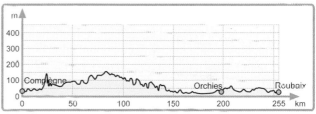

Picardy is known for its almost exclusively crop-producing farmland, with wheat, barley and rye fields sometimes interspersed with sugar beet. The road stretches out as straight as a die, past fields that at this time of year are lying fallow. Occasional splashes of colour from the fields of yellow oil-seed rape, green meadows and isolated groups of trees manage to break up the monotonous surroundings a little.

The first pavé sections

After about 80km you reach Bohain-en-Vermandois. Here the first checkpoint for cycle sportives takes place (see

Paris-Roubaix

In 2010 the Tour de France used the Roubaix route: here Lance Armstrong grits his teeth against the dust.

'Cyclists, check this out!', page 53), so after that you can slowly get used to the fact that the long time just bowling along is coming to an end. This is where the favourites among the professionals sort themselves out in front of the field and get into a good position for the first of the pavé sections. You eventually reach this shortly after Troisvilles (96km) – and at 2km long this really is the acid test.

A sudden branching off to the right from the main road onto a path through the fields brings you onto this section. Your first thought is: this is awful! Anything that isn't securely attached to your bike with rivets or nails goes flying off through the air – bicycle pumps and water bottles are obvious candidates for free flight. You bounce up and

down on the saddle like a rubber ball, but you mustn't be put off by this. The faster your speed, the easier it is to ride on the pavés. You should also push a high gear. If you once lose your rhythm, it's extremely painful, because you then have to use all your strength to keep the bike, which is bucking in every direction, in a reasonably straight line and at the same time relax your body, arms and legs as much as possible so that the impacts aren't too painful.

Those of you who are daring enough can try cycling on the narrow, unsurfaced earth strips at the side of the path, as you see the professionals doing on the TV broadcasts.

You must also find the right line to ride. Whether you manage better on the raised middle section or at the side of the path is a matter of personal preference. Those of you who are daring enough can try cycling on the narrow, unsurfaced earth strips at the side of the path, as you see the professionals doing on the TV broadcasts. Even here it's a question of greater skill in steering and powerful pedalling, but at least you'll be spared the worst of the jarring shocks. But when it's raining and muddy these side strips can't be used.

After just this first section you're glad to feel normal tarmac under your wheels again. So how does it go on from here? There are still 26 sections to be overcome further on. There's another one immediately after you've done 104km: the section is called Viesly to Quiévy, which at just under 2km long is not easy either, particularly because as soon as you join the Quiévy to St Python section there's a stretch that is almost 4km long – a real acid test. As well as a great deal of strength you also need a high degree of concentration in order to get over the cobblestones – and that exhausts riders even more.

Half-time in Solesmes

And so it goes gaily on: the next section of cobbles follows in Saint Python (115km), after which the professionals are given refreshments in Solesmes at 120km. A stop in the little municipality won't do any harm – it gives your wrists a chance to rest. The 130km of the course still to go, of which just under one-third is over pavés, will eventually push the riders to the limits of their performance several times over.

You now have the feeling that the cobbled sections aren't following each other so quickly any more. There is also a

The sprint to the finish in the stadium – you only get that in the Paris–Roubaix.

change in the landscape: it appears now to be more built-up, crowded and not so open as at the beginning of the tour. When you started, some of the sections were still gently climbing and then going down again; now they're as flat as a plank, although this doesn't actually make them any more pleasant. In fact, you've had enough of them already – you know now how it feels to ride on them and so you can join in whenever the conversation in cycling circles gets round to them. However, you don't want to give up now under any circumstances, and so it's worth gritting your teeth and riding to the end of the tour.

You've covered exactly 164km when one of the highlights of the race (and probably the hardest section) arrives: the forest of Arenberg. In the TV broadcasts of the professional race you can see densely packed spectators here, with the peloton chasing through at a hair-raising speed, which often results in serious accidents. But as you go through there are only a couple of walkers at the side of the road, who observe you with as much indifference as they earlier watched with interest. Thankfully you

Fabian Cancellara celebrates his win in the Paris–Roubaix in 2010.

can't read the word 'weirdo' in the speech bubble over their heads – you're focusing too hard on not having an accident on this formidable bumpy stretch. Basically you just want to survive!

You wish you had a fully sprung mountain bike with the cushioned saddle of a ladies' bike, you're bouncing around in the saddle so much.

This section continues for 2.5km, which, because of its fame, is like a scheduled Monument. In addition, with five stars it's one of only three sections which has acquired the hardest rating. There is a reason for this: even though the pavés here were refurbished by a local horticultural society a few years ago, you wish you had a fully sprung mountain

bike with a well-cushioned saddle, you're bouncing around in it so much. For the professionals this is where the outcome is decided, 90km before the finish line: if you lose contact with the leaders in the forest, the race is usually over.

Recovery time between the pavé sections is now shorter, and suffering increases. In Beuvry-la-Fôret, after 191km, the professionals have their second feeding station. Even though there are 'only' 67km to go to the finish line, you still have only half the pavé sections behind you– 13 of them still lie in front of the riders, including Mons-en-Pévèle and Carrefour de l'Arbre, the other two five-star stretches.

Cancellara's unbelievable attack

You have to conquer the section at Mons-en-Pévèle after 210km. To start with, a 3km-long bumpy stretch leads gently upwards before going just as gently downhill again. The road is extremely narrow and rough. This section is well known, in one respect, from the often-repeated story of George Hincapie, who, on his way to making his dream of a Roubaix victory come true, suffered a broken fork here, fell heavily and sustained a serious injury to his shoulder. In 2010 the Swiss Fabian Cancellara launched the attack that brought him victory on this stretch. He rode away from the leading group with such incredible speed and in such a high gear that many people even voiced the suspicion that he was powered by a hidden electric motor. Subsequently he was a whole 2 minutes ahead of his strongest opponents – an impressive solo victory.

There's no way you'll be able to fly along; somehow you'll just have to try to ignore all those aches and pains, both big and small, in your bottom and the back of your neck. The game repeats itself with each new section of cobblestones. The last five-star stretch of cobbles is called Carrefour de l'Arbre, which is reached after 242km. The beginning of it in the woods is very hard and strenuous, then, after a good half of the 2km stretch, the flat ground opens out and the pavés are a little more bearable again.

In the context of a sportive you also get to know the famous showers in the bowels of the stadium.

Once you've finally overcome this section, there are just three more sections to come: Gruson (244km),

Willems à Hem (250km) and Roubaix (257km). But being on average a kilometre long, each of these stretches is essentially easier to ride, and also the quality is markedly better than the worst stretches.

Next you go straight to the Velodrome, situated in a park. You are officially only allowed to ride this in the tour version, but do look inside; in this context you also get to know the famous showers in the bowels of the stadium, where the shower heads are operated by means of metal chains. Naturally the changing cubicles are also a part of this experience, and you get to know the great names in cycling, since each cubicle is named after a former winner.

So what do you think now? Do you have your own love–hate relationship with the Paris–Roubaix?

2011 results <<

1 Johan Vansummeren (Belgium), 6 hours 7' 28"
2 Fabian Cancellara (Switzerland), + 0' 19"
3 Maarten Tjallingii (Netherlands), same time

Cyclists, check this out!
The Paris–Roubaix Cyclo for sportive cyclists takes place every two years, usually in June. This doesn't start in Compiègne, but in Cambronne les Ribcourt, 15km to the north. The main course covers 255km, of which 49km are over pavés. There are also two further routes of 98 and 173km. For more information go to www.vc-roubaix-cyclo.fr.

Cycling and sightseeing
Highlights of the race are definitely the Arenberg Forest and the Velodrome in Roubaix. You're only able to ride in the latter officially during the tour version of the race, but nevertheless you can still have a look at the building after a successful tour. Roubaix has had a velodrome since 1895. The first

one had a track 333.33m long, which was surfaced in wood in 1910. But this was dismantled by the Germans in the First World War. Finally, in 1936 the track we have today was opened in the Parc des Sports. In addition to the Paris–Roubaix the velodrome is used as the finishing line for other road races such as cyclo-cross events.

Background
Roger de Vlaeminck is still the king of the Paris–Roubaix. Between 1972 and 1977 the Belgian triumphed no less than four times in the 'Hell of the North'. Not for nothing has he been nicknamed 'Mr Paris–Roubaix'. That de Vlaeminck has coped so well with the adversities of the race is down to his penchant for muddy conditions. Because of this, de Vlaeminck, who was born in Eeklo, has also been successful in cyclo-cross, and has even been World Champion twice. In other classics, too, he is among the best of his time and was Eddy Merckx's constant rival. Together with Rik van Looy and the 'Cannibal', he is one of only three riders to win all five Monuments in his racing career.

TOUR PROFILE <<

Race date: Easter Monday

Type: Professional race (semi-classic)/sportive

Start: Gummersbach (Germany)

Finish: Cologne (Germany)

Distance: 201km (suggested route 110km)

Total vertical climb: 1900m (1250m)

Riding time: 8 hours (4 hours)

URL: http://arturtabat.online.de/ruk_neu/

Route: From Gummersbach you go straight across the Bergisches Land towards Cologne; the course runs continually up and down. Because the course overlaps several times it's also possible to shorten it. Beware: the start and finish lines are situated more than 50km apart, so you should make the appropriate logistical arrangements in advance (preferably by rail).

Fitness: The route includes many small climbs, but these are all easy enough to deal with. The only climb you need a certain amount of strength for, to push on up the cobblestones while staying seated, is at Schloss Bensberg. If you don't feel like doing 200km, you can shorten it on the way so that an 8-hour slog quickly becomes a more pleasant 4-hour excursion.

Equipment: Because of the many shorter, but nonetheless steep climbs, such as the incline up to Schloss Bensberg, you should fit a 27-tooth sprocket or a compact chainset. You also have to take the weather forecast into account – even in April the heavens can quickly give you a watery surprise.

The peloton fights its way through the Bergisches Land in the Rund um Köln.

'Round Cologne roll the riders' – so goes the refrain of a song that the singer Joe Fernando and ex-sprinting star Marcel Wüst recorded some years ago in honour of this traditional race in the cathedral city. When a race gets its own song that's not just a sign that the cycling event is being celebrated as an important festival, but also that the competition can look back on a long tradition. This is exactly the case with the Tour of Cologne. First held in 1908, this road race, which goes through the Rhineland capital and the surrounding countryside, is the second oldest German classic still in existence, after the Rund um die Hainleite.

Initially, the Rund um Köln went over bumpy roads and tracks, yet the race also met with great enthusiasm from spectators right from the start, and quickly experienced a rise in the international calendar. In particular the 1920s are regarded as a golden age for the race, and to give but one example, as famous a race rider as the three-time Road World Champion and five-time winner of the Giro d'Italia, Alfredo Bina, rode to victory on the banks of the Rhine.

In the following years the race was run many times as an amateur event, until it was reorganised in the 1990s as a race for the professionals. Still the tradition grew. Professional races in recent years have once again highlighted famous race riders such as Udo Bölts, Frank Vandenbroucke, Erik Dekker, Steffen Wesemann, Jan Ullrich (*see* 'Background', page 59) and Erik Zabel.

Changes in the last few years
Upgraded now to the most important category in the continental race series of the World Association UCI (1.HC), the race has experienced a setback in the wake of the doping incidents during the Tour de France. The race organised in 2008 was greatly reduced

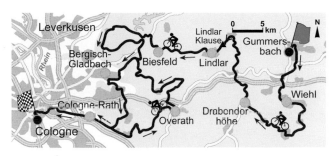

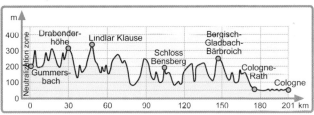

– most of all in the course. Wintry weather meant the centenary edition of the race was cancelled. In 2009 national teams lined up at the start, and since 2010 normal running of the race has resumed. The route has also experienced some changes in the last few years. Until 2008 the race started in Leverkusen; in 2009 it started in Wehnrath; and in 2010 and 2011 the starting line was in Gummersbach, the Oberbergischer district seat.

This is also where you click into your pedals for this particular tour. From the former site of the Steinmüller company you leave the handball town in the direction of Vollmerhausen. (For the professionals the race is neutralised up to this point and finally begins with a flying start in the Vollmerhausener Straße.) After a short downhill slope the climb towards Wiehl (4km) is the first peak in the profile that you have to overcome. A vertical climb of just under 100m over 3km is not much of a problem before you can ride bravely and cheerfully through the historic town centre with its half-timbered houses.

The next stretch of the route leads towards Nümbrecht, taking you first to the village of Gaderoth (13km), then later crossing the Bröl and passing farm meadows and little woods before going straight to Nümbrecht (19km). There follows a little downhill slope past the Homburg paper mill and a little later you cross the Bröl again to finally tackle the climb up to Marienberghausen (25km) with its vertical climb of 90m, along a winding road that even has two hairpin bends.

Once you've got up to the village, a short section of cobblestones by the church awaits the rider. After you've left the last houses behind there's a short dip downhill, then you go up the next slope

with a vertical climb of 80m to the Drabender-höhe (30km).

Gently undulating but descending a little overall, the route goes along a wide main road through a wooded section, interspersed here and there by meadows.

Having headed south all the time to Nümbrecht, the route now goes back north. The next major destination is Engelskirchen, which you reach after 38km. The route there leads through a landscape typical of this region: gently undulating but descending a little overall, it goes along a wide main road through a wooded section, interspersed here and there by meadows. Just before Engelskirchen you go under the A4 motorway, and arrive in the little town soon afterwards over a modern bridge over the River Agger. However, you barely pause there before going north again on the wide (but unfortunately busy) roads until you reach Freilingsdorf. A pleasant alternative would be to turn off onto smaller side roads here – for example, left to Remshagen or right to

Though the racers have no time for looking around, tourists can enjoy the town with its famous cathedral.

Flaberg – where the countryside is that much more attractive.

Though at first the roads are relatively flat to undulating, from Kaiserau (44km) the route begins for the first time to climb for a very long time. The road leads on further uphill through Freilingsdorf (45km) until after a left-hand turn in the village you set off for the Dimsberg – the first mountain test is waiting. In all you'll have coped with a vertical climb of 150m when, through open fields, you approach the top (46km), which is crowned with a little wood. Now you go downhill for some time until you reach Lindlar (48km). Through a small valley with wooded sides you get to the villages of Linde (54km) and Reudenbach (56km). The scenery here is typical of the whole of the Bergisches Land:

alternating dry hills and damp river valleys with wooded sides.

The junction at Odenthal

Further on, the route starts off more steeply, then later slopes more gently upwards in the direction of Kürten, and at Biesfeld (61km) the next climb is waiting. Then comes a downhill slope in a westerly direction. In Bechen (67km), take the first exit from the roundabout in the middle of the village and a little later on turn right to go downhill again into the still wooded outskirts of Odenthal. A descent improved by four hairpin bends brings you down into the green valley of the Dhünn.

You reach Odenthal after 74km and join the route of the all-comers race (see 'Cyclists, check this out!', page 59), which started out from Bayenstraße in Cologne and has covered 20km to get here. Then turn eastwards again and go along the road that takes you uphill back to Bechen (85km). If you leave out the Odenthal–Schliefe section you can save yourself 18km of the tour here.

At Bensberg Palace you get that authentic classic-race feeling – during races, spectators are kept behind barriers to make sure there's enough room for the riders.

In the southern part of the town of Spitze (89km) the first part of the tour is over and you start to do one and a half laps of a 59km long circuit. That'll bring you one step closer to the finish line in Cologne. You can already feel that the traffic is getting much heavier, especially on the outskirts of Bergisch-Gladbach, which you reach after 94km. At the edge of the city the next climb starts with the short but winding ascent to Dombach–Sander–Straße.

You go south again along the Hüttenstraße ('Humble Hovels Road') until you reach Bensberg – as the name suggests, the Rund um Köln's famous climb up to the Palace (101km) is not far now. Left from the Buddestraße the climb begins, and is twice as difficult because of its cobblestones. But in return you get that authentic classic-race feeling – during races, spectators are kept behind barriers to make sure there's enough room for the riders.

Through Forsbach (106km) the road leads further on south until you reach Kleineichen (110km). Here – as the shorter course of the All-comers' Challenge demonstrates – you can turn right immediately to Cologne, and you'll have just 20 more kilometres to go to the

Top sprinter André Greipel poses with the organiser, Artur Tabat.

The climb up to Bensberg Palace is the killer climb of the race.

finish line. But the professional race keeps to the left on towards Rösrath, in the centre of which (119km) you go over undulating areas gently sloping downwards to the A3 motorway. Now you turn again into rural fields and come to Overath (125km) over a steep climb to Lüghauser Straße, and then over a partly wooded hill. Then there's a short but sharp slope down towards the River Agger winding down into the centre of the village before you go left up to the village of Ferrenberg (127km), where the next climb has to be tackled.

You now remain on the high ground and head through the Bergisches Land to Hohkeppel (133km), a village of half-timbered houses and surrounding pasture land characteristic of the region. Seven kilometres further on a gentle downhill slope brings you to Immekeppel (141km), and from here in the direction of Bärbroich your abilities as a mountain rider are tested once

more: you have to face a vertical climb of 150m over 4km.

Riding along high ground, you eventually reach the summit again after 151km – the first circuit is complete. Now the same route as before goes to Bergisch-Gladbach (154km), up the steep climb to the Bensberg Palace (161km) and through Forsbach (165km) to Kleineichen, which you reach after 169km.

Here you turn right and head straight for Cologne. Those who are keen on the middle of the road come into their own on the gently descending course. In the area of the city called Rath, after 174km, you get to ride past the famous 'Schmitzebud' (see 'Cycling and sightseeing', opposite). The first houses of Cologne (which since 2010 has been the fourth-largest city in Germany, with more than a million inhabitants) are quickly reached, and you approach the Rhine through Vingst (179km) and Kalk (181km). The traffic dominates here

Cyclists passing the Kranhäuser (literally 'crane houses') on the banks of the Rhine in Cologne.

and doesn't make cycling very easy, so you should appreciate the beauty of the previous ride through the Bergisches Land.

Over the Severin Bridge (184km) you finally go along the banks of the Rhine to the home straight at the Holzmarkt, and there at the top of Dreikönigen-straße (186km) is the finish line. The professionals now have two more circuits to do around the town centre, which thankfully are on streets closed to traffic. It's generally a good idea to take part in the race that's open to everyone – streets that have been closed off are considerably nicer than pushing and shoving your way through roads blocked with traffic!

Jan Ullrich riding to his comeback victory in 2003.

2011 results

1 Michael Matthews (Australia),
   4 hours 50' 50"
2 Marcel Kittel (Germany), same time
3 Giacomo Nizzolo (Italy), same time

43 Mark McNally (Great Britain), same time

Cyclists, check this out!

During the Easter weekend cyclists bowl around right in the heart of the cathedral city for two days on Sunday and Monday. Both professionals and those riding in the race that's open to all come into their own. And successfully: over 3000 participants lined up for the 2010 edition of the Tour of Cologne Challenge. There were two routes on offer: an easy one over 67km and a demanding one over 126km. For more information see the organisers' website (see 'Tour profile', page 54).

Cycling and sightseeing

Cologne is incidentally not just the home town of one of the most famous cycle races in Germany, but also of one of its best-known cycling clubs: the one at the 'Schmitzebud'. Located at the entrance to Cologne's Königsforst, it's been a meeting place for cyclists of all age groups since the 1920s.

Famous professionals like Karl-Heinz Kunde (who wore the yellow jersey during the Tour de France in the 1960s) and Linus Gerdemann have also put in an appearance here. Since then a real cult has grown up around this club, and in 2010 the organisers of the Rund um Köln included the 'Schmitzebud' in their race with a time trial. Find more information – including a permanent RTF-Route – at www.schmitzebud.com.

Background

In 2003 the public in Cologne witnessed the unbelievable comeback race of Jan Ullrich. Only the year before, the former German cycling idol had made negative headlines because of injury and a positive test for amphetamines. After moving to Team Coast, Ullrich contested his first race for a long time on German soil on the Rhine. About halfway through the race the then-29-year-old attacked for the first time and after a further acceleration 50km from the end he began a solo that eventually ended in a famous victory. Long before the finishing line the former Tour de France winner clenched his fists and did high fives with the spectators. It was the beginning of a successful season: in July he had to admit defeat to Lance Armstrong in the Tour de France by just a hair's breadth.

8 AMSTEL GOLD RACE
On the zigzag course through Limburg

Route: This beautiful route runs through the province of Limburg for a little over 250km. Unlike the Liège–Bastogne–Liège race, which goes along the length of the Ardennes, the 'beer race' wanders about through the foothills from west to east and back again. At the same time it also goes continually uphill and down. Even when the vertical climb is no more than 150m at a time, it adds up to more than 3000m overall. The finishing line in Valkenburg is just over 10km away from Maastricht.

Fitness: The Gold Race is one of the most demanding classics, which only well-trained athletes can manage all in one go. But because the route overlaps several times and leads in a continual zigzag you can shorten it any way you like and put together your own 'beer race' from the map. Those who follow the official tour version (see 'Cyclists, check this out!', page 65) have a choice between six different distances.

Equipment: The roads, most of which are in good condition, don't present any particular challenge to your equipment. You should be fine throughout with a 27-tooth sprocket or a compact crankset.

Cycling and the Netherlands go together. And no wonder – from a statistical point of view every one of the nearly 17 million inhabitants owns a bike. This bond is also clear in the professionals, since time and again the Netherlands has produced great riders: Joop Zoetemelk, Jan Raas, Gerrie Knetemann, Hennie Kuiper or Erik Dekker and Michael Boogerd (see 'Background', page 65), to name just a few. They've also put their stamp on the Tour de France – not for nothing is the L'Alpe d'Huez known as 'Dutch Mountain'. All the Netherlands lacks are its own important races. Even though a professional event takes place there almost every week, they only have one world-format classic: the Amstel Gold Race. The 'beer race', as it's called because of its main sponsor, a Dutch brewery, belongs with the most important one-day races, after the five Monuments. It's thanks to the single-minded work of the organisers since its first edition in 1966 that the Gold Race today holds a permanent place among the 'big' races.

From sprint classic to hill climb classic

Over the years the route has experienced a character change to make it more attractive to riders and spectators. For a long time the Gold Race was a race for sprinters. Victories by riders such as Jan Raas, a sprint star of the 1970s and, with five successes to his name, the Gold Race record holder, and Olaf Ludwig and Erik Zabel in the 1990s, are evidence of this.

Since the turn of the millennium, more and more hills have been incorporated into the profile to make it more difficult for those who are fast at the end to make a final sprint to the champagne. Some 31 climbs are now part of the route. They may not be long, but continually going up and down is extremely tiring. As the demands have changed, we can see from the latest victories by riders like Alexandre Vinokourov, Frank Schleck, Damiano Cunego and

In good weather Limburg is a dream.

Philippe Gilbert that athletes who can push on strongly over such cracking short climbs are successful.

Since enthusiasm for cycling is as great in the Netherlands as in Belgium, crowds of spectators gather at the start in the Market Square in Maastricht. When you're in the large square it's very easy to imagine the fans crowding in, and for once it's not the founding of the EU (which made the town so famous) that's important, but the cycling. When you follow the route you should therefore definitely factor in extra time in addition to the tour to get to know Maastricht with its medieval buildings, parks, bridges and beautiful squares.

The scenery quickly becomes rural, and in good weather, in spite of the coolness of the morning, anticipation increases for the tour that includes practically every climb you can find in the Netherlands.

You go over the Wilhelmina Bridge along the Maas and head north, where the official start takes place at the Beatrix Harbour. Accompanied by the Maas and the Juliana Canal to the left, you keep going north. The scenery quickly becomes rural, and in good weather, in spite of the coolness of the morning, anticipation increases for the tour that includes practically every climb you can find in the Netherlands. After 10km the initial stage is over. You can see on the right-hand side the green Kasteelpark in the town of Elsloo, at the end of which the first of the 31 climbs begins: the Maasberg. It may be short, but it's a foretaste of what's to come in the next 250km: nothing but going up and down through the Dutch province of Limburg.

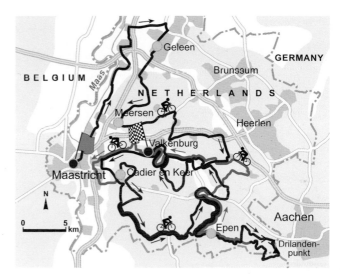

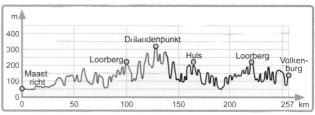

You ride through the little town of Elsloo and its immediate neighbour Stein (14km), past numerous clinker-brick buildings with their immaculately kept front gardens, until just before Sittard you reach the northernmost point of the race and turn south again towards Geleen (23km). Cycle paths marked in red on the right-hand side make it easier to cycle in the still flat countryside.

Little undulations, short hills

As you leave Beek (29km) the next short hill, the Adsteeg, is waiting. However, people who live in the Alps will consider it to be a hillock, at most. The road is well tarmacked and wide.

The countryside is now more open. It goes gently downhill past green

The peloton on the first climb of the Cauberg.

The previous ride to Valkenburg has incidentally already shown why it's really great to ride the Gold Race: the continually zigzagging route and the repeated overlapping sections allow you to create a circuit of any length you like.

Going over the Cauberg for the first time

Now the route leads between fields through Valkenburg, where with the Sibbergrubbe (66km) and the Cauberg (71km) the next two climbs are waiting. The first climb – two mostly tree-lined kilometres long, with a 90m vertical climb – is absolutely exhausting, a fact which becomes noticeable on the Cauberg, which follows immediately. This climb is very steep in the middle, with a gradient of 12 per cent, but basically shorter. However, you'll have to get used to both climbs because they both occur again later on in the profile of the race.

meadows and fields and the occasional tree. In Oensel (33km) you turn right past Maastricht Airport to the north and so on to Meerssen (36km). Here the third climb, the Lange Raarberg, is waiting. With a vertical climb of 60m and an average gradient of 5 per cent, this is an uphill section to be taken seriously.

Having reached the top, you get a wonderful view of the surrounding villages nestling in the valleys of the foothills of the Ardennes.

It continues to be rural for a little longer. The road runs past more fields along avenues past Raar (39km) and Arentsgenhout (44km) in the direction of Valkenburg. However, before you reach the town – which will later take on greater significance – turn sharp left towards Kunrade (54km), and a few metres after leaving the village you're upon the Bergseweg. With a vertical climb of 90m over 2.7km, it's the hardest climb so far. Having reached the top, you get a wonderful view of the surrounding villages nestling in the valleys of the foothills of the Ardennes.

Without realising it you've got close to Maastricht again. You go southwards through its suburbs and soon make your way into the fields of countryside again. This region, also known as Mergelland, is incidentally not just the venue for the 'beer race': other events are also held in the region, such as the De Hel Van Het Mergelland – which is open to tourists as well as to professionals.

From now on there's no let-up and the hills come more or less in a steady stream.

If the last few kilometres have been relatively relaxed, it now gets more hilly again. The Wolfsberg, a two-stage climb, marks the start of this. From now on there's no let-up and the hills come more or less in a steady stream. In idyllic

Slenaken (96km) the climb to the Loorberg starts: curving to the right, the road hugs the wooded slope and you then ride on the spine of of this towards Gulpen. But before you start to go down the Gulpenberg you turn right towards Partij (105km). There is a feeding station here for the professionals.

Very soon you come to hill number nine: the Schweibergerweg behind Mechelen (108km) climbs for 3km with a vertical climb of a whole 120m. You go uphill mostly through open country past a couple of isolated houses. The next downhill slope over the Eperheide leads to the Camering, which you reach after 115km.

Now you go uphill along a narrow road for 4km. The gradient may not be in double figures, but the length makes the Camering demanding. Once you get there, the route leads north again to Vijlen (121km), where you take a detour to the right and finally reach the most southerly corner of the Netherlands.

Away game in Belgium

The Drielandenpunt is situated – as its name suggests – exactly at the three corners of the Netherlands, Belgium and Germany. At 321m above sea level it's also the highest point of the race. The route follows a narrow path through the woods in a series of bends for 3km and with a vertical climb of almost 150m to the summit. Then follows a short excursion onto Belgian soil, which ends with a gentle climb to Gemmenich (131km). A short section through open country finally ends with the climb to Vijlenerbos (134km). This is steepest of all at the end, where for a short time the gradient even reaches double figures.

You ride on now through the wood for a few kilometres until you reach the

Camering again, which you've only just conquered, and you come down the same route you went up, but in the opposite direction. The same is true of the Eperheide (144km). The zigzag course now takes a right-hand turn-off towards the north to the Gulpenberg (152km) – which you missed out a little while back – with its narrow but tarmacked farm track. This leads in a long drawn-out left-hand curve upwards until you ride over several hairpin bends down to the village. Near neighbouring Wittem (155km) you finally begin the van Plettenbergweg climb, a broad slope through fields which leads to Eys (157km).

Only after you've overcome the short but steep Vrakelberg climb at the 168km mark can you relax a little.

The first climb over the Eyserbosweg appears. The narrow road above the village leads through a wood to Eyserheide. Though the Eyserbosweg, here in the middle of the race, initially has the job of sorting out the riders, the

The Belgian Philippe Gilbert was able to secure victory in 2010.

Michael Boogerd regularly put his stamp on the 'beer race' at the turn of the millennium.

vertical climb is only 60m, riding really starts to hurt.

Every corner enjoyed to the full

You head for Maastricht (190km) again and from there to Cadier en Keer (193km), where the Bemelerberg marks the beginning of the 23rd climb. Along the edge of the wood a relatively easy climb goes gently uphill. Noorbeek (214km), followed by Wolfsberg (215km) and Loorberg (221km), are already known to you, as is the road to Wittem, which you reach after 233km. You notice that the route planners were very thorough, and through their planning every corner of Limburg is explored.

After 235km The Kruisberg represents a new development. This time on the way to Eys (236km) you leave out the van Plettenbergweg climb and ride to Wahlwiller (234km) on a narrow road. Very steep – in places more than a 10 per cent gradient – it winds its way upwards, which is real torture. For the professionals the hard section starts now.

And it continues on the Eyserbosweg (237km). Zigzagging curves, ascents and descents come one after the other the whole time, and you get used to expecting another nasty surprise around every corner in the form of a vertical climb. And that's just what happens when you've left the wood at Eyserheide and ridden through Elkenrade (239km): the Fromberg is the 29th climb. Perhaps you shouldn't count the climbs when you're riding – this can have a demoralising effect, especially on the first half of the tour.

You really don't need to look at the sign at the side of the road to know that the gradient you have to tackle here is 22 per cent.

second time around it plays a decisive role: from the ramps with their gradient of well over 10 per cent to the finish line it is only 20km.

Once you reach the summit you come to Simpelveld (162km). Here in front of you stands the steep St Remigiusstraat, with a vertical climb of 80m. And only after you've overcome the short but steep Vrakelberg climb at the 168km mark can you relax a little. At least the next 9km go gently downhill.

Now you push on again up the familiar section of the route in the direction of Valkenburg (176km), where the Sibbergrubbe (177km) and Cauberg (182km) have to be climbed again. And, even though it seems like it, no, the climbs haven't become longer. It's increasing exhaustion making itself known – you've been on the road now for more than 7 hours. There the added climb to the Geulhemmerweg offers no let-up compared with the precious road straight after you left Valkenburg – quite the opposite. Even though the

The narrow descent to Schin op Geul (244km) gives you only a short time to recover then a real wall rises up in front of you, perhaps the hardest of the whole Gold Race: the Keutenberg. You really don't need to look at the sign at the side of the road to know that the gradient is 22 per cent. Every step of the way is harder and you'll curse every single per cent. One motivation should be that from this point you only have another 12km to go to the finishing line in Valkenburg.

Travelling through several small villages on narrow country roads, you get nearer to the final section. After 254km you'll finally be in Valkenburg. It goes quickly: 2km before the finishing line the ride up the Cauberg hill begins, then the gradient slowly increases. Just where the red devil's cloth to signal another lap would normally be hanging, it's not there: this is the third time that you've climbed this hill. The steep middle section really takes some strength, then the road becomes flatter. The invisible finish line is 100m after the top of the hill. At this point it may be you're not able to do Philippe Gilbert's famous 2010 burst of speed – but you can celebrate just the same. You've still finished one of the most difficult classics!

2011 results

1 Philippe Gilbert (Belgium), 6 hours 30' 44"
2 Joaquin Rodriguez (Spain), + 0' 02"
3 Simon Gerrans (Australia), + 0' 04"
...
57 Steve Cummings (Great Britain), 6 hours, 33' 30"

Cyclists, check this out!

The day before the Amstel Gold Race for the professionals, a version for sportive cyclists takes place. The organisers offer no fewer than six distances: 65, 100, 125, 150, 200 and 250km. On each circuit through the province of Limburg not only is your own personal time recorded on a chip, but also photos of the competitors are available to purchase. For further information on the race click on the 'Tour Version' tab at www.amstelgoldrace.nl.

Cycling and sightseeing

Valkenburg was the home town of Jan van Hout, a Dutch cyclist who was successful (particularly on the roads) before the Second World War. Among other things, he set a new world hour record. But van Hout deserves our attention not just as an athlete, but also as a committed anti-fascist who during the German occupation of the Netherlands was a member of the Resistance. A few months before the end of the war, however, he was captured and sent to Neuengamme concentration camp, where he eventually died. On 15 May 2006 a monument to his memory was unveiled on the Cauberg in Valkenburg.

Background

Even though in the course of his career Michael Boogerd was known as 'the perennial second place man', he undoubtedly belonged among the most successful riders at the turn of the millennium. In this period he regularly put his stamp on the Amstel Gold Race. The Dutchman, born in the Hague in 1972, was considered at the beginning of his career to be a future Tour de France winner. And with fifth place overall in the 1998 edition he appeared to be on his way to fulfilling this promise. Though from then on 'Boogie' certainly developed into one of the very best professionals in the peloton, he lacked what might be called the qualities of a winner. Successes such as that of the 1999 Gold Race remained a one-off, and he achieved second place or a place in the Top 10 much more often. Boogerd stood on the podium of the 'beer race' a whole six times more – he was second all three years from 2003 until 2005. In the equally demanding Liège–Bastogne–Liège race he climbed onto the podium four times – without once winning the race. In the whole of his career he only won two stages in the Tour de France.

9 LA FLÈCHE WALLONNE
The 'Walloon Arrow'

TOUR PROFILE <<

Race date: Mid-April

Type: Professional race (semi-classic)

Start: Charleroi (Belgium)

Finish: Huy (Belgium)

Distance: 198km (suggested route 134km)

Total vertical climb: 3200m (2200m)

Riding time: 8 hours (5 hours)

URL: www.letour.fr/indexFWH_fr.html

Route: After a relatively unspectacular start the climb up the Mur de Huy (Wall of Huy) and the hilly second half make up for all the effort. It's advisable to start the tour in Huy; that way you'll shorten the route to a comfortable 134km and you won't have the logistical problem caused by the start and finishing lines being so far apart.

Fitness: Although at 198km the Arrow isn't the longest of the classics, it's one of the more difficult ones because of its numerous climbs and total vertical climb. You should also be comfortable with hill climbs and be in peak condition.

Equipment: Since you have to be ready for a maximum gradient of up to 20 per cent on the Mur de Huy, you should choose a set-up that can cope with this: a 29-tooth sprocket or a compact crank are obligatory – but it goes without saying that you'll be pushing the bike on the steepest section.

The mid-week Walloon Arrow, as the Flèche is called in English, is one of the most important spring classics in cycling and, along with the Amstel Gold Race (which takes place the Sunday before) and the Liège–Bastogne–Liège (which is held on the Sunday after), it is part of 'Ardennes Week'. The name 'Ardennes' comes from 'Arduenna', the Celtic word for highland, but in comparison with the passes through the Alps these hills aren't really mountains. But anyone who now thinks that riding here should be easy is mistaken. Because just as in Flanders it's the apparently innumerable short climbs one after the other that finish you off. Not for nothing is the Arrow one of the few classics in which genuine mountain specialists have a chance of winning.

A quick look through the list of winners makes this clear: the Australian Cadel Evans, Kim Kirchen from Luxembourg and the Spaniard Alejandro Valverde are examples of riders who have put their stamp on the race recently, all of them riders who have also been involved at least once in the difficult mountain stages of the Tour de France. The Italian Francesco Casagrande in particular was counted among the strongest mountain climbers in the 1990s, and also a certain Lance Armstrong was included in the list of winners. Other well-known names that crop up are Laurent Fignon, Bernard Hinault, Raymond Poulidor, Ferdy Kübler, Fausto Coppi and – last but not least – Eddy Merckx, who with three wins is one of the record holders of the race.

World cycling in Wallonia

The Arrow starts in Charleroi, a town with a cycling history. It's not just associated with the Walloon Arrow, it's also a part of the GP de

On the narrow roads of the Ardennes the field can be seen stretching out to its full length.

On the Walloon Arrow it's straight down to business, particularly in the second part.

Wallonie, a major professional race which takes place in autumn. It has also hosted the Tour de France and once even the Giro d'Italia, which finished a stage here in 2006.

But back to the Arrow: after the start the route runs relatively quickly towards Osten, and after 70km the race has its proper start in the Ardennes with the first climb of the famous Mur de Huy. The Wall is also the hill that makes the event so famous and gives it its character – one of those climbs that every cyclist should have under his wheels once in his lifetime. But more about that later.

In order to manage a distance of just under 200km reasonably you should set out early in the morning. However, you'll hardly be able to avoid the traffic chaos in Charleroi. With more than 200,000 inhabitants the town is the biggest municipality in the Walloon region of Belgium and the third biggest in the country overall – so proportionally there's a lot of traffic on the streets. You leave the town in the direction of Fleurus and ride further on to Onoz. Now the traffic decreases noticeably. It's early in the day, the sun is shining in your face and you can enjoy the task in front of you.

A plateau with enormous fields stretching as far as the eye can see now opens up in front of the rider.

Just before Onoz there's a short curving downhill slope into a wood, but because of the wide roads and the good quality of their surface this presents no problem. The road soon meanders through a little valley: left and right of the road skirts a little wood before it climbs gently up with a gradient of roughly 2–5 per cent and you reach Spy (20km). Now for a short time there's

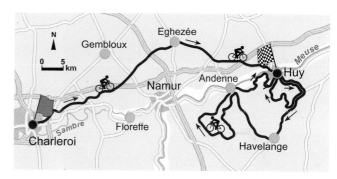

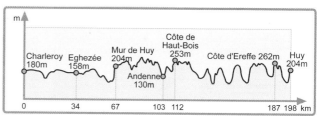

more traffic. You cross the A15 motorway by means of an underpass and follow the well-signposted road in the direction of Eghezée. Saint-Denis (26km) is a picturesque and very green village. Many trees surround the typical little houses. As you ride further on a plateau with enormous fields stretching as far as the eye can see now opens up in front of the rider. The road leads largely straight on.

Shortly before Eghezée (34km) the traffic increases again. But you can escape from it on the cycle path that starts here, before turning right in the town towards Fernelmont with its castle of the same name built in the 13th century. You go through Forville (45km) and Bierwart (48km), and follow the signposts in the direction of Huy. The area is still very rural and the flat terrain proves to be ideal for bowling along. Just before Huy there's an easy downhill slope, which time-trial specialists will be especially pleased about. With a gradient of 2 or 3 per cent in places, the road will tempt you to really push on.

The leading group on the climb up to Huy.

The riders on the famous Mur de Huy.

Welcome to the Ardennes!

Once you reach Wanze (60km) it quickly becomes clear that the route up to now was just a warm-up. It may be going gently downhill now, but in front of you the Ardennes are looming up. It's hilly – that's no secret. But before you get there you can enjoy the slope downhill into the valley where the Meuse meanders towards the sea. Over a suspension bridge – incidentally with separate cycle lanes – and two roundabouts, you approach Huy (63km) on the right bank of the river. Just as you're passing the welcome sign a glance at the old stone fortress dating from the early 19th century will give you a sense of the romantic charm of the area.

You should stop in Huy in any case. After all the town is the hub of the Flèche Wallonne: you go through it three whole times during the race. Refreshment in one of the narrow cobbled streets or at the Li Bassinia fountain in the town centre is a must. The market is also worth a visit, as is the whole town. You can, and in fact you should, consider starting the Flèche Wallonne here – that way you also avoid the logistical problem of the start and finish lines being so far away from each other.

You quickly get an inkling of why seasoned professionals like Cadel Evans can only keep riding by standing up out of the saddle and pedalling squares.

Suitably refreshed, you can set off eastwards from the town centre to the hill that is certainly one of those most steeped in cycling history: the Mur de Huy. At a length of 1.3km and with an average gradient of 9.3 per cent this climb certainly doesn't look all that bad at first glance – but with a maximum of over 20 per cent it will almost make you despair as you ride up it. There's a very good reason why this climb is closed to cars. In all, riders on the Flèche Wallonne have to contend with this three times, and the first time it's already incredibly hard because of the steepness. You quickly get an inkling of why seasoned professionals like Cadel Evans can only keep riding by standing up out of the saddle and pedalling squares. All the riders say that the crowds of spectators shouting encouragement here just cannot believe that they've actually managed to cope with the Wall. But now you're riding it alone and have to do it without this support – you'll be so much happier once you've got this section of the route behind you.

Once you've dealt with the first of the three climbs of the Mur, two circuits of Huy follow – a long one and a short one. And there's only one adjective to adequately describe the remaining route: hilly, for the cols and côtes that are typical of the region start here. But once you leave Huy it'll be a little flatter for a short time. Turn right after Pont de Bonne (79km) and on to Pailhe, where the next climb follows with the short Côte de Pailhe.

Hills, hills, hills

You then leave the little village of Evelette lying on your right and set a course for Andenne (103km). Past Evelette there follows a long downhill slope, and it may briefly occur to you that where it goes downhill it'll also soon start going uphill again. And indeed the hills follow just around the next corner. So instead of enjoying the peace and quiet of the beautiful little towns along the Meuse you turn sharp left in the direction of Sainte-Begge. The Côte de Peu d'Eau (106km) and the Côte de Haut Bois are the next two Ardennes

The Spaniard Alberto Contador (in front) and Igor Anton battle it out on the 'Mur'.

Cadel Evans (Australia) wins the 2010 race.

the N942 and wind your way round two further bends towards Faulx-des-Tombes. From here on you keep to the N941 and go past Goyet (131km) to Groynne (135km), where the next climb presents itself with the Côte de Groynne. But this one's simple too, and you can easily cope with the vertical climb of 160m. The gradient keeps to mid-single figures, only moving into double figures for a short time at the end.

After a short connecting downhill slope comes the Côte de Bousalle. Although it's a little longer, it's not as steep as the ones before.

The next downhill slope finally leads you back to the banks of the Meuse and you also reach the centre of Andenne, which you didn't do before. But the peace and quiet doesn't last long: with the Côte de Bohisseau you go straight past the last houses and onto the next climb. The 1.3km-long climb is steeper than its predecessor and you now slowly begin to feel the distance you've covered so far. But it's not over yet: the Côte de Bousalle comes after a short connecting downhill slope. Although it's a little longer, it's not as steep as its predecessor.

hills you have to deal with. But both of them prove to be very moderate. The first stands before you with a length of 2.7km and an average gradient of 4 per cent, and the latter with a length of 1.6km and an average of 4.8 per cent.

Next, continue on in the direction of Gesves. You ride past little woods and meadows used for agriculture over narrow little roads. It's continually undulating there until you hit the N946, where you keep to the right towards Gesves (121km), which you reach after another right-hand turn at the next crossroads onto the N942. You stay on

There follows a downhill slope enlivened with a sharp bend, after which you turn back to the beautiful banks of the Meuse. That's the end of the first circuit, and with it Huy is no longer that far away. But before you reach the town another climb is waiting with the 2.3km-long Côte d'Ahin. But you quickly deal with the relatively even 150m vertical climb, so that after a short series of hairpin bends downhill you can gather your strength on the relatively flat section that follows. This is an absolute necessity, since the second crossing of the Mur is coming up.

Up the Wall a second time

Now you have 165km in your legs and already the first third of the Wall is hurting. After you've turned right again it'll be even worse. The accumulated vertical climb on the first circuit has already driven lactic acid into your muscles. But somehow or other you sweat it out to the top – now you've got 80 per cent of the route behind you and so you can motivate yourself a little. Once you've got up to the Wall again there's only 30km to go to the finish line. Now it's time for the smaller circuit.

You leave Huy along the same route as on the first circuit, but at the crossroads at Pont-de-Bonne (181km) turn right rather than going straight on. Near Le Hoyoux you turn left in the direction of Ereffe where the next climb follows with the Côte d'Ereffe. You have to contend with another vertical climb of 150m along the

narrow street, and then you'll be 13km from the finish line. This is the last incline before the final climb of the Wall. You pass through Marchin (189km) with its typical Gothic church and arrive at another winding stretch over the N641, a narrow little Ardennes road which brings you to Huy – again.

The Wall follows one last time. That damn Wall. You can't think of it any other way. You keep staring at the clock, counting down the number of metres to go to the summit. You can mitigate the effects of the 23 per cent gradient a little by weaving from side to side. Just another 500m, the last bend. This is where in 2010 first Andreas Klöden and then the Spaniard Igor Anton suffered for their earlier burst of speed. Cadel Evans caught up, passed them and secured victory. The last 100m, and then you've done it: the Flèche Wallonne is over!

2011 results

1 Philippe Gilbert (Belgium), 4 hours 54' 57"
2 Joaquin Rodriguez (Spain), + 0' 03"
3 Samuel Sanchez Gonzalez (Spain), + 0' 05"

Cyclists, check this out!

Although there's not a real Arrow for tourism cyclists, there is the Flèche de Wallonie, a very similar event, which uses many of the same parts of the course. The start and finishing lines are in Spa. Three routes are on offer: 130, 166 and 220km. For information visit www.cyclo-spa.be.

Cycling and sightseeing

The famous landmark of the Flèche Wallonne is and always will be the Mur de Huy. Tourists can also visit this steep hill on foot. For convenience there's even a cable railway that runs to the top of it, taking you straight to the church of Notre Dame de la Sarte at the summit. But as a cyclist you should do without this easy option of the cable railway – there's only one way to do it: head down,

grit your teeth and ride to the top on your bike!

Background

The spectators experienced a memorable Flèche Wallonne race in 1994: in that season the outstanding Gewiss-Ballan team had it all their own way and dominated the field. A good 70km before the finish the Italians Giorgio Furlan and Moreno Argentin, and the Russian Evgeni Berzin, who were all wearing Gewiss jerseys, broke away from the field. Nobody was able to follow the three of them, who then didn't leave the competition any chance at all and extended their lead even further. At the finishing line in Huy, Argentin won in the end over Furlan and Berzin – a sequence that was determined by team order. The team doctor at the time was incidentally a certain Dr Michele Ferrari – because of their dominance, it's hardly surprising that while the team existed they had to fight accusations of doping.

TOUR PROFILE <<

Race date: Mid-April

Type: Professional race (Monument)

Start: Liège (Belgium)

Finish: Ans (Belgium)

Distance: 258km

Total vertical climb: 3600m

Riding time: 11 hours

URL: www.letour.fr/indexLBL_us.html

Route: After the start in Liège you travel the length of the Ardennes from north to south and back again. Because of this the course, surrounded by numerous woods, proves to be ideal for discovering the beauty of the region. But watch out: there's not much time for relaxation …

Fitness: Although there are not any long climbs in the profile of this race, it's a match – when measured in terms of the total vertical climb – for any of the high mountain stages. This vertical climb is 3600m – it's no surprise that those who are known as climbing specialists are often included in the list of winners as well as the classics specialists. That's the result of the long distance of 258km: you need tremendous endurance to be able to complete the course in one day. An overnight stay – for example, in Houffalize after 114km – is an ideal solution.

Equipment: Since the roads are generally in very good condition, you only have to worry about the set-up. You should be fine with a 27-tooth sprocket. And even in the sunshine you should pack a waterproof jacket – the weather in the Ardennes can change unbelievably quickly!

Not for nothing does the Liège–Bastogne–Liège race carry the nickname 'La Doyenne', for the race has been run through the Belgian Ardennes since 1892 – so it belongs to those cycling events in general which are the richest in tradition. It's true that Paris–Brest–Paris and Bordeaux–Paris are both older competitions – but since these are no longer part of the professional calendar, the LBL is justifiably 'the oldest' of its kind.

However, this classic can also be called 'the toughest'. It's distinguishing feature is that it has a hard route: the organisers send the riders over an extreme distance of 258km and also put numerous cols and côtes, which are typical of the region, in the way. Although they don't look as difficult individually as the big Alpine passes, together they gradually suck the strength from your legs. The total vertical climb of 3600m on this circuit speaks for itself. And on top of that there's the treacherous weather in the Ardennes that can very quickly give you a nasty surprise.

Foggy mists and a liking for woods

In the course of the history of the race the riders have also had to contend with snow – even though the middle of April is relatively late in the year to hold an early classic. For example, in 1980 it was so cold that only 21 professionals reached the finishing line (*see* 'Background', page 77). Bernard Hinault was the winner of that memorable race; it was the first of his two wins of the LBL. However, the holder of the record number of wins is someone else: Eddy Merckx. He won five times between 1969 and 1975, mostly in the role for which the 'Cannibal' is best remembered – as a solo rider with a big lead on the field.

In the recent past Moreno Argentin (four wins between 1985 and 1991), Michele Bartoli, Paolo Bettini, Alejandro Valverde and Alexandre Vinokourov have distinguished themselves. So far only

La Redoute is the best-known climb of the LBL.

two Germans have won: Hermann Buse before the Second World War (1930) and the 'blond angel', Didi Thurau in 1979.

Like the Flèche Wallonne, the Liège–Bastogne–Liège makes its way through the Belgian part of the Ardennes. As a result it's the Ardennes once again that give the route their typical atmosphere: thick fogs which rise up over the woods in the early mornings and whose mists produce an almost depressive general mood, and at the same time the unmistakeable beauty of the deep still woods which spread themselves like a blanket over the characteristic landscape.

Passing along several main roads you then come to Sougné-Remouchamps, which acts as a hub in the race.

This romantic aspect of the Ardennes isn't much in evidence in Liège when you click into your pedals in the Place Saint-Lambertin. You leave the town in a southerly direction in heavy traffic. There are two reasons to refrain from a relaxed cruising pace here and immediately step on the gas instead: first, to get away from the busy town; and second, because it's still cold in the early morning. You soon get to the southern part of the town of Embourg and immediately reach the suburbs of Beaufays (4km), where you've already left the hectic rush of the town behind to a large extent. You go over towards Sougné-Remouchamps (20km), which acts as a hub in the race: you cross the small stone bridge over the Amel both going and coming back.

Once you've crossed the river you come to the age-old forest of the Ardennes. Aywaille (22km) is a typical little town in the Ardennes with a

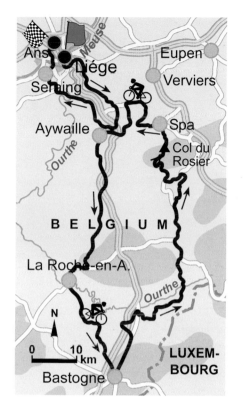

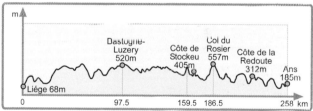

wonderful historic town centre. As you leave it the route starts to climb for a kilometre, and you leave the valley of the Amel. The roads runs further south to Harze (27km) and soon afterwards along an undulating section of the route you reach the southern Belgium province of Luxembourg. The next places you come to are Oster (48km) and Lamormenil (52km), before you turn left near Dochamps (55km) towards Samree (58km). After a right-hand turn in the town centre there's a

The little town was hard fought over in the Second World War as an important junction and later played a big part in the Ardennes offensive. The Mardasson Memorial still bears witness to that today. For the Liège–Bastogne–Liège the real starting signal for the race is given here: although in the first part the riders from the local teams try to hog the limelight, the return leg now belongs to the favourites, whose teams now try to reduce the lead of the breakaway groups little by little.

Because of the 144km still remaining, you should consider looking for accommodation in Houffalize.

In the darkness of the Ardennes forest a creepy atmosphere prevails.

longer downhill slope, which leads down to the valley towards La-Roche-en-Ardenne. Those interested in culture should take a look at the ruins of the castle. The Baraque de Fraiture, the highest peak of the Ardennes at 652m, is also close by.

Half-time in Bastogne

The clock shows 66km. Up to now the road's been undulating through a landscape of woods and meadows, but now you come to the first real hill on the programme. Once you've crossed the Ourthe as it meanders through the valley you climb a 5 per cent incline for almost 3km to the Côte de la Roche-en-Ardenne. It's the only appreciable climb on the way to Bastogne, which is not far off now. Past Ortho (74km) the route brings you Bertogne (83km). Shortly before you reach the town a small downhill slope takes you across the Ourthe and then you have to contend with an equally small uphill slope on the other side of the valley. In Bertogne you go straight over the big roundabout to Longchamps (87km), Savy (92km) and finally Bastogne. You've reached the halfway point of the race – time for something to eat and drink.

You leave Bastogne, which incidentally is also the birthplace of the Belgian professional cyclist Maxime Monfort, and after a sharp left-hand turn at the crossroads head immediately north again. Straight away the N30 runs parallel to the motorway through fields, some of which are built on and some of which are used for pasture. You go past Foy (99km), Noville (103km) and Mabompré (108km) and finally reach Houffalize after 114km. This idyllic village of 5000 souls lying on the banks of the Ourthe is well known to insiders as the venue for the World Cup mountain bike race of the same name. Because of the 144km still remaining, you should consider looking for accommodation in Houffalize. But you should have reserved it well in advance – places to sleep are extremely few and far between.

The route then leads on from the town to the second hard climb: the Côte de Saint Roch is only a kilometre long, but devilishly steep. On a gradient of up to 12 per cent you'll arrive on the main road round a long drawn-out left- and right-hand bend. After that you turn left towards Vissoule (119km) and ride along eastwards over narrow little streets. After a kilometre you turn left again near Tavigny and then continue on your way in a northerly direction.

Solitude on the way to the north

The next waypoints are Cetturu (124km), Steinbach (129km) and Curtil (139km). The road there winds in a series of bends and you cross the Salm, a tributary of the Amel, which you will follow now for some time. From now on you'll also be accompanied by the railway line, which you have to cross repeatedly. Those three villages are like little islands of civilisation. There's not much going on here. There isn't even any traffic – most of it is on the motorway a little way away.

In Salmchateau (146km) you go past the castle of the same name and finally dip into a wooded valley that ends 2km later in Vielsalm, the next large village. You ride further northwards past the lake in the town centre; the landscape remains hilly. After Grand-Halleux (155km) it gets really serious: you're only 100km from the finishing line, but along this stretch, as well as numerous small climbs that are part of the landscape, there are also a total of eight hard climbs waiting for you.

The little side street leads up an incline of seven per cent, before it goes over an equally narrow little street further on to Stavelot.

The climb up to Wanne – also known as the Côte de Wanne – is a foretaste of what's to come. The little side street leads up an incline of 7 per cent, before it goes over an equally narrow little street

further on to Stavelot, which you reach after 164km. This little town is one of the oldest places in Belgium, with a history stretching back as far as AD 648. A downhill slope runs into the town and you have to be careful not to miss the sharp right-hand turn onto the Côte de Stockeu, the next climb.

And there it is: the first ramp with a gradient of 13 per cent right there in the town. With the hillside on the left, and the houses of Stavelot on the right you fight your way to the top. The road soon becomes rougher and narrower; there's just room for a car. The gradient now increases to 17 per cent, before you leave the wood and climb past meadows on a gradient that is now only 8 per cent. After a little over a kilometre the Eddy Merckx Memorial on the right-hand side finally signals the end of the climb (166km). Once you've got to the top you turn left again down into the valley beyond Stavelot (167km). Incidentally, the Formula 1 race track Spa-Francorchamps isn't far away. Now you ride west towards Trois-Ponts, where you begin the longest climb of the race over La Gleize (177km).

Alexandre Vinokourov triumphed twice in 2005 and 2010.

The Highroad team training on the 'Redoute' in 2008.

The highest point of the race

At 6.4km the Col du Rosier is long by Belgian standards, with a vertical climb of 262m over an average gradient of 4 per cent. At 557m above sea level – there is actually a plaque to confirm this – the pass also represents the highest point of the race. Round a few more bends (including two hairpins) and you arrive at the centre of the little town of Cour. It's worth taking a look at the surrounding hills of the Ardennes before you plunge into the wood again. Once you've reached the top the road goes straight to Spa, which you reach after 191km.

The town, which is best known for its mineral springs and therefore also as a spa town, positively invites you to pause – perhaps to take the waters as well – before you leave it and go west again to climb the Col du Maquisard. This is not quite so long at 2.8km and also not so steep. The road runs past a few houses up along a narrow right-hand hairpin bend (198km) before going down after La Reid into the valley of the River Hoëgne to Theux (205km).

But you only skirt round the self-styled Walloon 'crayfish capital' and arrive at the seventh mountain climb, Mont Theux. The climb rises in height by 160m over 3km. It starts with a gradient of up to 10 per cent, then levels out in the middle before rising sharply again at the end.

The Côte de la Redoute, the most famous climb of the LBL, is waiting.

The next few kilometres of the road now stretch out from the summit, before you reach Sougné-Remouchamps after 210km, the place you've passed already on your way out to Bastogne. Riding through it this time is far more important: the Côte de la Redoute, the most famous climb of the LBL, is waiting. The reason is that the outcome of the race is often decided here, primarily because attacks are the order of the day in the middle stretch of the 2km mountain, which has a gradient of up to 21 per cent.

'La Redoute' is soon signposted and is not to be missed: after you've left it, the whole road is decorated and you can easily imagine what happens here on race day. In the middle you reach a maximum incline of 21 per cent – enough time to read the individual signs. The sign with the name of the pass, which is a thing seldom seen in the Ardennes, isn't at the summit of this climb, but in a slab of granite near the end of the first third of the climb on the right-hand side. The greatest effort is over now and you come to a little tarmacked square at a height of 294m. You only have to struggle a little further straight on and you've beaten the Redoute.

After that you follow the Rue de Warnoumont to the right and go past Florzé to reach Sprimont and the côte of the same name. But that's a doddle compared with the Redoute and you get through that in a couple of shakes of a lamb's tail.

Now the road goes down a winding slope to Esneux (235km), where you find not just the biggest sequoia tree in Belgium, but also the climb to the Côte de la Roche aux Faucons (238km) shortly after crossing the Ourthe. The first half of the 10 per cent hammer lies nearby in the town, the second follows after a right-hand bend in the forest. After that the road goes along the summit for a short time until the downhill slope to Serraing (245km) finally follows. It's not much further now to the finishing line, for you've already reached the outskirts of Liège.

There are just two more climbs in the remaining 13km – and they really hurt. After you've crossed the Meuse and reached the Tilleur district of the town (251km) you come to the penultimate

killer climb, the Côte de Saint-Nicolas. The professionals arrive in the Place Ferrer via the Rue Chiff d'Or in the direction of the famous and distinctive completely red Standard Liège football stadium. They continue down the Rue Piron and arrive in the centre of Liège by way of the Rue des Grands Champs.

Until 1991 the race ended in the town centre. From 1992 the finishing line was moved to the north-western suburb of Ans so that for the last few kilometres riders have to deal not only with the traffic in the town centre, but also with one final climb there. Along broad streets the route climbs a gradient which at times is in double figures before you finally reach the top of the hill and the wide home stretch on the Rue Jean-Jaurès. A long tour now lies behind you – but 'La Doyenne' (the oldest – and perhaps also the hardest) has been beaten!

2011 results
1 Philippe Gilbert (Belgium), 6 hours 13' 18"
2 Frank Schleck (Luxembourg), same time
3 Andy Schleck (Luxembourg), same time
...
37 Steve Cummings (Great Britain), 6 hours 15' 49"

Cyclists, check this out!
There are two events open to all-comers that come very close to this race: one is the Liège–Bastenaken–Liège organised by the Dutch promoter Le Champion, and the other is the Tilff–Bastogne–Tilff. The first is run over most of the original course and also uses quieter roads. Three routes of 130, 170 and 245km appeal to all levels of performance. The second race starts a little to the south of Liège in Tilff and also offers three tours of 78, 136 and 244km, over a similar course. Find more information at www.lbl-lechampion.nl and http://sport.be.msn.com/cycling/tilffbastognetilff/.

Cycling and sightseeing
Eddy Merckx, who won the Doyenne a record number of times, accompanies you long after the end of his career on the edge of the course – on the Côte de Stockeu, that is. A monument was erected at its highest point to that most successful professional rider of all time.

Background
In the course of more than 100 years of history the LBL gave rise to numerous anecdotes and heroic tales. The year 1980 in particular stays in the memory. On 20 April that year it snowed right at the start of the race and it was so cold that after 2 hours two-thirds of the riders had already given up. At the front in the leading group came the high point of the competition for Bernard Hinault. He shook off his rivals 80km before the finish and produced an incomparable solo ride. In the end he won, with an unbelievable lead of 8 minutes, a race which might well have been called the 'Snow-Bastogne Snow'.

TOUR PROFILE <<

Race date: 1 May

Type: Professional race (semi-classic)/sportive

Start: Eschborn (Germany)

Finish: Frankfurt (Germany)

Distance: 202km (suggested route: 111km)

Total vertical climb: 1700m (1150m)

Riding time: 8 hours (4 hours)

URL: www.eschborn-frankfurt.de

Route: A varied course, which runs from the municipal districts of Eschborn and Frankfurt into the mountainous forest of Taunus. Several climbs make sure that you occasionally feel like you're high up in the mountains. In particular the short but steep Mammolshainer Berg (over 20 per cent) represents a challenge. While the professionals complete two circuits through the Taunus, in this description the additional circuit and the section through the busy streets of the municipal districts are omitted. Anyone who wants to experience the feeling of being a professional without the stress of the traffic is strongly advised to take part in the all-comers event (see 'Cyclists, check this out!', page 83).

Fitness: Riders of all levels of performance should have no problems with the 111km circuit described here. Anyone wanting to follow the complete professional route should be able to complete 200km and the total vertical climb in one go.

Equipment: The steep climbs require a compact crankset or a 27-tooth sprocket. Since you are never further than 30km from the starting line in Eschborn you can also spare yourself the bother of taking heavy waterproof clothing with you in the right weather conditions.

The date 1 May is associated with tradition in German cycling. One of the most important races in Germany, the Rund um den Henninger Turm, has taken place in and around Frankfurt on this day since 1962. Founded the year before by the brothers Hermann and Erwin Moos, the event sponsored by the Henninger Brewery soon established itself as an important permanent fixture in the international race calendar. Successes by great sportsmen such as Hennes Junkermann, Rudi Altig, Eddy Merckx, Johan Bruyneel, Olaf Ludwig, Michele Bartoli, Davide Rebellin and Erik Zabel testify to the positive development of the race since its founding. In 1995 the event was even part of the World Cup. But the traditional date of 1 May, which more often than not falls during the week, meant that a longer guest appearance in this series wasn't possible. Because the date of the event was fixed it couldn't be included in the UCI Tour either. Yet it's kept its important position in the racing calendar – to this day.

New sponsors, new concept

However, in the last few years the Henninger Tower race has experienced a renaissance. Witness the new name of the event, which is now run as the Rund um den Finanzplatz Eschborn–Frankfurt. The reason for this reorientation was the withdrawal of the Radeberger Gruppe, who ended their sponsorship in 2008. When this became known there was even talk of this being the end of the traditional race. Eventually it was the two towns of Eschborn and Frankfurt that stepped into the breach and saved the 'Henninger', as it was known by fans and riders.

The course was also redesigned. Now the two towns share the start and finishing lines. Most of the course, however, continues

Riders climb the Feldberg

to run through the famous loop of the Taunus, where the numerous climbs provide a selection process for the riders. It starts in Eschborn, and the finishing line is in Frankfurt at the Alte Oper.

Anyone who wants to follow the course as a tour, however, should bear in mind the volume of traffic in the region. Since the route runs through the centre of Eschborn and Frankfurt participation in the partially cordoned off all-comers race, the Škoda Velotour (see 'Cyclists, check this out!', page 83), is advisable in any case. Otherwise you have to ride on roads which are not really suitable for cyclists or even where cyclists are not allowed. In the following description a 111km circuit is envisaged, on which you can avoid the worst of the traffic, yet still get to know all the important places in the race.

It's a good idea to steer clear of at least the first city-centre circuit.

The tour starts on Elly-Beinhorn-Straße near the Eschborn-Süd railway station. Under normal circumstances you would then follow the professionals along Lorscher Straße (5km), the Breitenbach Bridge (9km) and the Mainzer Landstraße (13km) to pass the finishing line at the Alte Oper (16km) in Frankfurt for the first time. But it's a good idea in fact to steer clear of at least the first city-centre circuit. You want to get under way without putting yourself at risk from the heavy traffic.

One possibility would be to shorten it this way: go straight from Eschborn-Süd onto the Frankfurter Landstraße via Steinbach and Weißkirchen, and rejoin the professional course. This has made another circuit beforehand through the suburb of Riedberg, past the Johann

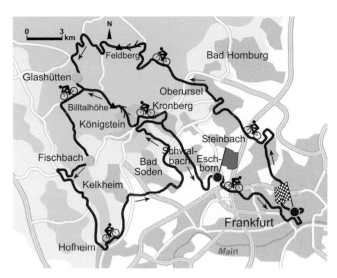

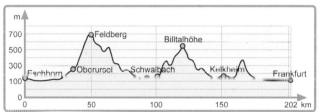

The race is an experience for all-comers too.

Wolfgang Goethe University and then northwards past Weißkirchen (30km) in the direction of Oberursel. If you take the

The route continues through colourful fields – but Frankfurt's skyline is already waiting in the background.

short cut it'll save you 22km – and a lot of stress.

Just before you get to Bommersheim you turn left onto Gablonzer Straße (31km), accompanied by the railway line on your right, where you're getting close to the first real climb of the day. The first mountain classification has already been passed previously, but the easy hill isn't big enough to mention. An underpass beneath the railway line and the left-hand bend following it introduce the climb in Bommersheim. You clear a vertical climb of just under 50m over the next kilometre. Along the Oberhöchstadter Straßethrough a densely populated residential area you finally reach Oberursel (36km), without losing much height, and here the first sprint classification is held for the professionals.

Welcome to the Taunus!

There is something on offer for those who are interested in history when they

get to the beautiful square with its old town hall and the St Ursula fountain: the tower of the Church of St Ursula, one of the main attractions of this town in Hesse rises on the right-hand side in the background between the half-timbered houses.

You go further down the Altkönigstraße until you come to the railway line again on Hohemarkstraße. You can now easily make out the Feldberg. After 40km you're still riding through an urban area, before the crossroads at the edge of town marks the beginning of the Taunus landscape with its hills and forests. In addition, the wide main road is slowly beginning to climb.

It continues to climb, first 2 per cent, then with an average gradient of 4–5 per cent. And you're continually surrounded by the forest. Trees to the left, trees to the right and the road in the middle. This road nestles against the mountain, with relatively few bends. You don't reach the

first sharp right-hand bend until you've done 45km. By the Hotel Sandplacken (48km) you finally turn left to tackle the last 2km before the mountain classification, which takes place after almost exactly 50km. By then you're completely surrounded by the forest – pure Taunus.

The forest finally opens out a little after 2km going downhill and down a steep 11 per cent descent you reach Oberreifenberg – incidentally the highest village in the Taunus at 683m above sea level.

Be careful: the first part of the descent of the Feldberg is quite steep and full of bends. If you're in control you can risk a calm glance to the left. There lies the Großen Feldberg plateau.

Only speed specialists should let rip on the steep downhill slope to Schloßborn.

Bends to the left and the right follow, before you turn left in Niederreifenberg (54km) over the bridge across the Weil, which rises nearby, and head for Oberems. A short vertical climb of 60m opposite to the next mountain classification on the Kittelhütte is quickly dealt with, and three downhill hairpin bends later you find yourself in Oberems (59km). Shortly after leaving the village you finally branch off towards Glashütten (63km), a former Roman boundary town.

Down towards Schloßborn (66km) caution is called for: only speed specialists should let rip on the steep downhill slope – they can really have fun on the steep descent. A sharp bend to the left in the town finally brings the fun to an end and you go on to Ruppertshain.

Not long afterwards another well-known climb in the Taunus loop begins with the mountain of the same name. Under the thick leafy roof you quickly

The Austrian Josef Benetseder was part of a breakaway group that dictated the race for a long time in 2010.

change onto the small chainring – the 'Ruppertshainer' is one of the hardest stretches of the whole race. It goes uphill at an incline almost constantly in double figures for just under 2km, then a sharp left-hand bend marks the mountain classification and going down riders can let rip once more. The sharp and also very steep right-hand bend which now follows is the only braking point, then it's full speed through the town – obviously with consideration for other road users.

The Eppstein Wall

From Ruppertshain you go on to Fischbach (73km). The road keeps going gently down and the legs are enjoying this welcome respite. This comes just at the right time, because in Eppstein (75km) the next climb begins. However, you must be careful not to miss the right-hand turn into the Burgstraße, where the climb to the 'Eppstein Wall' begins. There's a reason for that name: it climbs up a kilometre and a half with inclines of up to 19 per cent in places to its peak in the Bergstraße, where the next mountain classification sprint takes place.

This picture explains, if it's not already clear, why the event is called the Rund um den Finanzplatz ('Circuit round the financial centre').

Back down in the town centre you head now towards Lorsbach along by the waters of the same name, which you reach after 83km. The gentle downhill slope makes you want to bowl along. You find yourself once more in the southern foothills of the Taunus, and it's no secret that not only the return leg but also the next few kilometres of climbing will soon follow. In Hofheim (89km) it's all set: after branching off left the road goes northwards up over a gentle hill and through a residential area.

Then you ride past isolated farms along wide main roads through fields with agricultural buildings to Münster (94km), then finally reach Sulzbach (98km). Then you pedal immediately to the fringes of the forest of the southern Taunus. After that you leave Schwalbach to the right to ride past more farmland to Mammolshain. You get there after 105km – the next mountain classification and one of the absolute highlights of the route is waiting.

In Mammolsheim a wall rises up in front of you out of the forest.

Already on the way there the road begins to climb gently until finally when you get to the first houses a wall rises up in front of you out of the forest. You're not officially allowed to ride on the steepest part – a one-way street in the opposite direction, which is closed off during the race – but there is a detour along the Hauptstraße with a hairpin bend there: a total vertical climb of just under 130m over a length of a little more than a kilometre – here even the professionals suffer.

After a long drawn-out bend to the left you finally reach the highest point in the forest (107km). After that a short descent brings you at least a little relaxation. At an extremely busy roundabout you turn right, before turning right again at the next crossroads below the Falkenstein towards Kronberg (110km), and then you have to decide: do you ride straight to the finishing line in Frankfurt or left to take on another mountain classification over the Billtalhöhe (120km) to Glashütten and start a second circuit? This would take you once more over the climbs at Ruppertshain (128km) and Eppstein (136km) and also the steep Mammolshain mountain (165km) …

Homewards in a high gear

If you give the second circuit a miss you'll save yourself 58km – and in principle you've already done it: in fact the ride continues from the 168km mark. Then comes a section for those who are keen on time trials, and you approach the starting line in Eschborn again on the big chainring, going gently downhill all the time. The tower blocks on the horizon show that the finishing line in Frankfurt is also not far away. Meanwhile you leave the Taunus behind you, a green mountain landscape.

At Niederhöchstadt (172km) you should leave the busy main road (and also the original route) and ride through the town alongside the railway line – that's much more pleasant. You eventually reach the starting point of the tour after 176km. If you've taken both the big short cuts, the clock now stands at 96km.

And having kept out of the way of all traffic difficulties until now you should consider the section of the route through long lines of traffic to the finish as an easy ride. Though many streets have a cycle lane, quite a few do not. However, it's worth joining in with the stop-starting: after all you've taken in more or less all of the highlights of the Eschborn Frankfurt City Loop. And although the Alte Oper is still 15km away, a coffee there will make up for the strain you've been through. You can make the journey back to Eschborn on a suburban train.

2011 results

1 John Degenkolb (Germany), 4 hours 50' 49"
2 Jerome Baugnies (Belgium), same time
3 Michael Matthews (Australia), same time

Cyclists, check this out!

Sportive riders and amateur racers also get a lot out of the Eschborn–Frankfurt City Loop: altogether three routes of 42, 70 and 103km are on offer within the framework of the pro event. Like the rest of the all-comers' races, the Škoda Velotour abides by the road traffic regulations. Find more information at http://www.velo-tours.net/.

Cycling and sightseeing

For some years the Henninger Tower was the symbol of this race. Even though the route no longer passes directly in front of it you can still have a look at it: the former grain silo of the Henninger Brewery in the Frankfurt-Sachsenhausen quarter of the city is easily recognisable from a distance and comprises the silo as well as what looks like an added-on television tower. The 118.5m-high building was once used as an observation platform with a restaurant. But the tower has not been used since 2002. There are currently plans to convert it into a residential building.

Background

Eric Zabel, who won in 1999, 2002 and 2005, is the current record winner of today's Eschborn–Frankfurt and the former Henninger Tower race. But hot on his heels is the German classic specialist Fabian Wegmann. In the last two editions the 30-year-old had his nose in front and therefore has a good chance of catching up with the former world-class sprinter in the future. The two wins in Frankfurt count as the greatest successes so far in Wegmann's career.

SUMMER SPECIALS

12 GRAN FONDO FELICE GIMONDI

Following the 'Phoenix' round Bergamo

TOUR PROFILE <<

Race date: Between the end of April and the middle of May

Type: Marathon sportive

Start/finish: Bergamo (Italy)

Distance: 165km (alternatively either 89 or 129km)

Total vertical climb: 2950m

Riding time: 7 hours

URL: www.felicegimondi.it

Route: The course weaves its way from Bergamo through the mountains of the Lombardy province. The difficulty lies in planning, for you have to know exactly how to judge your reserves of strength through the numerous medium-size mountains. In particular you have to save some scraps for the last two climbs. In some places the downhill slopes are dangerous, narrow and pitted with potholes. Here you should ride with enormous care! On the map the short route is marked in green and the medium-length route is marked in red.

Fitness: Because there are three variations of the Gran Fondo Felice Gimondi, participation is open to everyone. Anyone who wants to try the full distance must be in very good physical condition, though, as the cycling time can come to anything up to 7 hours.

Equipment: Because the climbs are not very steep you can take part in this tour with a standard set-up of 39/25. But those who want to change gear more easily on the mountains should fit a compact chainset or a 27-tooth sprocket.

When a race is named after someone then this sportsperson must really belong to the great and the good. And as far as the Gran Fondo Felice Gimondi is concerned, that much at least is true. The 'Phoenix', as his fans affectionately call him, is still counted among the most successful riders of his day: as early as 1965, in his first year as a professional cyclist, Felice Gimondi managed to win the Tour de France. In 1967 and 1968 he was overall winner of the Giro d'Italia and the Spanish Vuelta. Gimondi is therefore one of the few cyclists who managed, in the course of his career, to win the historic triple: all three of the great Grand Tours. The northern Italian, now aged 68, has many other great successes to his name, including the title of World Cycling Champion in 1973.

For the Italians there were many reasons to be proud of their 'Phoenix', which is why a marathon was dedicated to him. The Gran Fondo, in and around the Bergamo region, is virtually the backyard of the ex-professional who comes from near Sedrina. In all, participants have a choice of three routes of 89, 129 and 165km. Of course the most beautiful tour of them all is the longest – you'll get the best impression on this one of the beauty of the province of Lombardy.

Felice Gimondi is an Italian cycling legend.

On the starting line in Bergamo things are still calm.

Starting point: Bergamo

You start in the northern part of
Bergamo, on the Via Marzabotto
opposite the sports centre. If you want
to do the whole race you should set
your alarm clock early since the starting
signal goes off at seven in the morning.
If you also want to be placed highly in
the field you must be prepared for a
short night. Tour cyclists who simply
want to get to know the route have an
easier time of it. They also spare
themselves the pushing and shoving,
particularly in the back part of the
peloton, caused by numerous traffic
jams during the first few kilometres of
the Gran Fondo.

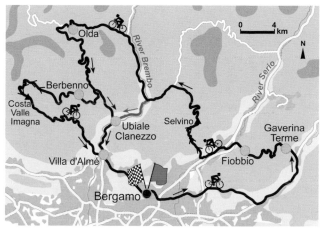

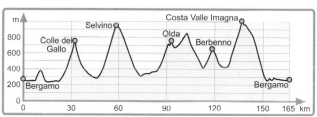

The crowded peloton doesn't thin
out at all until after you cross the short
but gorgeous Colle di Pasta which you
reach 11km later via the towns of Gorle
(4km) and Negrone (8km). The great
crush is hardly surprising: the 'Gimondi'
is, after all, part of the UCI Golden Bike
Series (see 'Cyclists, check this out!', page
91) and so belongs among the greatest
marathons in the world. Nearly 4000
cyclists push and shove their way over
the north Italian streets on the day of the
start.

After the descent from Colle di Pasta –
given the steep gradient and the open
course of the road the fearless can reach
a top speed of over 80km/hr despite its
shortness – you come to Trescore
Balneario (16km). This idyllic little place
is perhaps still known to die-hard fans as
a stage town in the 1987 edition of the
Giro d'Italia. The stage winner at that
time, Giuseppe Calcaterra, is no longer
well known, but perhaps the wearer of
the pink jersey and later the overall
winner is remembered: the Irishman
Stephen Roche.

In the town you turn left and follow
the gently climbing road signposted

towards Casazza (24km). Anyone who is
on the tour as a tourist and would like to
see the typical stone buildings of the
region must make their way straight to
the town centre. However, the original
course of the Gran Fondo doesn't go
that far: riders turn here just at the
entrance to the town to get onto the Via
Drione and fight it out for position in the
front of the field on the way to Gaverina
Terme.

*You go very smoothly past the
numerous houses of the town on
the way to the top, then you cover
the last few m of the climb in the
forest.*

The time for bowling easily along is
now over, for from this point on it's
uphill all the time. With the 763m-high
Colle del Gallo comes the first real long
climb on the programme. And the

and into Albino (41km). You go alongside the Serio, one of the rivers characteristic of this region, through the valley of the same name to Nembro. Once you've reached the village, after 44km, you have to be careful that you don't miss the correct turning: shortly before the town centre you turn right onto the Via Torquato Tasso. Now the next mountain awaits you with its climb up to Selvino.

The Italian professional Michele Scarponi attacks on the Colle Gallo.

mountain is no stranger – not to the professionals' peloton: the 2010 'Lombardy Week', for example, started here with a preliminary mountain time trial. The winner, Michele Scarponi, took just 14 minutes 55 seconds for the 6.6km-long climb – an average of almost 27km/hr! However, this fact can also give you courage: that is, you'll not find any really steep sections here.

Still relatively straight at the beginning, the road soon weaves its way in narrow hairpin bends from Gaverina Terme up the side of the mountain. The gradient is always comfortable. You go very smoothly past the numerous houses of the town on the way to the top, then you cover the last few metres of the climb to the top of the pass (31km) in the forest. However, caution is necessary when going downhill: this is just as full of bends as the climb and the road surface leaves a lot to be desired because of the many potholes!

Once you're down in the valley the course continues past Fiobbio (39km)

Refreshments in Selvino

At 946m this climb is the second highest of the day – because of its average gradient of 6 per cent, it's as pleasant to ride up as the Gallo. Only at the beginning, just after the first bend, is there a short section with a gradient in double figures. The rest rolls on, and if you've found your rhythm you can enjoy the wooded scenery to the full.

You leave Nembro behind you quite quickly before fighting your way up quite a straight stretch to the top. Only a couple of bends interrupt the flow of the ride until you reach San Vito. Now the road weaves its way round many beautiful hairpin bends up to Selvino – only the end bit runs straight again, but by now you've almost done it all. You've covered 56km to get to Selvino and the little mountain town invites you to make a short stop for coffee: an excellent idea. A feeding station is also set up here for the Gran Fondo.

It's worth being alert again during the descent: some hairpin bends, particularly in the upper part, are not easy to judge and require a high degree of concentration!

Down below on the flat it's the competitors turn again. From now on the route glides gently uphill with a 2–3 per cent gradient. And so you reach Ambria after 71km, where you could turn off onto a short course back to Bergamo – to do that simply turn left in the village towards Sedrina. However, all those on the middle and long-distance course turn right at the crossroads and arrive not long afterwards in San Pellegrino Terme (76km), the origin of the famous mineral water of the same name. The road continues to climb gently until you reach San Giovanni Bianco. With just over 80km in your legs you've now done half of the Gran Fondo.

It's one of those unpleasant climbs that sucks the strength from your legs.

As you leave the town, turn onto the Via San Carlo, a little road that soon begins to climb more steeply. The Costa d'Olda, 806m in height, is a foretaste of the next mountain. It's a difficult climb, which isn't really steep but stretches over the wooded spine of the mountain. Shortly after Sottochiesa (89km) the trees thin out a little. You may have reached the top of the pass (91km) for the moment, but the descent that follows towards Olda brings little relief. Through Peghera and Forcella di Bura, the road continues to climb gently on for another 10km. At 2 per cent, sometimes 4 per cent, it's one of those unpleasant climbs that sucks the strength from your legs.

Past Forcella di Bura (100km), the next descent arrives. This winds its way down round narrow and at times blind corners to Brembilla (111km). Incidentally, you look in vain for any flat stretches on this part of the route as it's continually going

The idyllic roads in northern Bergamo are a joy even during the race.

uphill and downhill – typical Lombardy. Meanwhile the 113km you've already done are also beginning to make themselves felt in your legs. But there's no time to rest. Only those who chose the medium-length course can to go straight on in Brembilla and take a short cut. The rest go to the right through Loxolo and up to Forcella di Berbenno (117km).

Strawberries for hunger

At 5.5km this mountain is actually one of the shorter climbs, but with its gradient of a good 8 per cent in comparison with the previous climbs it's a good deal more demanding. Several hairpin bends in the middle section offer a bit of a break, then it gets steeper again. Don't let yourself be taken in by the first houses in Berbenno, you still have a good kilometre to climb after that. The next descent follows past Chiesa Selino (121km) down to Sant'Omobono (126km), the last possibility for a break before the climbing starts. In the Gran Fondo the last feeding station here is a must: the sweet strawberries have got many a participant out of a dip in performance!

And that's important: for with the Costa Valle Imagna comes the last and also the hardest mountain of the day. The road winds upwards to a height of 1036m – and that's with a continual gradient of around 8 per cent. As soon as you're out of Sant'Omobono the climb begins with a left turn into the Viale alle Fonti, a narrow little road that is now surrounded by trees. It's particularly difficult to get into a rhythm until you've left Valsecca (129km) behind, which you pass after a third of the route.

Once you've finally reached the top of the pass it's almost all downhill to Bergamo.

As the road levels off it makes the descent easier – but still the suffering increases proportionally. It's simply built up over the many climbs you've done so far, which add up to a total vertical climb of almost 2500m! And what's more you've already got 130km in your legs. This is where you have to find the tempo that makes the climb bearable. And there's an extra motivation: once you finally reach the top of the pass (135km), which is 1036m high, it's almost all downhill to Bergamo.

And you can enjoy this! Although the bends are tight you're well used to this after the descents you've already made.

There's still the odd tunnel or two waiting for riders on the route.

Rough tarmac on many sections means you have to be careful.

In Capizzone turn right to go beyond Strozza and you'll eventually reach Villa d'Almé (155km), where the short and medium-length courses link up again with the long course. Here there follows just a short climb up the other side, but at 500m you can cope with that. Then you've done it: the signposts already say Bergamo, and you follow them along the straight road until the first houses of the provincial capital appear on the horizon. You do a short winding section through the streets, go along the Via Cristoforo Baioni, and after 165km you reach the sports centre on the Via Marzabotto.

In the Gran Fondo the remaining groups get that good old final spurt feeling – as happened in the Giro d'Italia: as the 2009 Tour of Italy entered the final stretch in Bergamo, a good 40 riders from a strong field fought it out for a place in the rankings.

Bergamo has often been a stage town for the Giro d'Italia. The last time it hosted this was in 2011.

2011 results

1. Antonio Corradini (Italy), 3 hours 37' 04"
2. Davide Tongi (Italy), + 2' 57"
3. Andrea Natali (Italy), same time
4. Matteo Zannelli (Italy), same time
5. Tiziano Lombardi (Italy), same time

Cyclists, check this out!

With around 4000 participants, the Gran Fondo Felice Gimondi ranks among the biggest cycle marathons on the Italian boot. But it is also as one of the most exclusive marathon series worldwide, the UCI Golden Bike Series. Altogether six races from New Zealand to the Swiss Alps make up this series – which includes the Flandernrundfahrt in Europe, which is described in this book. Through their support UCI guarantee participants quality organisation above everything. More information at www.ucigoldenbike.com.

Cycling and sightseeing

Chapels dedicated to cyclists are a characteristic of Italy, the land of cycling. So, too, at the roadside of the 'Gimondi' there's a place of worship dedicated to athletes on two wheels and to protecting them when they're riding. You'll find the Madonna dei Ciclisti on the way to Colle del Gallo in Gaverina Terme.

Background

One of the most spectacular accidents in the history of the Giro d'Italia happened quite near the route just described: on the eighth stage of the 2009 edition of the Tour of Italy the Spaniard Pedro Horrillo misjudged a corner on the descent from the Culmine San Pietro pass and plunged over the guardrail. He fell nearly 80m down the mountainside – and survived. Just four months later Horillo, who at that time was 35 years old, started training again. But he never resumed his career – the memories of his accident went too deep.

TOUR PROFILE <<

Race date: Mid-May

Type: Marathon sportive

Start/finish: Cesenatico (Italy)

Distance: 205km (alternatively 131km)

Total vertical climb: 3840m

Riding time: 8 hours

URL: www.novecolli.it

Route: From the Italian Adriatic coast this circuit goes through very attractive scenery into the hinterland of Emilia-Romagna. In the course of the 205km you get to know the merits of this region kilometre by kilometre. The course of the Nove Colli runs for the most part along quiet roads so you can really enjoy the ride.

Fitness: Apart from needing a good level of endurance you should be able to manage this race with its many mountains one after the other – but you hardly ever get into a proper rhythm. The road continually goes up or down, and you search in vain for longer flat stretches for some relief. Those who can't spend so much time sitting in the saddle can turn off at Barbotto onto the smaller circuit – at 131km it is quite long enough.

Equipment: Although the mountain climbs on the Nove Colli aren't very long, they're often blessed with very steep sections. Maximum gradients up to 18 per cent (at Barbotto) represent the greatest difficulty. So at least a compact crankset or a standard set-up with a 29-tooth sprocket is advisable.

Cesenatico is the home of Marco Pantani. 'The Pirate' is everywhere here.

Emilia-Romagna ranks among the most beautiful cycling regions of all. The lush green plains near the Adriatic coast alternate with the gentle mountains of the Apennines in the hinterland to produce a unique landscape. Add to this the typical Italian cuisine, which naturally tastes so much better in these surroundings, and the outstanding hospitality of the locals. No one who travels here should leave his bike at home under any circumstances because there's so much to discover. Above all, there's one route that really cries out to be cycled: the Nove Colli.

This Gran Fondo now counts as one of the biggest and best known of its kind in the whole world. In Italy it fights it out for the top spot with the Dolomites Marathon. A good 11,000 cycle maniacs tackle both courses over 131 and 205km every year, and by the middle of February all the places on the starting line have already been taken. It wasn't always like this: when the first edition took place in 1971 there were just 17 riders who met in front of the Del Corso bar in Cesenatico, the place where the idea for this long race came into being, and took up the challenge of the Nove Colli.

The event takes its name (which means 'Nine Hills') from the route of the course: it's a very good description of the profile since it consists, at a rough glance, of exactly those nine peaks separated only by the descents in between. So you shouldn't expect an easy ride along the coast of the Adriatic, but a rather more strenuous collection of climbs in the Apennines instead.

Bowling along after the start

At the beginning the Nove Colli is still being good to us. The first 25km are almost exclusively flat and perfectly suitable for a warm-up ride. However, before you start and ride past the harbour channel of Cesenatico, built according to the plans of Leonardo da

Vinci and alive with the colourful sails of the fishing boats, you should pay a visit to the statue of Marco Pantani in the town centre. 'The Pirate', one of the most charismatic professional cyclists in history, lived here (see 'Background', page 97). Also during the coming 205km spare a thought for the climbing specialist with the prominent ears – for until his death in 2004 this section of the Nove Colli was Pantani's usual training ground.

After the start you go inland. You soon find out how well known the Nove Colli is for there are frequent signs at the side of the road that show the way. Beyond Borgo Campone and Montaletto you go past many green meadows to Martorano (17km), where you reach the commuter belt of Cesena. The 'city of three popes', as the town is also known – Pius VI and Pius VII were born here, and Pius VIII had his episcopal seat here – is incidentally also the birthplace of Marco Pantani. You don't ride through the town, but around it to the north. Beyond Diegaro (22km) you get to Forlimpopoli (28km), which is the starting point for the first of the nine mountains.

In Bertinoro the gradient increases noticeably, and you have to really sweat to make any headway between the Mediterranean-style houses.

Nine seems to be the fateful number of the tour since that's exactly the number of kilometres for the ride to Polenta (37km). Although you only have to reckon with a total vertical climb of 280m, with its maximum incline of up to 13 per cent, this climb is not to be underestimated. At the beginning you make your way to the top round gentle bends, slowly at first then faster and

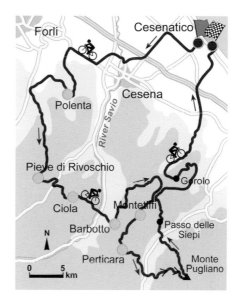

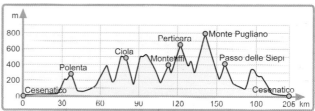

In the coastal town there's even a special museum dedicated to climbing specialists.

Bewitching – this is the first word that comes to mind when you see the scenery of Emilia-Romagna.

faster later on. In Bertinoro (32km) the gradient increases noticeably, and you have to really sweat to make any headway between the Mediterranean-style houses.

A bend to the left finally brings relief, and you can get your strength back on a downhill slope in between before the last part of the mountain lines up ready. After 500m you go left to Polenta, which you finally reach after two ramps along the narrow road. The last kilometre leads through the town and you soon find yourself on the winding and at times very steep descent.

You go downhill past a red-brick church on a road with ramps in double figures in places. Keep an eye out for traffic at all costs on this mad rush between the bushes! That's because the road is so narrow you can have problems with oncoming traffic on the bends. (Incidentally this is also true for all sections of the course – many Italians are

not exactly known for their defensive style of driving.)

Hairpin bends and panoramic bliss

When you reach the bottom the road is flat past Fratta Terme (42km) and on to Meldola (47km), where the route turns sharp left to follow the idyllic road to Pieve di Rivoschio, the second mountain of the day. The next 10km go gently uphill and the surroundings also become more and more hilly. Finally a signpost marks the turning to Pieve di Rivoschio: now you go uphill for 8km. The average incline comes to a comfortable 5 per cent.

And it's even more bearable when after a kilometre the trees thin out and an impressive view unfolds on the right-hand side: green rolling hills, towering cypresses, umbrella-like pines, olive groves and isolated farms – a really evocative picture of the region. As well as the wonderful panorama, numerous hairpin bends make the ascent over an ever-narrowing road easier. After a flat section in the middle there's just the final section to go. However, you're fresh and fit again, so that presents no problem.

Once you reach the top (65km) you plunge to the left into the descent to San Romano (69km), which is very steep at times. On the 20 per cent incline and narrow hairpin bends keep both hands tight on the brake levers, particularly in the second half. Speed freaks will definitely have a great time here! A speed of 90km/hr with the appropriate safe riding and road safety is well within the bounds of possibility.

In San Romano you turn sharp right towards Linaro (71km) where you tackle the next of the nine hills with a climb up to Ciola: 6km with an incline of 6 per cent. Soon after the beginning the markings in the middle of the road disappear and the road gets narrower. Protected by a leafy roof of trees you wind your way round hairpin bends up to the top. A rock wall on the right-hand side, 3km before you get to Ciola, finally signals the end of the sharp bends. One kilometre before you reach Ciola it even starts to go gently downhill again.

Idyllic Mercato Saraceno invites you to stop for coffee.

The next descent leads down to Mercato Saraceno. By now there are 87km on the clock, and the idyllic town with its cobbled pedestrianised zone invites you to stop for coffee. This is a good time to collect your strength – the Barbotto

follows immediately, the hardest and also the best-known climb of the Nove Colli: at 5.5km it's not long, but a maximum incline of 18 per cent makes it a tough nut to crack. Anyone who isn't in shape will quickly pay the price.

The aqueduct-like bridge as you leave the town marks the start of this mountain, which gives you no chance to establish a rhythm. Even the professionals on the Giro sweat here. At the beginning you should save your strength, because 3km from the top of the pass it gets really serious: the first ramp, with a gradient of 14 per cent, is followed by a second with a gradient of 18 per cent – and it's about as much fun as having a tooth out. The last kilometre is pure torture! A café on the right-hand side finally comes to your rescue and marks the end (91km).

Here you turn left and after a short winding section on the far side of the mountain make the next descent towards Sogliano al Rubicone (103km). The road is nice and wide, and has a good surface. Just before the village

The Barbotto is the best-known mountain of the race. The Giro also goes up and down it.

Nove Colli

With over 10,000 entrants the Nove Colli is a really major event.

leads to the summit (122km) round several hairpin bends.

Just 3km from the top of the pass there's a shrine to the Virgin Mary on the right-hand side. Since you now have many vertical-climb metres in your legs – in particular those of the Barbotto – making this climb is a real torture, and you may want to send a quick prayer heavenwards. The view just before Perticara (122km) compensates for your efforts.

However, you still have three mountains ahead of you. The road goes past the cliffs framing the town down a 6km-long descent until at the crossroads beyond Sartiano (128km) you turn onto a wide road. A bend to the left finally marks the beginning of the climb to Monte Pugliano.

you go off to Ponte Uso (107km). If you notice that you're already running out of strength here you should keep going straight on and use the short course – it's only 25km to Cesenatico, and downhill all the way.

Everyone else turns right in Ponte Uso and follows the signposts to Monte Tiffi. The fifth mountain is again somewhat shorter, and more manageable at 3km long. Nevertheless, you shouldn't be taken in by the easy start: in the shadow of the trees the incline rises to 16 per cent. However, at the top you're treated once more to a beautiful view over the landscape as a reward. A well in the town below (113km) invites you to take a rest and fill up your empty water bottle.

A single up and down

Immediately after that the road goes downhill. By now at least you must have resigned yourself to the fact that the Nove Colli has hardly any level sections. With wheels humming you reach Serra (113km), from where you go to the sixth mountain: Perticara. At 7km it's the longest climb so far today. Beneath the shade of the trees you make good progress. But a sharp right-hand bend at 118km ends this easier section: a 12 per cent ramp starts here, which eventually

Four kilometres before the summit of the Pugliano you get to the village of Maiolo, from where the climb gets a little easier.

The highest mountain of the day takes its conquerors up to a height of 791m. The climb continues for 11.5km – a generally beautiful climb to ride, which allows you to get a good rhythm going. Four kilometres from the summit you reach the village of Maiolo, from where the climb gets a little easier. The road goes up an incline of 4–6 per cent until you reach the highest point at 142km.

Now you've survived the worst. Rimini is already signposted and after a left-hand turn the road goes downhill for 10km to Secchiano (152km). This is a lovely descent on a well-surfaced wide road. And a view of the fortress of San Leo perched dizzily on a cliff offers a real highlight.

Even though the Passo delle Siepi, which you have now reached, is only 4km long and relatively flat, it still hurts.

The increasing distance and the climbs so far have left your legs like jelly so that the 6 per cent incline feels like the earlier 8 or 9 per cent climbs. The road surface gets a bit bumpier again, needing careful cycling, just like the descent from Ponte Uso did. You ride through the town for a second time and approach the last climb of the day, the Gorolo, on a gentle downhill stretch surrounded by fields and woods.

Anticipation of the evening meal

Just like the Siepi, this climb measures only 4km, but it's noticeably harder. A section with a gradient of 17 per cent makes It into a real killer, which hurts at least as much as the Barbotto. It's the last kilometre in particular that hurts because of that maximum gradient – but then suddenly you've done it, and after a quick descent you go from the top of the pass (177km) to Borghi (184km) and Savignano sul Rubicone (192km), and back to Cesenatico.

After 205km you're finally back on the promenade of the seaside town from which the tour of Emilia-Romagna started. You can clip out of your pedals proudly – the nine mountains have been vanquished. Now it really is time to enjoy a little of what you've been looking forward to throughout the tour: the culinary specialities of the region.

2011 results

1 Antonio Corradini (Italy), 5 hours 58' 23"
2 Michele Rezzani (Italy), + 1' 59"
3 Ersilio Fantini (Italy), same time
4 Stefano Nicoletti (Italy), + 2' 02"
5 Raimondas Rumsas (Lithuania), + 8' 02"

Cyclists, check this out!

While the Nove Colli established its link to Marco Pantani, particularly through his home town of Cesenatico, in the last few years there has been another cycle marathon associated with 'The Pirate': the Gran Fondo Marco Pantani. At 175km long and with a total vertical climb of 4500m it will please all those riders who, like Pantani, loved fighting their way uphill best. The Gavia and the Mortirolo, two of the passes the 'The Pirate' loved best, have been included in the race. From 2011 the race has been known as the Gran Fondo Internazionale Giordana. In addition to the long course, a Medio Fondo (155km long/3600m-total vertical climb) and a short Fondo (85km/1850m) are also offered. Find more information at http://gsalpi.com/de/gf-giordana/editie 2011.

Cycling and sightseeing

In addition to the memorial in the centre of Cesenatico there is also a museum dedicated to Marco Pantani. This deals with his career and his greatest successes, and also with the fall from grace of this charismatic sportsman. A must for all cycling fans! Find more information at www.spaziopantani.it.

Background

The routes of the Nove Colli were the main training roads for Marco Pantani. Born on 13 January 1970 in Cesena, 'The Pirate' was one of the best cyclists of the 1990s and quickly rose to be the darling of the public with his lightning-speed attacks. The climbing specialist experienced the highlight of his career in 1998 when he won the rare double of the Giro and the Tour de France in the same year, dropping out of sight only one year later after a positive drugs test. He came back In 2000 and won two mountain stages of the Tour de France – among other things he beat Lance Armstrong on Mont Ventoux – and was considered to be the future challenger of the Americans. However, a new doping scandal engulfed him in the following year. From then on the headlines about him were almost always negative. Another comeback in 2003 only lasted a short time. There were more and more reports of Pantani's depression. On 14 February 2004 he was found dead in a Rimini hotel room. Ten thousand people paid their last respects to him at his funeral. If you want to find out more about Pantani you should read John Wilcockson's biography *Marco Pantani: The Legend of a Tragic Champion* (Velo Press).

14 MARATONA DLES DOLOMITES

On the road in the heart of the Dolomites

Route: A circuit that includes all the well-known mountains in the region. Beyond Corvara you tackle the Sella Ronda which is subsequently extended to the Giau, Falzarego and Valparola Passes. Scenery-wise the circuit is an absolute dream. In addition to the long route there are also two shorter distances of 106 and 55km (marked in green on the map).

Fitness: Even if 138km sounds like rather an easy proposition for classics conditions, you should only tackle the Maratona as a mountain-hardened endurance specialist – the reason for this is a total vertical climb of almost 4200m. However, there are two alternatives in the medium and short routes.

Equipment: A mountain stage like this cries out for a light set-up. A compact crankset or a 29-tooth sprocket are required if you are to complete the seven passes successfully. In addition it's important to take weatherproof clothing with you.

In summery conditions the beautiful scenery of the Dolomites is a dream – and an absolute must for every cyclist.

The area around the Sella mountain group ranks as the favourite region for cyclists in the mid-European Alps. Nowhere else do the Alpine passes crowd together more thickly, and there are few places where the mountain scenery is so impressive that it compensates for the efforts expended here on the border between the South Tyrol, Trentino and Veneto. Pordoi, Giau, Falzarego and, last but not least, the Sella Pass itself – fans of the Italian tour will immediately recognise the names of these passes where the professionals have become heroes over many editions of the Giro. It's the interplay of all these factors – spectacular views, sporting demands and cycling history – that makes this region so popular. And it's for exactly these reasons that, by popular consent, the event that enjoys the highest popularity is the Dolomites Marathon.

The first edition in 1987 saw 166 cyclists taking part. And like its counterpart on the Austrian side, the Ötztaler, and also the Nove Colli on the Adriatic coast, this ride quickly developed into a major event, which today is one of the biggest in the region, with up to 9000 participants. The route of the 'Maratona', as the Italians like to call the event, is not the longest, at only 138km, nor is it the hardest of its kind, with a total vertical climb of just under 4200m – but it is perhaps the most beautiful.

And this doesn't really depend on the time of year in which you're cycling. In spring, when the roads are free of snow for the first time and the banks of snow tower several metres high on the climb to Pordoi it's just as attractive as in summer, when golden eagles circle high in the sky and you get the feeling that they're just waiting until you're all alone and then you're going to be their prey. And in autumn the larches turn golden yellow in the Gardena Pass, and snow poles on the side of the road announce the coming of winter.

Great crowds

The 'Maratona' itself takes place every year in early July – probably the best time to tackle the pushing and shoving from the point of view of the weather. If you want to take part in the Dolomites Marathon you should, however, make preparations as early as October of the year before since, as is the case with the Ötztaler Radmarathon, there are always twice as many inquiries as there are places on the starting line, and you need a bit of luck to be able to get onto this dream event. Anyone who wants to ride the route as a tourist instead will avoid these difficulties – but you'll be all on your own.

The starting line is in La Villa, an idyllic little mountain village not far from Corvara, or 'star'. On the day of the 'Maratona' a long colourful crowd, seemingly consisting solely of cyclists, snakes

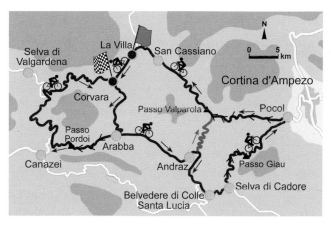

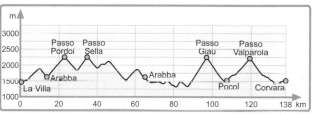

Cyclists as far as the eye can see – together with the Nove Colli the 'Maratona' is the biggest marathon in Italy.

endlessly through the village before the start. Although the countdown to the Marathon starts as early as 6 a.m., a later start around 9 is fine for tourism cyclists. So it's much easier to have breakfast, and the mountain air is no longer quite so cold. But anyone who expects to be able to bowl along will be disappointed: because immediately after the start the road is already climbing – a foretaste of the 138km to come. The whole route doesn't contain more than 10km on the flat in total.

The Campolongo is the starting point for the tour around the Sella mountain group, which is so popular with cyclists.

At the beginning you head south and follow the signposts to Corvara, which you reach after 4km. From here the climb up to the Campolongo Pass (1875m) begins, which at the same time is also the starting point for the tour around the Sella mountain group, so popular with cyclists. You have to conquer a vertical climb of 350m over 6km. This isn't a problem; numerous hairpin bends and easy bends make the climb more comfortable, and at 5.5 per cent it counts as one of the easier ones anyway. On the 'Maratona' most of those who started further behind get caught up in a traffic jam here – this problem doesn't affect the tourism cyclist.

Once you've ridden over the first pass of the day there follows a 4km-long descent with hairpin bends down to Arabba (14km), where you follow the signpost indicating the Pordoi Pass (2239m) to the right. Your legs are still fresh and the prospect of an amazing tour in this wonderful scenery, which incidentally is a UNESCO World Heritage Site, has you positively flying up this mountain. After the easy bends and hairpin bends of the first part of the

Shortly after the start the riders are still closely packed together, snaking endlessly up to the Campolongo Pass.

climb – there are 33 altogether over 9km – when you leave the village you follow the mountain road, which climbs at an easy 7 per cent. It's in good condition, and so after about 45 minutes and two short tunnels you arrive at the end of the top of the pass (23km). The fastest riders fly up here in 25 minutes – unbelievable!

In the shadow of the mighty Marmolada

You only stay on the summit for a short time enjoying the view towards Sassolungo and Piz Ciavazes, then you start on the 6km-long descent down a road just as winding as the climb up, first in the high mountain region and later in the forest. At Plan de Schiavaneis you turn right to the Sella Pass, which at 5.5km and with a constant climb of 6–8 per cent can be ridden with a relatively

steady rhythm. Always in the shadow of the impressive Marmolada, and surrounded first by conifers, later by mountain pastures, you get nearer and nearer to the top of the pass, which you reach after 35km at a height of 2244m. It's hard to believe that you've already tackled a vertical climb of 1500m over this short distance.

After a 5km descent towards Wolkenstein you turn right by the Hotel Miramonti towards the Gardena Pass. After a short section with a gradient of 8 per cent you reach a longer straight stretch, which leads along the Sella mountain group to the top of the pass (2121m) over two final very winding kilometres.

Now you've completed 46km – and then there follows another descent which is long and, at the start, particularly fast. With hairpin bends come hidden dangers, so be careful! This heart-stopping descent lasts for 9km until you finally reach Corvara (55km) again. Riders on the short course have now reached the finishing line, while the rest turn right in the village: the Campolongo has to be tackled a second time.

By now it's midday and the sun is shining. You can easily imagine that the next pass will be a sweaty and exhausting affair.

This time the climb turns out to be more difficult. By now you've tackled a vertical climb of 2000m and your legs feel like jelly. However, when you reach Arabba again (65km), you can cheer yourself up a little with the thought that

you've done almost half the tour. Now comes the 10km-long section to Andraz, which is mostly flat and allows you to pump your legs more easily again. By now it's midday and the sun is shining. You can easily imagine that the next pass will be a sweaty and exhausting affair.

In Andraz (75km) you ride up to the Falzarego and Valparola Passes, but after 1km you turn right up an 8 per cent climb to Cernadoi (76km) to tackle another downhill section. (Those taking part in the medium-length race, keep to the left here instead.) When you reach Rucavà (81km), you follow the signposts to Colle Santa Lucia. You eventually reach this Ladin commune after a further 2km with a good 7 per cent incline. The descent that starts now in the direction

In the course of the 'Maratona' you come out above the treeline more than once.

make the climb more difficult. It's broken up by a few hairpin bends, but this doesn't make it any easier. The Codalonga stream is a constant companion from the very beginning. You also have to cope with three tunnels and a road surface that is bumpy in places in the upper section. The last 3km are the most beautiful – but also the most difficult. Unfortunately, decreasing strength and the battle with the climb hardly give you a chance to glance back at the valley, which would be really worthwhile because of the dream view.

You've left the forest far behind when the road curves round to the right and you have a clear view of the top of the pass. After a left-hand bend and a total of 97km you've finally done it: you're at the top of the Giau Pass and can reward yourself with an incredible panoramic view – including the Nuvolau Massif. Then comes a winding and very steep descent with ramps in high double figures, which are only fun if you're a speed specialist. You're heading for Pocol (107km), which also marks the beginning of the seventh and last climb of the day: the combination of the Falzarego and Valparola.

If there's nothing to distract you it makes the physical agony even worse.

The Dolomites are the home territory of the South Tyrolean climbing specialist Alexander Zelger (among other things the Amateur World Mountain Champion in 2007). He does the Sella Ronda up to 30 times a year. 'For me, the route of the Maratona is the most beautiful of all,' he says.

of Selva di Cadore to Codalonga (87km) is then the last chance to rest your legs before the Giau Pass, a real killer, is on the agenda.

The killer climb up to the Giau Pass

This journey winds its way up to a height of 2236m over exactly 10km and a vertical climb of over 925m. It's the most difficult climb of the 'Maratona'. Starting off in the forest, the road climbs continually with a gradient of 9–10 per cent. Ramps of 14 per cent in places

Only 12km and a total vertical climb of no more than 750m remain to be overcome. To begin with the road goes round a few easy bends with a gradient of 5 per cent, but soon you're into 2km of flat road from which you can easily see where the top of the pass will be. As you go further on the climb remains relatively smooth and goes into the forest with a gradient of 6 per cent. Naturally you are now somewhat spoiled by the impressiveness of the scenery so far, so that this climb seems rather boring. And when there's nothing to distract you, apart from signs at the side of the road every now and then giving the actual height, this naturally makes the physical agony even worse.

In the end you're glad to tackle the final bends on the way to the top of the pass, which lead past a large car park and a restaurant to the top of the pass (2117m) with the cable railway station. When you reach the Falzarego (118km) the best part of the descent is over. Now you turn right to Valparola. After a short smoother section with a gradient of 5 per cent there follows a short ramp with a gradient of 10 per cent, which leads eventually, after 1km, to the top of the final pass at 2200m. As a reward there follows the longest descent of the day, a whole 14km. Beyond San Cassiano (130km) – incidentally there's an interesting museum here of Ladin culture and tradition – the road leads further down to La Villa (133km) and you arrive back at the place you started.

However, anyone who wants to put their feet up is mistaken because there's still another tough 5km to go on the programme: the finishing line of the Dolomites Marathon is in Corvara – and that's a 110m climb. The tough unpleasant climb of 2–4 per cent causes two and three times the pain of the climb so far. It's the fact that after the Valparola you have, in principle, written off the course in your mind as 'done and dusted' that makes the last section so difficult. Or is it down to the pangs of hunger you're feeling? You ponder that until you come out of the forest and catch sight of the first houses in Corvara: then it really is over and you've successfully completed the Maratona course – and discovered one of Europe's most beautiful cycling regions!

2011 results
1. Mazzocchi Sorrenti (Italy), 4 hours 33' 55"
2. Michel Snel (France), + 5' 23"
3. Luigi Salimbeni (Italy), + 8' 20"
4. Andrea Beconcini (Italy), + 9' 51"
5. Bart Bury (Belgium), + 9' 54"

Cyclists, check this out!
To prepare for the Dolomites Marathon you can take part in an open mountain time trial from Arabba up to the Pordoi Pass. The Sella Ronda Bike Day at the beginning of July is also a car-free Sunday on which the Sella Ronda can be ridden without traffic. And those who can't get enough of the beauty of the South Tyrolean mountain scenery should take a close look at the Giro delle Dolomiti: this stage race, which starts and finishes in Bozen, takes place in the first week of August and takes its participants over several Dolomites classics in a day; that way you'll meet the requirements of both the RTF (Radtourenfahren/German tourist cycling association) and amateur racing. Find more information at www.girodolomiti.com.

Cycling and sightseeing
On the way from the Pordoi Pass to the Sella Pass you go past a monument dedicated to one of the greatest stars, Fausto Coppi. It recalls both his great successes and crossings of the Pordoi Pass on the Giro.

Background
The passes you ride over on the Maratona are also regularly mountain stages of the Giro d'Italia. So you'll find numerous road paintings – mostly of the Italian heroes of the previous year – on the ground to reflect on as you climb. During the race the enthusiasm on the passes is just as gripping as on the famous Tour de France. Because of its geographical proximity, every cycling fan should see the Tour of Italy live – and best of all combine this trip with a tour through the South Tyrolean mountains.

TOUR PROFILE <<

Race date: End of June

Type: Marathon sportive

Start: Trondheim (Norway)

Finish: Oslo (Norway)

Distance: 540km. Shorter distances are also on offer: these start in Dombås (350km), Lillehammer (190km), Hamar (130km) and Eidsvoll (60km)

Total vertical climb: 3400m

Riding time: 21 hours

URL: www.styrkeproven.no

Route: From the profile of the route the tour doesn't appear to be difficult. The total vertical climb of 3400m does sound a lot given the long distance over a predominantly flat course. The main factor is the long time it takes to ride – above all endurance, and also psychological staying power, will be severely tested.

Fitness: Endurance, motivation and the ability to stay in the saddle are the three key elements in undertaking the Trondheim–Oslo. You can only get through 540km with the right preparation. The shorter courses on offer make participation possible for everyone, but it's the actual 'test of stamina' which makes the TO so interesting.

Equipment: A 39/25 set-up is enough for cyclists who have trained well. To be on the safe side you can fit a compact chainset. A triple chainset isn't necessary because the course profile is so flat.

A team meeting before the start.

It's normal for ambitious cyclists to set themselves ever-higher targets. If you've successfully completed the Ötztaler Radmarathon (*see* pages 142–147), participating in the Trondheim–Oslo cycle tourism event, also known as the 'Store Styrkeprøven', would be a possible step up. If the total vertical climb of 5500m of the Ötzi was capable of inspiring respect, then the 540km route from Trondheim to Oslo takes things to another level. On one hand, you'll be attracted to its magic, while on the other you'll always have doubts as to whether you'll be able to rise to the challenge. Not for nothing does the nickname of the race translate as 'the big trial of strength' ...

In the imagination of most cyclists 540km is the distance covered in a week of training in Majorca – in good weather and with a hotel where after finishing the ride you can hit the beach. There's no way the Trondheim–Oslo can fulfil this ideal. You have to do the whole lot in one go; if you can snatch a couple of hours on a mattress in a crowded gym in the evening and if the daytime temperature reaches a high of 15°C and the rain decreases from your own personal shower to a light drizzle, then you can count yourself lucky. (Of course there will always be editions without any rain, but you shouldn't count on it.)

Numerous undulations at the start often make standing up out of the saddle necessary.

A logistical marathon as well

There's only one way to find out whether you can stand up to all these demands: you hand over the entry fee, wait for all the documentation and in the time left over from training get busy with all the logistical tasks a journey to the far north entails so you can arrive in Norway's third largest city in good time for the midsummer solstice, when the race is always held.

Just like the Ötztaler, the 'trial of strength' also exerts a great attraction for many participants: Axel Fehlau from Cologne, for example, has completed the Store Styrkeprøven 17 times so far. He sums up his fascination with the event as 'Scenery, cyclists and suffering: the experience stays with me for the rest of the year.'

The starting line for the 540km is the Munkegata, one of the two main streets in Trondheim, which leads up from the market to the famous Nidaros Cathedral, which has stood there solidly since the 12th century and is considered to be one of the most important church buildings in Scandinavia. All Norwegian kings have been crowned here since 1814, in accordance with the constitution. Modern times are in evidence here on the Trondheim–Oslo in the time-keeping chip attached to the bike. This has replaced the old barcode on the competition number that was read and noted down at the finish.

Once your pack of about 100 cyclists starts to move, all the tension falls away and all doubts as to whether the training kilometres on the bike since spring were enough just evaporate.

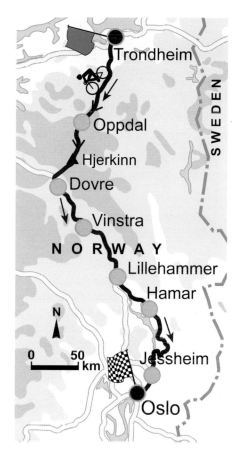

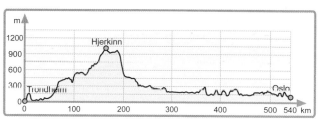

Frame material has also noticeably changed from chrome-molybdenum to aluminium, and carbon can also be seen. But touring bikes with good old steel frames have also survived – in some cases equipped with mudguards and saddlebags, which mean abandoning all thoughts of light weight – and their owners are noticeably carrying a few too many kilos to be able to pass as cyclists

down the other side again with a similar downhill gradient. In this way you cover some 25km to Kvål before you can draft again on the more even route on the following 40km to Soknedal.

The Norwegian forest

From now on the green fields at the beginning of the race give way to thick forest leading into the Gaula valley, which isn't particularly wide and in places is strewn with boulders. On the whole the surroundings appear rather less than spectacular and the route profile doesn't promise any particular difficulties either. Here and there the road climbs by 2–3 per cent, sometimes by as much as 4 per cent, and then sustains this climb over long sections, but the major part of the route to Garli, where the first feeding station is waiting, runs on the flat.

And the profile of the route to Driva and the next 'Matstasjon', as the feeding stations are called here, doesn't change significantly. Gentle climbs alternate with flat sections and a few gentle descents. So far you have 127km and a total vertical climb of 550m in your legs and the information board which announces the next feeding station in 52km time is gratefully noted. However, what isn't mentioned anywhere is that the largest part of the uphill section of the route so far – up to Dovrefjell – now lies in front of you. (In the Scandinavian countries the word 'Fjell' refers to every area above the treeline.)

If you weren't so stressed because of this distance you'd certainly be able to take more pleasure in the exotic, almost prehistoric appearance of the scenery.

Drafting is particularly important on the Trondheim–Oslo. It saves your strength and increases your speed.

who have trained for the event. But it's precisely these riders who make a lasting impression, which for some reason or other is rather reassuring.

Once your pack of about 100 cyclists starts to move, all the tension falls away and all doubts as to whether the training kilometres on the bike since spring were enough just evaporate. All your attention is directed towards your fellow cyclists so you don't get caught on those overtaking or riding next to you and thus perhaps run the risk of an accident. That would be all the more unpleasant so early on in the race.

You leave Trondheim on the wide four-lane E6. You cross the River Nidelva, which meanders between the warehouses of the metropolis and soon come to the edge of the city – and here's the first climb. The 2km-long climb with a gradient of 5 per cent is quickly seen off and is followed by a longer, gentle descent, which leads to a crossroads: the way to Oslo is signposted here. However, the fact that it's 527km away is rather less than encouraging.

The next few kilometres demand constant gear-changing. The road climbs up little hills 100–200m long with a gradient of some 7 per cent, then goes

But the road is still running on the flat and you're making good time when, after about 150km, the valley becomes considerably more narrow. The road is also climbing, but not over 5 per cent. It drags on noticeably for a good 10km. With the arrival of a plateau the incline decreases markedly and, over gentle ascents and descents, you approach Hjerkinn, the 'roof' of the route at 1022m above sea level. By now you've done 165km and actually you could stop now – but there's still more than two-thirds of the way to go to the finishing line. If you weren't so stressed because of this distance you'd certainly be able to take more pleasure in the exotic, almost prehistoric appearance of the scenery.

That scenery is predominantly low bushes, wind-blown trees, rocks covered in moss and lichen, and little lakes, behind which rise mountain ridges with isolated patches of snow. In Norwegian mythology this region in known as 'Utmark': the 'land beyond the influence of man'. Those who have read books by the famous Norwegian writer Henrik Ibsen (author of *Peer Gynt*, published in 1867) know that the legendary trolls are also supposed to live up here.

Rather more real, however, is the population of some 23 musk oxen established in this area, which is partly designated as a national park. But you see these shy animals as rarely as you see trolls. What is noticeable is the heavy traffic, which is not at all pleasant. Not long after leaving Trondheim the E6 goes down to two lanes and isn't as wide, so drivers mostly see cyclists as a nuisance.

Battling with the traffic

Larger groups have a better time of it here, since they can rarely be overtaken because of the oncoming traffic – but cars push past smaller groups and solitary cyclists, sometimes with very little room to spare. So it's a good idea to

The landscape, which in the course of the race offers a wide spectrum of Norwegian vegetation, appears wide and mysterious.

In 1993 Oslo hosted the UCI Road World Championships. The winner of the amateur race was the German Jan Ullrich.

thickly forested then wider again and with enough room for green fields, fertile farmland and impressive towns. If it wasn't for the unfamiliar timber houses in the towns, the scenery would make you feel you'd been transported to a low mountain range in Germany.

There are no difficulties on the road waiting for you here. Mostly flat, at times also gently descending, the route continues with not a single climb along the way. Instead there's a different problem here: while the fastest have already reached the finishing line in Oslo, darkness is slowly stealing over the majority of riders, who are still on their way. As it's midsummer's day it's not completely dark, but visibility is now so bad that speed and in particular safety are no longer guaranteed.

Those for whom the time taken isn't the highest priority would do better to spend the hours between midnight and about 3 a.m. in the morning at one of the feeding stations, which offer secure accommodation. You can have a shower, perhaps, or a massage, and even try to get a little sleep there – rest and relaxation are called for in any case. You reach the feeding station at Kvam after about 270km, and the next one in Kvitfjelltunet after some 320km.

use the narrow strip marked off at the side of the road as a cycle path, which will at least give the traffic a little more room.

The road keeps to the plateau for a good 30km before it goes down to Dombås on a 5 per cent descent. You've already done 200km once you turn into the Gudbrandsdalen. In the Middle Ages the king was taken from here to Trondheim for his coronation, while today riders on the 'trial of strength' want to take the 'crown' for their passion for cycling in Oslo at the other end of the route.

If it wasn't for the unfamiliar timber houses in the towns, the scenery would make you feel you'd been transported to a low mountain range in Germany.

The road now goes southwards through the valley carved by the Lågen river flows for 150km. The surroundings reflect the rural side of Norway in particular: in places it's narrow and

More and more hills

Shortly before you get to Lillehammer you leave the E6 and the valley, and encounter once more an agricultural landscape with meadows, woods, settlements, farmland and pastures. But the road's climbing again. Not bad climbs, mostly only from 3–4 per cent, increasing at one point to 6 per cent at the most. Many are only 100m long, but others stretch out for 2–3km. However, by far the greater part of the route is flat, in places even downhill, and if you were on a section like this on a training circuit at home you'd certainly try to set a good pace.

Here, with 350km already in your legs, it looks different, because every climb on the road, however small, makes the number on the speedometer drop noticeably. While the fastest reached the finishing line long ago, for most people the real suffering starts here. And everyone will suffer, sooner or later, more or less, and every kilometre that you put in when training will pay off now.

You have to find your own rhythm here and distract yourself: with the scenery, by thinking or by talking to other participants.

Feeding stations are situated about 40km apart, and every 10km signs tell you how far you still have to go, but the distance to them decreases excruciatingly slowly. You have to find your own rhythm here and distract yourself: with the scenery, by thinking or by talking to other participants. Sixty kilometres after Lillehammer you reach the feeding station at Rica Hamar Olrud (420km) and after 480km you get to Eidsvoll Verk, which you get to along the Trondheimsvegen. The final spurt is coming closer, and thinking about it brings new strength.

However, it's the city sign for Oslo that really puts you out of your misery. For now there are only some 15km to the finishing line. Increasing traffic doesn't make the ride any easier. Just one last climb about 2km long, then there's a lane reserved for cyclists to the finishing line. Exhaustion doesn't allow for great emotions, but joy and also pride are experienced by all at their achievement. And rightly so, because you've successfully ridden the 'great trial of strength', one of the greatest in cycling!

2011 results
1 Ove Matland (Norway), 13 hours 17' 58"
1 Arne Kettedal (Norway), same time
1 Helge Løge (Norway), same time
1 Olav Tu Husveg (Norway), same time
1 Rune Holmen (Norway), same time

Cyclists, check this out!
For those who like cycling in the Norwegian scenery, the all-comers' stage race the Viking Tour is recommended: for a whole week the fjords on the west coast and their hinterland are not safe from cyclists. You'll be surprised not just by the numerous mountain passes but also by the incredible highlights of the scenery. Find more information at www.vikingtour.no.

Cycling and sightseeing
In August 1993 the UCI Road World Championships took place in Oslo. Since the World Association at that time still divided cycling into amateur and professional classes, there were two winners of the difficult circuit of the Norwegian capital: Lance Armstrong and Jan Ullrich. Nobody thought at the time that later on both of them would come to win the Tour de France over the years. The Ekeberg was the killer climb of the course at that time, and this is worth a visit the day after the Trondheim–Oslo. You'll find it in the south-east of the city, near the coast.

Background
Specialists have emerged for long-distance races such as the Norwegian 'trial of strength'. For such randonneurs, as these riders are called, who happily cover more than 200km at a time, there are now quite a number of events that carry the name 'Brevet' (French for 'exam'). Here it's not so much the time as completing the course that counts. The best-known example of this type of race is certainly the Paris–Brest–Paris (*see* chapter 'Further classics', page 175), which is run over 1200km in France. London–Edinburgh–London (1400km) and Madrid–Gijón–Madrid (1200km) are also well-known events of this type.

TOUR PROFILE <<

Race date: Early to mid-June

Type: Marathon sportive

Start/finish: Beaumes-de-Venise (France)

Distance: 170km (75 and 102km versions are possible)

Total vertical climb: 3500m

Riding time: 7 hours

URL: www.sportcommunication.info

Route: A very charming tour round bare giant mountains. The most difficult part, the climb on the Ventoux, comes immediately after the first 30km. Once you've survived that the second climb to Chalet Reynard isn't a problem, and you can quietly enjoy the scenery of Provence.

Fitness: Mont Ventoux demands every mountain-climbing quality – a climb of 1700m in one go speaks for itself. However, with the appropriate level of training this circuit is possible without any problems. For those who can't spend so much time in the saddle, La Ventoux offers versions of 102 and 75km. On the former you miss out the second big climb up to Chalet Reynard and on the latter you also miss out the loop over the Col de Veaux.

Equipment: Whatever else you do, pack your mountain set-up at all costs: a 29-tooth sprocket and/or a compact chainset are obligatory here. Otherwise you'll run out of breath on the higher reaches – and then this climb will feel like you're on a merciless desert planet.

Mont Ventoux is one of the hallowed mountains of the Tour de France.

You recognise it as a hazy blue silhouette on the horizon. This mountain rises up all on its own and its bare peak, worn down over centuries by the wind, towers above the landscape which is otherwise characterised by green forests and brown fields. Some people call it the 'barren giant of Provence', others the 'hallowed mountain'. However, it's usually known by its proper name: Mont Ventoux.

This 1910m-high summit in southern France is linked inseparably with the history of the Tour de France. Together with the Col du Galibier, the Col du Tourmalet and the torture of the ski station on the Alpe d'Huez it's counted as one of the four 'hallowed mountains' of the Big Loop. The reason for this is the dramas that have been played out on its scree-strewn slopes over the years since its first edition in 1951. Often enough a preliminary decision is made here about the overall outcome. Certainly the 1967 season is remembered as a tragic highlight when the Brit Tom Simpson toppled dead from his bike just below the top of the pass (*see* 'Cycling and sightseeing', page 115).

Ventoux for everyone

But it's not just the professionals on the tour who can experience the Ventoux: this pleasure is also open to hobby cyclists. La Ventoux is a unique cycle marathon which, in the course of its 170km with a total vertical climb of 3500m, is dedicated to the bare giant. After you've climbed it from the classic Bédoin side – for the very first edition in 1951 the climb was tackled from Malaucène on the northern side, then for every later edition from Bédoin – you ride round it once and then you storm up the first half once more as far as Chalet Reynard.

The tour of Provence starts in Beaumes-de-Venise, a town typical of the region, which makes its living in particular from wine-growing and lies not far from the western side of the Ventoux. Once you've made all your preparations you leave the town to the east and follow the signposts to St-Hippolyte-le-Graveyron (5km). The road goes gently but continually upwards, past numerous fields and isolated farmsteads, to Caromb, which you reach after about 8km.

You now approach Saint-Pierre-de-Vassois (11km) over narrow little roads of rough tarmac, then turn north to Crillon-le-Brave (14km) and ride on from there to Bédoin (17km). The Ventoux is now directly in front of you and you know that it won't be long until the long hard slog begins. The mountain dominates everything. It also rules the lives of its inhabitants, who for one thing make a living from the tourism it attracts.

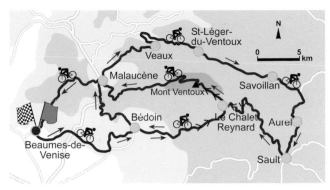

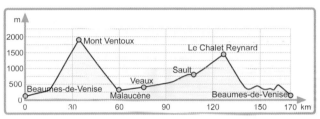

On the ride to the Provence colossus the peloton is still together. Soon the riders will go flying off one after another.

In good weather you can make out the summit with its huge aerial high up in the distance.

As you leave Bédoin you're finally there, and the torture begins. At first the road is still being kind. It passes numerous fields on the way to Sainte Colombe (22km), and you can get used to the climbing to come on a gradient that starts at 3, then 5 per cent. In good weather you can make out the summit with its huge aerial high up in the distance. So far you've climbed 1500m in the last 18km.

Finally the going really gets tough 3km later in Saint Estève. The forest begins, and after a left-hand bend the gradient leaps up to 9 per cent. It stays at this level for the next 8km. This is the hardest part of the climb. Surrounded by numerous trees you wish you were at the crossroads at Chalet Reynard (33km). Not just because it's a bit flatter there, but also because you've reached the treeline here and from now on you'll be rewarded with the typical barren, stony atmosphere of the Ventoux. And still you haven't reached the summit. But you're already two-thirds of the way up when you reach the turn-off for Sault. You can have a short rest here and fill your water bottle at the fountain.

A stony wasteland

The route has been gently winding up to now, but on the next few kilometres there are hairpin bends, which make riding easier. However, the gradient soon increases to 8 per cent. Even though it's still early in the morning the burning sun can really make you feel as though you're completely at its mercy. Not the smallest scrap of shadow, nothing. Just stones, stones and more stones. So you wind your way further along the moonlike

Lance Armstrong attacks –
but the American has never managed to win on the Ventoux.

Remembering a dark hour in cycling history: the memorial to Tom Simpson.

You've got to the summit. As a reward, a breakneck descent is waiting.

mountain ridge. The aerial on the summit moves slowly closer and your pedalling becomes more and more jerky. It's hard to imagine the high speed at which Marco Pantani, with his sustained climbing, and Lance Armstrong, with his staccato pedalling out of the saddle, fought their duel here in 2000. Two kilometres from the top of the pass you reach the memorial to Tom Simpson (*see* page 115). The last few metres are painful again: ramps with an incline of up to 12 per cent demand all your strength – and then comes the famous final hairpin bend. You have to muster all your strength one last time and pedal out of the saddle, and then after 39km you're finally at the summit, 1909m up.

Even the legendary Eddy Merckx must have experienced how merciless the Mont Ventoux can be.

Just want to get off your bike and lie down? You're not the only one to feel like that. Even the legendary Eddy Merckx must have experienced how merciless the Mont Ventoux can be. He won the stage in 1970, but he was so exhausted from climbing on that bleak giant that he collapsed before he reached the finishing line and had to be got back on his feet with the aid of a cylinder of oxygen.

But as a reward you can enjoy the magnificent panorama from up here. When the weather's clear you can see the Alps, the Cevennes and as far as the Mediterranean Sea – fantastic.

The breakneck descent on the northern side of the Ventoux down to Malaucène (60km) is your second reward for the hard climb: long straight sections, well-built hairpin bends and a relatively

Back down in the valley you cycle round the mountain. Even the professionals bypassed it in 2009 during the 'Paris–Nice'.

newer surface make for high speeds, and you arrive in the little village with its famous clock tower in next to no time. If you've already had enough you can turn off here onto the short route of 75km and bowl straight through the village back to Beaumes-de-Venise. The longer circuit, on the other hand, goes on after two right-hand turns in the direction of Veaux.

The beauty of Provence

The section of the route which follows is typical of Provence. It runs north around the Ventoux along an undulating little-used road, so you can really enjoy the beauty of the region. Riding is even more fun between the numerous arable fields and fields of lavender, and the hardships of an hour ago are soon forgotten.

Overall the road climbs gently, and after several bends and 72km you reach the beginning of the Col de Veaux (76km). Compared with the Ventoux the total vertical climb of just under 100m is nothing much. You go further on through St-Léger-du-Ventoux (84km) and St-Roch (90km) before you get onto a still gently climbing road after Savoillan. You now have 94km on the books, and just over half the course has been done.

Now you go on to Reilhanette (99km) where you work your way south again along the eastern side of the Ventoux. After 105km you arrive, on a narrow road, in the village of Aurel, built on the mountainside, and then not long after in Sault (107km), where the start of the village marks the second ride over the bare giant. Here you should definitely

16 La Ventoux

Inland numerous fields of lavender are characteristic of the region.

stop at a small café to have something to fortify yourself and to fill up your water bottles so that you don't end up helpless on the side of the road with your tongue hanging out during the climb, which doesn't lead all the way up to the summit but 'only' to the crossroads at Chalet Reynard.

The first 5km on the way to Sault lead through wonderful fields of lavender.

But that shouldn't happen in any case, since the ramp to the east of Sault is the easiest of the three climbs up to the Ventoux. On the 20km climb up to Chalet Reynard (129km) it's never steeper than 6 per cent. The first 5km

still lead through wonderful fields of lavender, before going into the forest on the climb from Bédoin. The road has more bends here, which makes riding easier. Seven kilometres before you reach the crossroads you've done the worst part and, despite increasing exhaustion, you can really enjoy the remaining part of the climb with a gentle incline of 2 per cent.

On the same route as the one you started the uphill climb on you now go down again to Bédoin, which you reach after 144km. There are now just 26km to go to the finishing line, and the tour is almost over. However, two small climbs remain: up to La Madeleine (151km) there is a vertical climb of 150m and you have to cope with tarmac, which by now has become hot with the sun. After that there's still the Col de la Chaîne, which comes just after Malaucène (154km), 4km long over narrow little mountain roads continually climbing at 5–7 per cent.

Then it's all over: through Suzette (163km) and Lafare (167km) you now go downhill until after 170km you're finally back where you started in the idyllic village of Beaumes-de-Venise. It's already late in the afternoon and fortunately, because you've finished you can turn round once more and look towards the east. There you'll see the hazy blue silhouette of the mountain that has kept you spellbound for the whole day: Mont Ventoux.

An unforgettable duel: Lance Armstrong and Marco Pantani battle it out for the stage win in the 2000 edition of the Tour de France.

2011 results
1 Jean Christophe Currit (France), 4 hours 4' 17"
2 Pierre Damien Clement (France), + 1' 09"
3 David de Vecchi (France), + 1' 04"

Cyclists, check this out!
Just like La Marmotte, La Ventoux has a mountain race called the Grimpe du Ventoux (for amateurs and all-comers) on the day after the long marathon. Cyclists tackle the 21.5km classic climb from Bédoin. If you want to compare your performance with that of the professionals, Iban Mayo holds the record. The Spanish climbing specialist took just 55 minutes 51 seconds to get to the summit in a mountain time trial during the Dauphiné Libéré in 2004 and was also almost 2 minutes faster than Lance Armstrong, who took part as well. A couple of days later Mayo was the overall winner of the tour.

Cycling and sightseeing
There's a memorial stone 2km from the summit in memory of Tom Simpson. He died on this stage of the Tour de France on the mammoth mountain in 1967. Shortly before he reached the finishing line Simpson collapsed and fell in a ditch at the side of the road. Trying to ride on he lost consciousness

again after a few steps and fell. A heart attack finally cost him his life. A post mortem a little later found stimulants and alcohol in his blood. Many cyclists who tackle Mont Ventoux use the memorial stone as an opportunity for a rest and leave something behind, such as a water bottle or some other gift.

Background
Traditionally, Mont Ventoux is the preserve of climbing specialists. But in 1994 a hitherto relatively unknown cyclist set out to disprove this: his name was Eros Poli. The Italian, nearly 6ft 4in tall and weighing 13st 5lb, was usually a member of the grupetto because of his size, and typically helped out his captain. But on that day he rewrote history. Early in the stage he started a long attempt to break away, and the fact that the peloton was tired by the previous day's stage allowed Poli to reach the foot of Mont Ventoux with a 24-minute lead. This cushion was enough to hold out against Marco Pantani and Miguel Induráin, specialists at forcing the pace: after a breakneck descent Poli, with tears in his eyes, held on to a stage win that had seemed impossible. His achievement impressed the tour organisers so much that they later named him the most aggressive rider of the Tour de France.

TOUR PROFILE <<

Race date: Early July

Type: Marathon sportive

Start: Bourg-d'Oisans (France)

Finish: L'Alpe d'Huez (France)

Distance: 174km

Total vertical climb: 5180m

Riding time: 7 hours

URL: www.sportcommunication.info

Route: La Marmotte is an impressive tour that combines the most beautiful Alpine classics of the Tour de France: from Bourg-d'Oisans you ride the Glandon, the Télégraphe and the Galibier one after another, and finish with the famous 21 hairpin bends up to L'Alpe d'Huez.

Fitness: If you haven't trained properly and turn the scales at a few kilos too many, you'll regret it every step of the way. Theoretically you can in fact avoid the final climb up to L'Alpe d'Huez and 1100m of vertical climb – but then you'd also have to give up on reaching the summit. You should also be used to long descents: the descent from the Galibier alone is almost 40km continuously downhill. So prepare yourself well!

Equipment: The total vertical climb indicates that you should use your mountain set-up here. A compact chainset or a 29-tooth sprocket will also be needed by good mountain riders to keep the legs relaxed. If you can do that the final torture up to L'Alpe d'Huez will be a little more bearable.

Tour de France riders in the Alpe.

If you were to do a survey into which of the mountain approaches on the Tour de France is the best known, you would very quickly come to a clear conclusion: L'Alpe d'Huez. From the point of view of cycling, this ski resort is legendary – for riders as well as for fans. Since its first edition in 1952 numerous epic stories have grown up around this climb, which, next to the Col du Galibier, is the most famous of all the French Alps. In fact, both of them are often combined into one stage, which makes this leg into the pinnacle of the Tour de France. So when riding La Marmotte you conquer both classic tours in one day.

This cycle marathon, the name of which means 'marmot', is one of the best known in the whole of France and, if you like, the blue, white and red counterpart of the Ötztaler Radmarathon in Austria and the Maratona dles Dolomites in Italy. On a 174km circuit around Bourg-d'Oisans riders have to contend with a total vertical climb of 5180m. And while you're doing it you're on the 'holy' ground of the Tour de France the whole time: the Glandon, the Télégraphe and the Galibier crop up in almost every edition of the great loop – as well as the crowning torment up to the Alpe d'Huez.

At the foot of the Alpe

The starting point for La Marmotte is Bourg-d'Oisans. This quiet little town at the foot of the Alpe hibernates for most of the year. It only wakes up in July – and then the cycling boom takes over. Because of the crowds expected here you should try to find accommodation in one of the many specialist boarding houses or campsites for cyclists well in advance. If you leave it too late there won't be anything left by July – the town will be bursting at the seams.

You leave the town going north. It's level for 10km, and you can bowl along until you get to Rochetaillée (7km). It's still early, and the valley is still mainly in shadow. The River Romanche murmurs quietly in front of you. It's going to be a long day in the saddle.

At the big crossroads you follow the signpost in the direction of the Col du Glandon and turn right. On the left now is the Verney reservoir, at the far end of which the climb begins up the first mountain of the day. The Glandon is really tough going: the road climbs for more than 25km, with only three short downhill sections to break it up, and has a total vertical climb of a good 1200m to conquer on your way up to the summit, which was crossed in the Tour de France for the first time in 1952.

In the course of climbing the Glandon you cross every climate zone in the Alps.

As you leave Allemont (10km) you enter a thick pine forest which will be with you for the time being at least. In the course of climbing

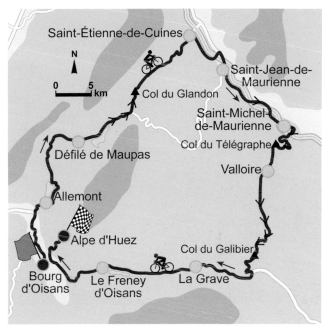

A participant in La Marmotte fights his way up the long road on the Col du Glandon. In the background you can make out the reservoir.

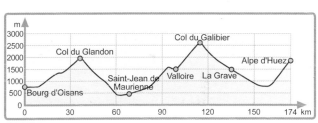

the Glandon (which turns out to be steep, with an incline of up to 11 per cent) you cross every climate zone in the Alps. Constantly riding along the slope you quickly gain altitude. To the left are cliffs and rock faces, to the right crash barriers. It continues like this to Rivier-d'Allemond, a little mountain village you go through after 20km. It's a little flatter here, and the decreasing incline even turns into a slight descent for a short time. Four narrow hairpin bends provide a bit of a breather. You'll need this because the route now switches to the other side of the valley and from now on you're pedalling up the mountain on the right.

You soon make up the height you've lost – an incline of 12 per cent over the next few kilometres sees to that. Another short descent ends the steep section. Then the road climbs again at a more bearable 8 per cent. The scenery becomes more barren and more and more alpine, and the quality of the road surface declines as well. Finally several

hairpin bends announce the arrival of Grand Maison lake (30km), whose reservoir walls had already been visible several kilometres away. It's not far to the summit now. You pass the treeline and a spectacular view opens up in front of you and you can see the pass for the first time.

There are just 5km left to the top. A short descent (31km) brings a bit of a break before you tackle another steeper section. A kilometre before the top of the pass the road turns towards the Croix de Fer which you have also been able to see for some time. Keep to the left. A little restaurant at the side of the road offers you a chance to fill up your water bottles.

During the tour a carnival atmosphere prevails on the Galibier. All the best spots have been reserved days before the race.

In the middle of the village you turn right at a huge crossroads and follow the signposts in the direction of the Col du Télégraphe. The road there is a typical link road, just like the Brenner on the Ötztaler. The very busy wide main road climbs quite gently and you keep to the left-hand side of the rushing River Arc all the time until you reach Saint-Michel-de-Maurienne (81km). There's an opportunity for refreshment here before you start the full 2400m climb over the Télégraphe up to the Galibier. The bridges decorated with flowers and the railway underpass later mark the start of the climb. You pass a few isolated houses on your way to Les Seignes (83km), when you enter the leafy forest.

A couple of hairpin bends follow before you finally reach the top of the pass (36km) at a height of 1924m.

Dangerous descent

However, the descent that follows is not relaxing: it goes steeply down the edge on the left-hand side. There are no road markings, but there is a rough, bumpy road surface again and many bends without good visibility. So you have to look out for traffic! On the lower section unlit tunnels make the chase much more difficult.

With the decrease in height the countryside quickly becomes greener again, and you arrive at the next village, Saint-Colomban-des-Villards, after 46km. Then it's fast down into the valley of the River Arc, which you reach at Saint-Etienne-de-Cuines after 57km. You should definitely watch out here: four speed bumps are built into the road surface to reduce speed. If you don't see them because you're going too fast, an accident is inevitable!

You shouldn't be tempted to use up too much energy – the worst is still to come.

Like the Galibier that follows, the Télégraphe was included in the Tour de France programme for the first time in 1911. In 2011, 100 years later, this was done again. The climb measures a good 12km. Its average incline of 7.3 per cent is not to be sniffed at. Because the whole climb remains relatively even you can find a good rhythm. Numerous hairpin bends and easy curves also help. But you shouldn't be tempted to use up too much energy – the worst is still to come. Three kilometres from the top of the pass the forest thins out and on the right you get a good view of the valley. A big wooden sign finally marks the 1570m high summit, which you reach after 93km.

Now there's a 5km long descent to Valloire (98km). There are already signposts to the Galibier next to the stone church in the village. A 17km climb with a total vertical climb of just under 1200m now lies in front of you. After a relatively flat start the climb rises at a constant 8 or more per cent. You quickly reach the treeline and with increasing exhaustion – by now you've a total vertical climb of almost 3000m in your legs – you soon begin to see why tour history is written on this alpine giant.

Riders on the snow-covered Galibier. In 2011 it had to be scaled twice.

Alpine panoramas and the last remnants of snow

At Plan Lachat (106km) there are still 9km to go to the summit. Everywhere you look there are green high mountain pastures and mountain peaks: an impressive panorama. If you're unlucky, you can run into a nasty crosswind here. A little mountain stream babbles down to the right, a couple of hairpin bends bring you higher up. It really is time to get to the top of the pass – your legs hurt and the height of 2000m is making itself felt too. During the Tour de France lines of caravans stand on the side of the road, the smell of barbecues hangs in the air and spectators form a narrow honour guard when the riders fight their way up the mountain.

Over the last few kilometres you're treated to an impressive view of the Galibier: below you winds the road that you've just climbed and you have a stupendous view over the surrounding mountains. Three kilometres before the summit the road becomes narrower and more exposed. Now the Tour professionals have to fight for the mountain classification. Patches of snow still lie at the edge of the road. Just one more kilometre, the last hairpin bend, and then the summit: you're 2645m above sea level and you've climbed the Col du Galibier (115km)!

Just like the descent from the Glandon, the descent from the Galibier has no crash barriers.

A descent follows that people like you yearn for: a whole 45km downhill to Bourg-d'Oisans – a rich reward for all that effort! But you should dress up warmly before you speed down because the wind chill factor makes the temperature noticeably cooler. Besides, the descent demands renewed caution: Just like the descent from the Glandon, the descent from the Galibier has no crash barriers! And to cap it all the road surface is worse

Even if the tour devil, Didi Senft, isn't at the marmotte, he belongs to this mountain just as much as to the Tour de France.

side, before you go downhill, after a short opposing climb, to sweep into Bourg-d'Oisans. If you have cramp in your fingers from braking so much, shaking them out helps!

At the turn-off to Les-Deux-Alpes, another famous mountain-top finish on the Tour de France, you go straight on and so finally arrive in the plain after 157km. But this pleasure doesn't last long: 4km later you pass the town sign for Bourg-d'Oisans. A big roundabout follows from which you exit right following the signposts – the final climb to l'Alpe d'Huez is waiting.

21 hairpin bends up to Olympus

L'Alpe d'Huez – a legend. The road winds up to the ski resort over 21 hairpin bends; 21 hairpin bends full of pain and history. Among other things the names the bends carry testify to this: each one is named after a winner on the Alpe d'Huez. Because of the frequency with which this mountain classification is included in the Tour de France programme, many bends are actually dedicated to two professional riders.

Once you've gone through Bourg-d'Oisans the bridge over the River Romance is the starting point for the adventure. If you were to ride this mountain on the day of the Tour, there would already be caravans, snack bars and T-shirt and jersey stalls at the side of the road. It's hard to imagine, but 1 million spectators crowd together here on race day. So the riders get the feeling that they're riding at a wall of people and they

in places and there are sharp bends, and decreasing concentration due to increasing exhaustion plays its part too.

After about a kilometre you reach a place where you can stop for refreshment. The famous memorial to Henri Desgrange (*see* 'Cycling and sightseeing', opposite) is here too. After 122km you get to the turn-off for the Col du Lautaret, which you don't take, but keep to the right instead. The road surface is better and the bends are bounded by crash barriers again. You reach the treeline and soon there are several small tunnels and two long ones. A light on your bike is definitely a good idea here.

Having almost arrived back down in the valley you discover another reservoir, the Lac du Chambon, on the left-hand just have to take it on trust that they'll jump aside at the last moment. The peeling slogans on the road testify to the carnival-like atmosphere of the last time they rode the Great Loop.

Do you remember the pictures of the US Postal Team that Lance Armstrong steered to their best time ever on the mountain?

The mountain classification stage starts out steeply. Do you remember the pictures of the US Postal Team that Lance Armstrong steered to their best time ever on the mountain? That's something you can only dream about. You need luck – 13.2km with an average incline of 8.1 per cent, and all with a total vertical climb of 4000m already in your legs!

In the forest one hairpin bend follows another, with only the sign boards with the names of riders on to distract you a little. Hennie Kuiper, Joop Zoetemelk,

Peter Winnen – now you understand why this climb is nicknamed 'The Dutchman's mountain'. In the 1980s they were the best mountain riders in the world – a time that is long past.

Hairpin bend number seven is dedicated to Gianni Bugno, who ushered in the 1990s. You've completed two-thirds of the climb now and it's a little flatter. From hairpin bend number three (Marco Pantani) the forest slowly thins out and the entry to Alpe d'Huez soon follows. Hairpin bend number two also belongs to Pantani and number one to his compatriot Giuseppe Guerini. The hotel appears, typical of a ski resort with its wooden facade. Just one more kilometre, a short underpass, it gets steeper again – and then it's all over: after 174km and a total vertical climb of 5180m you've conquered the 'Marmot' and you're standing in the finish area of the Alpe d'Huez: Mount Olympus on the tour de France.

2011 results «

1 Michel Snel (Netherlands), 5 hours 32' 23"
2 Jean Christophe Currit (France), same time
3 Bury Bart (Belgium), + 1' 32"

Cyclists, check this out!

If you haven't had enough of La Marmotte, you can do it all again the next day: the organisers also run the Grimpée de l'Alpe, a mountain time trial up to l'Alpe d'Huez. It's timed from the same starting and finishing points as the professionals use for the official record for the famous ride over 21 hairpin bends. The record holder is Marco Pantani. His time: an unbelievable 37 minutes 35 seconds!

Cycling and sightseeing

A memorial at the south entrance to the tunnel at the top of the Col du Galibier commemorates the creation of the Tour de France and its founder, Henri Desgrange. In

addition to the normal mountains classification the 'Souvenir Henri Desgrange' is held in his honour at each edition of the Tour de France. This special classification is awarded to the first rider to reach the highest point of that particular Tour. This is usually the Galibier.

Background

With 21 hairpin bends, the Alpe d'Huez is considered to be one of the most famous climbs of the Tour de France, along with the Col du Galibier, the Col du Tourmalet and Mont Ventoux. Why? Not just because of the difficulty of this mountain-top finish, but also because the greatest mountain climbers in cycling (with few exceptions) have found fame there after winning: Fausto Coppi, Joop Zoetemelk, Luis Herrera, Bernard Hinault, Gianni Bugno, Marco Pantani, Lance Armstrong and finally Alberto Contador. So for riders and spectators alike, success here is all the more important.

18 PAU-TOURMALET
A unique Pyrenean stage of the Tour

TOUR PROFILE <<

Race date: July

Type: Professional race

Start: Pau (France)

Finish: Col du Tourmalet (France)

Distance: 181km

Total vertical climb: 4400m

Riding time: 8 hours

URL: www.letour.com

Route: The unique route of the 17th stage of the Tour de France in 2010. From Pau it goes over the Col de Marie-Blanque and the Col du Soulor to the famous Tourmalet. When you ride the Pyrenean classic the second part in particular has very attractive scenery. Since the finishing line is more than 100km from the starting line you have to arrange for overnight accommodation (at the foot of the Tourmalet if possible).

Fitness: The distance and the total vertical climb are an indication that you have to be extremely fit. You'll curse every extra kilo on the climb. It might be a good idea to split the route in half or sign up for a tour in the Pyrenees.

Equipment: Because of the numerous climbs a 'pizza' cassette with a large 28- or 29-tooth sprocket is a good idea. So is a compact chainset. That way you can keep pedalling on the first of the two mountains and still have enough strength for the last bit.

It's been 100 years since the Pyrenees were part of the Tour de France for the first time. Since then many epic tales have been written in the mountain range between the Atlantic and the Mediterranean Sea. Octave Lapize, the first one to cross the Tourmalet and win the Tour de France in 1910, called the route planner a murderer; in 1913 Eugene Christoph had to repair his fork himself; Eddy Merckx set off on a solo ride of 140km, which was the cornerstone of his Tour win in 1969. And Jan Ullrich experienced his greatest moment here in 1997 when he took the yellow jersey for the first time on the Tourmalet. Now the Pyrenees are a classic of the Tour – and it's hard to imagine the route without it.

So it's hardly surprising that the most classic climb overall of the Tour is a pass through the Pyrenees: the Col du Tourmalet. Since it was first ridden in 1910 it has been on the Tour de France programme 76 times. (In comparison, the famous Galibier in the Alps has been included in the Great Loop 'only' 54 times.) In 2010 the riders even had to cross the Pyrenean giant twice – 'a wonderful idea' as Jens Voigt sarcastically described it. The 17th stage ends with the highest road pass in the region at 2115m. It should serve as a prime example of the beautiful tours in the mountain range in the south of France.

Sunny outlook

It starts in Pau, also a classic in the history of the Tour. After all, the little town in the north Pyrenees has been the start or the finish of the Tour 62 times; only Paris and Bordeaux have clocked up more appearances. You should be well prepared for the next 181km, for a good 4100m of vertical climb are in store for its conqueror. And then there's the pitiless sun, which can easily push the thermometer up to the 30°C mark at this time of year. But that's better than rain,

The Belgian Jurgen Van den Broeck on the Col de Marie-Blanque.

Pau is one of the best-loved places on the tour. The 'loop' has passed through here 62 times, so the town's in third place after Paris and Bordeaux.

you might think – but when the sun shines you'll need to be prepared to fill up your water bottle more than once.

Before you set out on your ride in Pau you should try to find accommodation at the foot of the Tourmalet. Since the route goes from A to B there's no chance of getting back the same day. You should also take a little time for sightseeing: the famous medieval castle in the town, among other things the birthplace of Henri IV, is situated just 1.5km from the starting line in the Allée Alfred de Musset. Once you've visited the museum, you can set off straight away.

But where the peloton weaves its way through cordoned off streets at 7 a.m. in the morning, you'll now have to fight your way through heavy traffic. Because the long ride takes more than 8 hours, an early start is advisable.

The mountains are still lying in shadow, but that will soon change.

You leave Pau and go to Laroin (10km), where you turn left onto the D217. Here the traffic becomes noticeably less, and because you're looking south you have the mountains right in front of you. The mountains are still lying in shadow, but that will soon change. After going through the unremarkable town of Saint Faust (15km) you come to the junction with the D24. Here you turn right and get ready immediately for the first climb to Côte de Gaye (23km).

Even though the first 50km on the elevation profile give the impression that it's relatively flat you shouldn't let yourself be taken in: there are numerous small hills to be overcome which definitely call for the small chain ring. But after two hairpin bends the Gaye is already history and you can once more

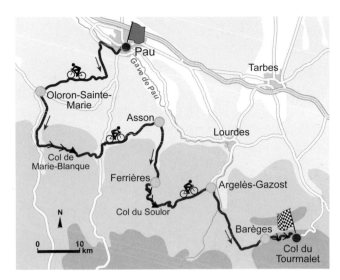

fight your way through a landscape of agricultural fields.

After Lasseube (28km) and Goès (38km) you go to Oloron-Sainte-Marie. You've already done 40km. The little town is divided in two by the Gave d'Oloron, where the Gave d'Aspe and the Gave d'Ossau meet. However, you don't cross the river, but turn onto the D238, which runs parallel with the bigger and very busy N134 along the river's eastern bank.

The road goes through Eysus (50km) and on to Lurbe Saint Christeau (51km) where you go straight over the crossroads with the D918. The Pyrenees are now so close you can almost touch them, and just a few kilometres further on you cross the boundary of the Parc National des Pyrénées. In Escot (55km), after you've turned left in the centre of

Narrow valleys, rocky cliffs: the wild side of the Pyrenees is on show here, particularly on this stage of the race.

the village, you reach the start of the first big mountain ride of the day: the Col de Marie-Blanque.

Very few bends, an awful lot of forest

This is a quite unremarkable Pyrenean pass, which links the Aspe and the Ossau valleys and isn't exactly a giant at 1035m high. But it is a mountain and, as such, a foretaste of all that's to come during the day: at 9.3km long and with an average gradient of 7.7 per cent you should conserve your strength here. The second half of the climb in particular with peaks of up to 13 per cent is not to be sniffed at. While you're pedalling up the road, which has few bends and has trees on both sides, you can tell yourself that the mountain – on the pass of which you reach your

highest point after 64.5km – is spectacular, as you realise that it has regularly been a venue for the Tour since 1978.

These days the Pyrenees in the south of France are one of the last largely unspoilt landscapes in Europe and the home of many rare animals and plants – a little wilderness.

The downhill side of the mountain is exciting: downhill specialists will love the narrow road with its newly tarmacked hairpin bends. After the Plateau de Benou (70km) the road goes down for more than 10km to Bielle (76km). In Bielle you turn left onto the D934, which runs alongside the dark-green shimmering Lac de Castet, before turning right at the roundabout in Louvie-Juzon (80km) to cross the lake and then immediately turning right again onto the D35.

Easy, hilly terrain follows and you get several opportunities to appreciate the southern French scenery. These days the Pyrenees in the south of France are one of the last largely unspoilt landscapes in Europe and the home of many rare animals and plants – a little wilderness. You can now think about a little snack, for there's already a good 3.5 hours on the clock. You bowl along more easily through Bruges-Capbis-Mifaget (92km) and Asson (97km), before turning right as you leave the village onto the D126, going towards the Pyrenees again. The traffic decreases noticeably and after a further 15km you reach Ferrières (113km), the starting point for the climb to the Col du Soulor.

Starting from 574m above sea level, this climb winds its way up to 1469m above sea level. But the incline is one of the easier ones: for one thing it never exceeds 9 per cent, and for another it always remains uniform. After Arbéost you work your way slowly upwards. Towards the end of the climb in particular a wonderful panorama unfolds in front of you: when the road turns from its previous northerly direction towards the east you get a magnificent view of the mountain scenery of the Cirque du Litor. And this scenery definitely distracts you from the prevailing heat – it's midday and the sun is scorching.

A good 6 hours of riding and a total vertical climb of over 3000m – everyone feels it in their legs in particular and the highest point of the day is yet to come: the Tourmalet.

Turn right again, please – the haul up to the Col du Tourmalet is waiting.

Once you've finally reached the top of the pass you can do up the jersey you completely undid earlier and keep to the left (you would go to the infamous Aubisque if you turned right). You turn onto the D918, where the descent to Arrens-Marsous (133km) and Argelès-Gazost (144km) begins, steep at first but gently sloping later on. Down in the valley you should think about refreshment again. A nice little roadside restaurant perhaps? A good 6 hours of riding and a vertical climb of over 3000m – everyone feels it in their legs in particular and the highest point of the day is yet to come: the Tourmalet.

As far as spectator enthusiasm goes, the Pyrenees can match the Alps anytime. The Tour is simply the Tour.

that you had the merest fraction at least of their strength.

Remembering the beginning of the Tour

You'll remember the many anecdotes of what happened in the early days of the Tour. Take, for example, the developer of the Pyrenean stage Alphonse Steinès, an employee of Henri Desgrange, who on the instructions of his boss looked at the feasibility of the Tourmalet for the first time. Although he got stuck in snow on his inspection in 1909 and the road was anything but suitable for the Tour, he sent the following telegram to Paris: 'No problem crossing Tourmalet. Stop. Road in good condition. Stop. No difficulties for riders.' Like the professionals in subsequent years you'll curse Alphonse Steinès too. Particularly once you've gone through Barèges (173km), the last village and therefore the last real chance for refreshment. Eight kilometres of utter loneliness follow.

Only the sound of a couple of cowbells and the whirr of the spokes can be heard when you get near to the top of the pass.

The approach to the Tourmalet begins after you've turned onto the D921 in Argelès-Gazost. You go through Lau Balagnas (146km), Adast (149km) and Soulom (151km) before you reach the starting point of the Tourmalet at Luz Saint Sauveur (162.9km). Despairing thoughts now flash through your mind. If you were fresh the Tourmalet would be hard going at a height of 2115m above sea level and with the road climbing continually over 19km. But with the previous difficulties you've already faced in your legs it seems an insoluble problem – that is, the climb offers no possibility of a breather.

While you're winding your way up the first kilometre it will be clear to you why epic tales have been written about the Tour. In 2010 the climb was the scene of a duel between Andy Schleck and Alberto Contador that they fought out right to the finishing line. But right now you won't be able to identify with either of this pair who positively flew up the mountain then. Rather, you'll just wish

The scenery, which was already barren, becomes even bleaker, the road surface rougher and the air thinner. The gradient increases to 10 per cent. Exhaustion sets in and so does the desire to zigzag up the course. If you glance behind you, you can see in the distance the road you've ridden up, as it goes past the rock walls into the last few kilometres. Still three to go; then two … Only the sound of a couple of cowbells and the whirr of the spokes can be heard when you get near to the top of the pass. Then the 181st and last kilometre. A long day in the saddle is drawing to a close, you can see the top of the pass. Just a few more metres and you've done it: the Tourmalet – you're at the summit of the Tour de France.

Members of the former Team Telekom pose in 1999 with the five-times Tour winner Miguel Indurain (second from right) in front of the Goddet memorial on the Tourmalet.

2010 results *

1 Andy Schleck (Luxembourg), 5 hours 03' 29"
2 Alberto Contador (Spain), same time
3 Joaquin Rodriguez (Spain), + 1' 18"
*only held in 2010

Cyclists, check this out!

The route described here was arranged for all-comers as a sportive within the framework of the 2010 Etape du Tour. This race has been organised since 1993 by the cycling wholesaler Mondovélo, and gives amateurs and hobby cyclists the opportunity every year to steal a march on the professionals and test out this unique route in advance. Find more information at www.letapedutour.com.

Cycling and sightseeing

Near the top of the pass on the Tourmalet is a memorial to Jacques Goddet, who was for many years the director of the Tour de France and from 1947 to 1986 skilfully supervised the greatest cycle races in the world. The best thing would be to plan for a stage ride lasting several days. Why? Simple: many more famous mountain classics of the Tour de France lie within easy reach and they are well worth doing. I'm talking about the Ax-3 Domains, the Plateau de Beille, Luiz Ardiden, the Col de Peyresourde, the Col d'Aspin, the Col de Pailheres and the Col d'Aubisque. Biarritz on the Atlantic coast or Perpignan on the Mediterranean coast, for example, could be the starting and finishing points for a Pyrenean tour like this.

Background

Since the Tourmalet is still used by the Tour de France, it's a real adventure. One story, which is told every time it's ridden over, is the drama of Eugène Christophe. He was wearing the yellow jersey in the 1913 Tour de France when his fork broke on the descent from the Tourmalet. To repair his bike he had to walk for 2 hours to the nearest blacksmith, and because of the rules he had to make the repairs himself without assistance. And as if that wasn't enough, because a boy worked the bellows for him the organisers even hit him with a time penalty …

AUTUMN
ADVENTURES

The sea is a constant companion on the 'Clásica'.

The Clásica San Sebastián is a one-day race that has taken place around San Sebastián in the Spanish Basque region in August every year since 1981. At just 30 years old it's not exactly the age that you expect of a classic race. But what distinguishes this circuit round the coastal town is not its history per se but the long tradition that links the Basque region with cycling. You could even call riding on two wheels a national sport here. Anyone who knows the wild crowds of fans on the arrival of the Tour de France in the Pyrenees knows what I mean. Whole passes were sometimes covered in orange, and you could hardly see the actual riders for all the Basque flags. A very special atmosphere! This tradition has been taken up by the Clásica: instead of a cup, the winner receives a 'txapela' – a Basque beret typical of the region.

Because of this enthusiasm for cycling in the Basque region it's hardly surprising that this region regularly produces powerful and talented cyclists. The five-time Tour winner Miguel Indurain has of course to be mentioned first. Jan Ullrich's former opponent Joseba Beloki, the time-trial specialist Abraham Olano and the king of the breakaway David Etxebarria are also Basques.

A large part of this veritable flood of professionals comes from the Euskaltel team, which since 1998 has been numbered among the largest and best-known professional teams in the world, a secret Basque national team, as it were – and because of the orange colour of its jerseys it also contributes to the spectrum of colours in the Pyrenean passes on the Tour. Since only Basque riders are allowed in the Euskaltel team, young talents also often get the chance to prove themselves here in the hard business of professional cycling.

More Basque than German races

And although the Tour of Spain has ignored the race for a long time because of political unrest and problems, the Basques can be proud of both their cyclists and their race: the national tour, a week-long tour of the Basque region which takes place in April, is part of the UCI's World Calendar and is an annual spring highlight.

Until recently there was even a second top-class stage race, the 'Euskal Bizikleta'. And the very important Bira Tour on the women's calendar shouldn't be forgotten either – in total the relatively small Basque region has more top-class race days than Germany. That should give you food for thought. In addition the San Sebastián has also been a stage of the Tour de France (see 'Background', page 135) as well as the venue for the UCI Road World Championships.

But now to the 'Clásica' itself. The race has been one of the most important on the calendar since its first edition and from the beginning has been part of the Road World Championships and later also of the UCI ProTour. The winners are also a testament to the top-class nature of the race. Because of the summer date they're often riders who hit their top form on the Tour de France: that's why Miguel Indurain has won his 'home' race, as well as the American Lance Armstrong, the Frenchman Laurent Jalabert, Paolo Bettini (Italy) and the Spanish all-rounder Alejandro Valverde.

Anyone who wants to ride the 'Donostia' – this is Basque for both San Sebastián and the race – should definitely take a couple of days to enjoy the tourist highlights of this coastal town: La Concha Beach, the Kursaal, the Buen Pastor Cathedral – there's more than enough to see. In addition there's the possibility of enjoying the sun – not for nothing is tourism the main source of income for the town.

What could be better than to start a ride by the sea – the taste of salt in the air, a cool breeze in your face and the prospect of a sunny day?

The race starts and ends at the famous La Concha Bay, the perfect place to set off for a beautiful tour. For what could be better than to start a ride by the sea – the taste of salt in the air, a cool breeze in your face and the prospect of a sunny day?

Once the water bottles are full and all necessary preparations have been made, you leave the promenade in a westerly direction and soon head inland. The first place you're aiming for is Usurbil, which you reach over a gentle uphill route. You mustn't get annoyed by the chaos on the motorway and main roads around San Sebastián – once that's behind you, you'll be fine.

Once you've passed the home town of Haimar Zubeldia, the mountain and

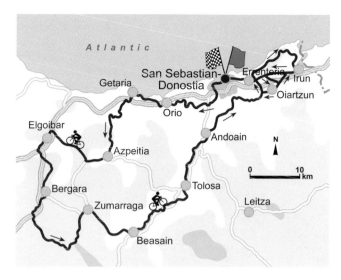

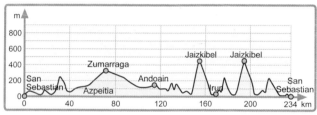

time-trial specialist, the route winds along the course of the River Oria which rises in the Sierra de Aitzkorri 50km to the south, through Aginaga (11km) and on to Orio (17km). There you cross the rushing water over a stone bridge. Left and right small green hills now rise. Soon you'll be climbing – that's for sure.

Although the road has been almost completely flat so far, the first climb comes after crossing the river at Alto Orio (19km). The vertical climb of 80m is spread out over just under 2km and so isn't much more than an easy warm-up. A right-hand hairpin bend and then it's more or less over and done with – then it's downhill again until you're almost at sea level and into the little town of Zarautz (22km) to ride along the coast of the Bay of Biscay again. It's now quite clear that the 'Clásica' is a route to enjoy.

Thereafter the route continues to wind along the coast until you get to Getaria (27km), a famous wine-growing region and the starting point for the next climb.

Back inland again

After the precipitous cliffs of the coast you wind your way inland: the Alto Garate with its climb of 250m now demands a little more of you. The average gradient of 8 per cent brings the riders round the first hairpin bend right out of the village and in a real sweat. Once you've done with the climb you soon get to Meaga (31km) and follow a line of hills and a river to Aizarnazabal (37km).

The little villages of Zestoa and Lasao are the next destinations, which you pass by in the valley of the Rio Urola. You stay with the gently climbing road for now and reach Azpeitia after exactly 50km. This little town has two museums – the Museum of the Environment and the Railway Museum. The latter is here because the first electrically powered railway line in Spain was built here.

The River Urola is still showing you the way. The road winds its way upstream between ever more overgrown and very green hills. You could really ride along round here for ever, and so the time passes until you come to the next town, Zumarraga (72km) just a short time later, even though you've had to make your way up 350m, which was barely noticeable. The road then goes just as gently downhill until you come to the next two towns, Ordizia (88km) and Legoretta (91km).

San Sebastián's La Concha Bay is the start and end point of the race.

The peloton climbs the famous Jaizkibel.

Incidentally, the first is the venue for the one-day race popular with cyclists, the Prueba Villafranca.

The gently rolling hills of the region and the peace here – it's something really quite special.

Now that there's a lot of traffic on the E5 you can ride relatively undisturbed on the country road that runs parallel to it. Near Tolosa you meet up with the River Orio again; you cross it, then ride from Irua alongside the railway line to Villabona (109km). After 116km you reach Andoain, a little town where you should have a break – after all, you've been on the road for a good 4 hours now. Then the little climb to Alto Irurain immediately after that will be that much easier. And after you've turned off to the right from Oria the next 10km to Astigarraga will just fly by. The gently rolling hills of the region and the peace

here – it's something really quite special.

Meanwhile you've slowly been getting closer to San Sebastián again. But then you bypass the town to the south and now turn slowly but surely towards the mountain that is the most famous of all the race: the Jaizkibel. Once you've dealt with another couple of hills, the Ventas de Astigarraga (130km) and the Alto Gainzurizketa (144km) after the ride from Oiartzun and Gurutze, you turn left to reach Lezo (148km), the starting point for what is the highest mountain of the day.

Now you're on the big final lap: while the peloton of the 'Clásica' has to make this climb twice, you can miss this out if one circuit is enough. Because of the length of the route the latter is a good idea – you will save yourself a not inconsiderable 40km, and a total distance of 194km is more than enough …

Basque fans provide their home race with a quite amazing atmosphere.

On the last circuit

The 8km-long climb up the Jaizkibel is certainly one of the most beautiful of this classic race. For one thing because it offers a magnificent view of the sea: first you see the Bay of Pasaia in the foreground and the houses of San Sebastián in the background, then further away you see the vast Atlantic. Then comes the climb: since the gradient is never steeper than 9 per cent, and this figure decreases significantly in the second half, it's easy to ride. Therefore, the speed calls the tune. But that's why you really mustn't bother about that on this tour. You easily wind your way up over the steep climb and the hairpin bends in the middle of the mountain ridges, over which you leave behind the final 450m of total vertical climb. You should never forget the view, with the sea to the side, the town behind you and

the green slopes all around. The professionals have to press on hard here to shake off the sprinters. Most of them manage to do that and one or two breakaways can race off 40km from the finishing line. But 2006 shows that this doesn't always work: on that occasion all 51 riders reached the home stretch and it was won by the Spaniard Xavier Florencio, a strong sprinter from the second rank who hadn't really been in the reckoning before.

The descent is quick and just as beautiful as the climb. The roads are in good condition and make up for the 170km that you've already covered. Once you've descended for a short time you even skim close to the French border, which runs through the mouth of the River Bidassoa. Now you turn towards San Sebastián again and have to deal with two more climbs: the Alto de Gaintzurizketa (173km), which you've already climbed once, and the Alto de Arkale (179km). From the point of view of the total vertical climb – the first is 70m, the second 170 – both are quite easy, but because of the distance you've already covered they'll hurt.

You've also been to the next town, Gurutze, once today already. However, now you turn off in the opposite direction and follow the road to Oiartzun, where you head for Errenteria again. Here you can decide whether you want to add on a second circuit.

Usually there are no more than 20 professionals fighting for position.

For those who are quite happy with just one circuit, these are now the last few kilometres; there are just eight of them to the finishing line. This is where the favourites among the professionals form a leading group. Usually there are no more than 20 professionals fighting for position. You leave Pasaia Bay to your right and reach San Sebastián again via main roads. The seashore is on the right, and the houses of San Sebastián on the left as you go down the long finishing straight on the promenade. You reach the finishing line after 194 or 234km, depending on whether you've ridden over the Jaizkibel once or twice.

When your each the shore, just be thankful that you don't have to fight it out at speeds of up to 70km/hr like the professionals do, but you can bowl down it at a comfortable pace instead. So you certainly won't be presented with the famous Basque beret for winning, but you can clip out of your pedals as soon as you reach the invisible finishing line, lean your bike against the seawall and get comfortable on the fine sand in the warm evening sun.

2011 results <<

1 Philippe Gilbert (Belgium), 5 hours 48' 52"
2 Carlos Barredo (Spain), + 0' 12"
3 Greg Van Avermaet (Belgium), + 0' 02"

Cyclists, check this out!

Unfortunately there is no all-comers' or amateur counterpart to the Clásica San Sebastián. However, anyone who still wants to take part in a big cycle marathon on the Iberian Peninsula should take a closer look at the Quebrantahuesos: starting in Sabiñánigo this goes north into the Pyrenees, where among other things you have to climb the Colmarie Blanque. The full distance comes to 205km; a shorter version of 90km is also on offer. Find more information at www.quebrantahuesos.com.

Cycling and sightseeing

Depending on whether time allows, you can also take a trip from San Sebastián to Pamplona, 80km away to the south. The suburb of Villava there is the birthplace of the greatest cyclist in Spain's history: Miguel Indurain. The five-time winner of the Tour de France is not just a freeman of the city, there is also a monument erected to him there. And every year at the beginning of April the Gran Premio Miguel Induráin, a one-day race named after him, takes place near Pamplona.

Background

For three days in the 1992 season San Sebastián was the venue for the Tour de France, which started there that year. The winner of the 8km long prologue round the city centre was none other than Miguel Induráin himself, the perfect introduction to what was almost his home game. The Spaniard lost out on the next mountain stage through the Basque countryside to his Swiss opponent Alex Zülle, but regained the lead after the 13th leg up to Sestrières. In the end Induráin won the Great Loop for the second time in his career.

TOUR PROFILE <<

Race date: Mid-August

Type: Professional race (classic)/ sportive

Start/finish: Hamburg (Germany)

Distance: 157km (the original distance is 217km; the route described is equivalent to the longest circuit of the sportive)

Total vertical climb: 580m

Riding time: 5 hours

URL: www.vattenfall-cyclassics.de

Route: After the start the route goes in a southerly direction onto the Lüneberg Heath. After going through Hamburg again, where it crosses the spectacular Köhlbrand Bridge, among other things, a second loop follows to the north-west, which returns to Hamburg along the River Elbe. The finishing line is on Mönckebergstraße. The route doesn't present any particular difficulties. Because of the high volume of traffic it's a good idea to do this ride within the amateur competition.

Fitness: The largely flat course suits cyclists. Endurance is the most important element because of the long distance. If you take part in the sportive – as advised – you should also be used to riding in a group or in a large field, as you'll be sharing the road with 22,000 other riders.

Equipment: The route doesn't make any particular demands on your bike; as a course for sprinters you don't need a mountain set-up. You should tackle the Waseberg with a 25-tooth sprocket.

The 'Cyclassics' is mostly for sprinters.

Currently, German cycling is suffering from a lack of high-profile stars, such as Jan Ullrich and Erik Zabel, who were great international advocates of the sport. And after Team Milram disbanded, for the first time in 19 years there was no German team at the highest level of professional racing in 2011. Even the race organisers are complaining: finding sponsors in the wake of the continual doping enquiries has proved to be increasingly difficult, and more and more events are disappearing. Since the demise of the Tour of Germany in 2008 the Bayern-Rundfahrt (Tour of Bavaria) is the biggest national stage race. There's only one black, red and gold single-day race left in the UCI World Calendar: the Vattenfall Cyclassics.

And this classic is the best example of what proper organisational effort can do to successfully counteract a trend like this. Even though the race, which was first run in 1996, can't look back on a long history, it has developed into a real cycling festival, perhaps the biggest in Europe. For a whole weekend everything in Hamburg revolves around cycling.

People of all levels of achievement come to fulfil their dreams. As well as the pros, within the format of the 'Cyclassics' set-up there are also races for young people, those with mental health problems and amateurs (*see* 'Cyclists, check this out!', page 141). Since a substantial part of the route takes place in the centre of Hamburg, there is a similarly large number of spectators at the side of the road. There's a good 800,000 of them on Sunday – as a result, the 'Cyclassics' are of a very high standard.

Amateur experience
It's a good idea to experience this route within an amateur competition just because of the great atmosphere. To do it any

After the start the course first heads south into the country.

other way turns out to be difficult because you have to ride through the centre of Hamburg or because some sections of the route, such as the Köhlbrand Bridge, are closed to cyclists. In addition many people think that a route other than the designated race roads in the city wouldn't show any special features – you only get these within the framework of the amateur race. The beauty of the race is that it follows substantial parts of the professional race. The only problem with riding this course is that you miss out on the Waseberg, the killer climb in the professional race (see 'Cycling and sightseeing', page 141).

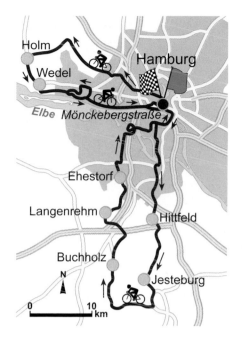

The Mönckebergstraße with its clinker-built buildings and its shopping facilities is a famous landmark in the city.

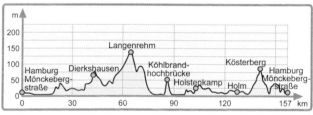

While the professional riders are clipping into their pedals on the Steinstraße by the St Jacobi church, the hobby and amateur cyclists are setting off from the famous Mönckebergstraße, one of the main streets in Hamburg. With its clinker-built buildings and its shopping facilities, this is a famous landmark in the city and later on the finishing line for the race too. Now you go in a southerly direction over the Freihafen-Elbbrücke to the Veddeler Dam, where the neutralisation ends and the real start follows. For amateurs the race here has already been a tough 5km.

The road continues through the harbour area until you turn right shortly before the Ellerholzbrücke and head south. Narrow winding streets with blind corners become fewer and you slowly get into an easy rhythm. Through the Wilhelmsburg district of the city, you're soon on your way to Harburg. At first the huge docks are everywhere around you, but the route becomes greener and greener as you go south. At the Harburg ring road (17km) the professionals have their first sprint classification, then 5km further on you cross over the Hamburg city limit past Wilstorf and Langenbek on your way to Niedersachen. Now comes the part of the route that's a joy to ride, the part away from the race's road closures that makes the race really fun.

But there's no flat land

The route goes past Hittfeld (25km) and Lindhorst (27km) over a rural plain. It is generally said that the north of Germany

is flat, but this preconception is not true either for Hamburg or for the part of the route over the Harburg Hills you're going through now: extremely hilly terrain attractively interspersed with wooded areas, treelined roads and flat sections over open fields. A few black and white cows are not infrequently seen in fields bordering the road.

Harmstorf (32km) is the next destination. Jesteburg (37km), known for its cultural life, and Asendorf (39km) come next. The undulating road goes on further south until you turn right in Dierkshausen (42km) and go west. You've reached the southernmost point and you weave your way slowly north again through the northern Lüneberg Heath, sometimes through woods, sometimes through open areas. Once

Are the cows at the side of the road interested in the race?

you're through the village of Holm-Seppensen you've finally done a third of the course. There are 50km on the clock. With Buchholz you arrive at a town where the professionals have held their next sprint classification. For the amateurs the first feeding station is here.

Up in the Alps, few people would take these 100m vertical climbs seriously.

You're now 20km from Hamburg and although the road remains undulating you begin to go slowly uphill in this hilly scenery of woods, heath and fields. You skirt Eckel to arrive at Nenndorf (62km) and Emsen (65km). Now Langenrehm (67km) lies in front

of you, forming the highest point of the Cyclassics with the huge Rosengarten telecommunications tower located on the Gannaberg Hill. Up in the Alps, few people would take these 100m vertical climbs seriously – particularly as they extend over 5km.

Going north you approach the Hanseatic city of Hamburg again, whose outline can soon be seen on the horizon. But first you have to deal with the wooded northern foothills of the Harburg Hills, which start at Ehestorf (73km). The road is easy to ride and leads mostly downhill to Hamburg which you reach again along the Cuxhavener Straße. In the amateur race the field now enters the Altenwerder district and then heads for the harbour. Before that you should take a quick look at the gigantic Köhlbrand Bridge, which rises above the city.

Climbing the Köhlbrand Bridge

The nearer you get to the bridge over the Elbe (which is usually closed to cyclists but open just on one side exclusively for cyclists during the race), the more insurmountable this seems to become. It's hard to believe that a bridge could be a mountain to climb, but that's what happens here: the structure rises up with a total vertical climb of 40m. On the wide road this becomes more and more difficult for the riders. Compensation comes at the highest point: you have a wonderful panoramic view over Hamburg up there, before gravity propels you down to sea level again on the other side.

Over the Veddeler Dam – incidentally this is where amateurs sometimes meet the elite riders, who started off later, coming towards them – and the road goes back to the city

On Cyclassics day the Köhlbrand Bridge belongs to the cyclists.

The amateur and professional pelotons are just a few traffic cones apart.

The professional peloton climbs the famous Waseberg.

centre. You cross the Deichtorplatz after 98km. The next destination is the Kennedy Bridge, and then just past Holstenkamp (104km) the next feeding station finally comes along. The professionals also come here a little later to collect their food. At the Volkspark in the Altona district (110km) you then go on to Lurup.

> *In the Blankenese district the professional riders finally have to climb the Waseberg – amateurs are spared this.*

You would do best to ride with the field along the dual carriageway that comes next. The same goes for the whole race, so that you can 'steal' a good many places by drafting and tactical skills.

Once you reach Pinneberg in southern Schleswig-Holstein after 120km you go through a rural area back to the Elbe again past Wedel (126km). You're getting close to the finishing line now and turn once more in the direction of Hamburg city centre.

In the Blankenese district the professional riders finally have to climb the Waseberg (*see* 'Cycling and sightseeing', opposite) – amateurs are spared this. Instead you have to get over the 70m climb of the Kösterberg (141km) once more; but this climb is as steady as can be, so you can get ready for a final spurt from the group you find yourself in.

It's worth giving it all you've got over the last few metres. The Elbchaussee brings you back into the Altona district of the city. You also ride past the well-known St Pauli with the Millerntorplatz (154km), and the finishing line is now within reach. The last 3km are in the city centre again and after several bends you go down the Mönckebergstraße to cross the finishing line after 157km. You have to really concentrate at the end in particular: a battle for position in a cramped space can often end up in the crash barrier!

Incidentally, if you take part in the amateur race or are there on race day as a spectator you'll experience the enthusiasm generated by 800,000 fans gathered in the streets of Hamburg and by more than 22,000 cyclists looking for victory. And that shows you something: even though it hasn't got the years of history of, for example, the Flandernrundfahrt – cycling in Germany is anything but dead!

Climbs of over 10 per cent lie in wait here for the riders.

2011 results

1 Edvald Boasson Hagen (Norway), 4 hours 49' 39"
2 Gerald Ciolek (Germany), same time
3 Borut Bozic (Slovenia), same time
...
31 Geraint Thomas (Great Britain), + 0' 8"

Cyclists, check this out!

On the day of the Cyclassics, Hamburg belongs to the cyclists. So amateur races are offered alongside the Vattenfall Cyclassics, just as with most classic races. But in comparison with other single-day races the sportive occupies a special position: with up to 22,000 entrants this is one of the biggest events of its kind in the whole world. The huge field sets off on their ride before the professionals. With the streets completely closed off, you really feel the intensity of the event with its three distances – 55, 100 and 155km. Up to 800,000 spectators see to that – it's a must for all amateurs! But you really must make arrangements in good time; generally two-thirds of the starting places are already booked up just 24 hours after online registration opens. Find more information at www.vattenfall-cyclassics.de.

Cycling and sightseeing

Although the Waseberg isn't part of the amateur race, it is the highlight of the professionals' race. This peak in the Blankenese district of the city is just about the only chance for cyclists who are strong mountain climbers to get away from sprinters. The road rises from the bank of the Elbe after a sharp right-hand bend up an average gradient of more than 10 per cent to the centre of Blankenese, and is thus the steepest climb in Hamburg. As it does so the road skirts the woods, which reinforces the feeling of a classic race.

Background

In the still-short history of the Cyclassics one rider has already won the race twice: the American Tyler Farrar. He won the Cyclassics in both 2009 and 2010 in a mass sprint. But Farrar is by no means unknown: in spite of his youth – he was born in 1984 – he has already won stages on the Giro and Vuelta and is counted as one of the best sprinters in the world. Incidentally, the last German victory in Hamburg was a good 10 years ago: Erik Zabel won the race – in a sprint finish, of course. In 2010 the black, red and gold flag fluttered overhead again: André Greipel, the most successful sprinter of recent years when measured in victories, secured third place, and in 2011 Gerald Ciolek went one better.

TOUR PROFILE <<

Race date: Late August

Type: Marathon sportive

Start/finish: Sölden (Austria)

Distance: 238km

Total vertical climb: 5500m

Riding time: 10 hours

URL: www.oetztaler-radmarathon.com

Route: A wonderful tour through the Tyrol, which will make a deep impression on you, not just from the point of view of your fitness, but also that of the scenery. It goes through the valley of the Ötz through Kühtai to Innsbruck, and from there over the Brenner Pass to South Tyrol. Then comes the Jauffen Pass, and finally the Timmelsjoch, slowly looming larger as you approach, before the course goes downhill at breakneck speed and back to Sölden again.

Fitness: Only those who have trained hard should take on this tour, otherwise the 'Ötzi' will very quickly turn from dream to nightmare. If you don't think you can do the tour in one go you could stay overnight in Sterzing after crossing the Brenner Pass.

Equipment: A mountain stage, which requires a set-up to match. This is not just because of the distance and the vertical climb, but also because of the steepness, which can be as high as 18 per cent (on a long stretch on the Kühtai). A compact chainset or a 29-tooth sprocket are absolutely necessary to get round this tour. And you should also take appropriate clothing with you: the area you'll be riding through is really big, and the weather in the Alps can change very suddenly.

It's the best-known sportive in the Alpine region, and with a distance of 238km and a total vertical climb of 5500m to deal with it's probably also the most difficult: first ridden over in 1982, the 'Ötzi', as it's known for short, developed into a Mecca for many hobby and amateur cyclists. Many people even say that every cyclist should get hold of a finishing jersey for this event once in his life, but that's not easy: generally the 4000 starting places are booked up the day that registration goes online, and even if you do get a place you still have to be able to cope with all the difficulties of the tour. Even the fastest riders need about 7 hours – however, these are performances at the highest level!

The cyclists who fight it out for victory here are often well-known faces who can either look back on a professional career or are pursuing their sport under professional conditions: the Swiss Gilbert Glaus, who won in 1992, won a stage of the Tour de France in his career; Valter Bonca (Slovenia), who won twice in the mid-1990s, also won a stage of the Sachsen tour in his career; and also Holger Sievers (1996), Patrick Vetsch (1997, 1998) and Mirko Puglioli (2003, 2004) were professional cyclists. So was Emanuele Negrini, a former stage winner on the Tour of Austria and, with three wins, the most successful participant in the 'Ötzi' in the last decade. But a shadow hangs over him – he was found guilty of doping in 2009 in Italy.

In 2010 the Italian Antonio Corradini won again – as he had done in 2008 – as an amateur. He fought a long battle with Philip Götsch from South Tyrol. With an overall win in the Jeantex Tour Transalp and numerous successes and course records for hill climbs throughout the Alpine region, he is also extremely successful in the amateur field.

The 'Ötzi', as the sportive is affectionately known, is the best-known event of its kind.

The hub: Sölden

Even though the start and finish of the Ötztaler have changed over and over again, in the course of its history this classic tour has for some years started in Sölden. You leave this tourist town in the early morning – because the ride will take so long it's best to set off by about 6 a.m. The 'Ötzi' also starts at about this time. It's not surprising – the slowest need nearly 14 hours and so get back to Sölden just as night falls.

The first few kilometres turn out to be ideal for bowling along. The road goes gently downhill from 1377m above sea level in Sölden to just 820m above sea level in Ötz. You can't get lost – there is only one road. It proves to be well constructed and runs down the treelined valley of the Tiroler Ache river which you cross several times. It's still quite cold, and the sun still needs a little time before it rises above the surrounding mountains, some of which are over 3000m high.

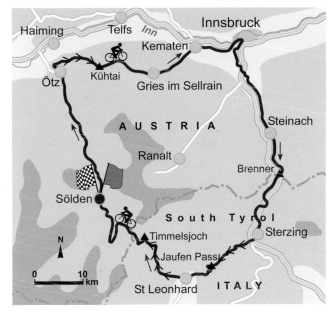

Gradients that are in double figures in places send lactic acid into your thighs for the first time.

Once you reach Ötz, follow the signpost at the roundabout just as you enter the village and go right to Kühtai for the first of four long climbs. The pass is 18.5km long and the total vertical climb is 1200m – this sets the standard. And the very first kilometres are the hardest: gradients that are in double figures in places send lactic acid into your thighs for the first time.

Although you're surrounded by houses at the start, the road, which is pleasant to ride, soon winds its way into the green mountain valley. The gradient levels out after the first few hard kilometres to a bearable 8 or 9 per cent.

Cycling along by the Stuiben stream you soon reach the top through deep woods.

Shortly before Ochsengarten (42km) a few hairpin bends make the ride a little easier, and it's a little flatter. To the left you could now ride over the Haiming mountain into the Inn Valley; but you stay on the road to Kühtai.

After another short flat section the road is now really steep. You have to fight your way up a ramp with a gradient of 18 per cent over a kilometre to kilometre 44 – that's quite something! The only consolation is the plateau that comes next, which then affords you a bit of a respite. At this point the trees thin out, and after another short ramp with a gradient of

12 per cent you reach the reservoir. Now the road's relatively easy for 2km, until after several easy-to-ride hairpin bends you finally reach the ski resort built on the Kühtai Saddle (51km) at a height of 2020m. There are several possibilities for refreshment and a short rest before you plunge down one of the fastest and most beautiful descents in the Alps.

Speed record on Kühtai

High speeds are possible here on the one hand because of the good visibility on the route and on the other the good surface and wide road. You only need to take care at the start because the name Kühtai (cow alp) is justified: that's to say

It's still early in the day when you arrive at the last hairpin bends on the Kühtai Saddle.

a cow or two often makes the tunnels at the beginning unsafe – either by their presence in the middle of the road or the slippery deposits they leave behind them. You should also take care over the cattle grids there.

Then you can really speed down to St Sigmund (58km); the road descends almost in a straight line at nearly 16 per cent, and you can reach speeds of up to 100km/hr. Then the road goes downhill over several relatively flat stages until finally after 66km you roll into Kematen. If you haven't eaten yet it's a good idea to stop at Ruetz the baker and then set out over level terrain via Völs (76km) to Innsbruck (86km).

You ride for a short distance past houses in the capital of the Tyrol, lying 600m above sea level with an historic medieval Old Town. Together with the Golden Roof and many other places of interest it positively invites you to look around. In front of Grassmayr's, the centuries-old bell foundry, you turn right onto the old Brennerstraße. By now you have 88km in your legs, and the sun has conquered the Inn Valley.

You leave Innsbruck's local mountain, the Patscherkofel, on your left and start the long climb to the Brenner Pass. You go uphill for a whole 39km, however the gradient stays within limits so that you can bowl along here. When riding in the Ötztaler it's very important on this section to ride in a fast group – that saves your strength and saves you time. Tour cyclists should choose carefully which day they ride here – at the beginning and the end of holidays there's more traffic here because tourists who want to avoid the toll on the motorway use this route.

The Inn Valley motorway hanging high over your head makes for impressive scenery during the climb.

The road goes on gently upwards, with a gradient of 2–4 per cent until you reach Schönberg (102km), where for a time the gradient even drops to 1 per cent and at times you seem to be riding along a plateau. The Inn Valley motorway hanging high over your head makes for impressive scenery during the climb, and just before Schönberg features the Europabrücke, the highest girder bridge in Europe at up to 190m.

You ride further along the Wipp valley until shortly before Gries am Brenner (121km) a 12 per cent ramp up to the Brennersee lake presents the greatest difficulty of the climb. After 127km you finally stand at the top of the Brenner (1377m) and you'll be disappointed: no panorama, just facilities for commercial traffic and bars. The only place of interest to cyclists is a shop on the left on the Italian side selling jerseys, which – when it's open – offers a wide range of cycling gear.

A well-constructed descent to Sterzing follows, which has several more hairpin bends at the beginning and is really fun. It's 19km long and drops down 450m – not much, but just enough for your legs to push on up the next climb more easily. By the time you reach Sterzing you already have an impressive 146km in your legs and so an overnight stay beckons for those who are not quite so fit. If you want you can also stay longer in this charming medieval town associated with the Fugger family. If you're riding the tour in one go, you should make sure that you take a midday break here at the very least.

Preliminary shake-out on the Jaufen Pass

But you shouldn't eat too much since the Jaufen Pass is waiting for you as soon as you leave the town. It climbs to a height of 2090m over 15km – a really hard

'This is what you've been dreaming about': once you've climbed the Timmelsjoch, it's nearly over and done with.

stretch. The Jaufen is the most northerly of the passes in Italy, lying in the heart of South Tyrol. To the north tower the mighty Ötztal Alps, to the south the equally vast Sarntal Alps.

The road is now climbing constantly at a good 8 per cent, and you spend most of the time climbing through the woods. This is where Corradini and Götsch made their first attack, which led to a preliminary shake-out in the race. Over many curves and hairpin bends you wind your way up at a constant 8 per cent until at Kalch (152km) – surrounded by alpine meadows – you can get some more sun again. After a short flat section the road goes immediately back into the wood and the gradient shoots up to 10 per cent.

You can only briefly enjoy the view into the Passeier Valley on the other side of the mountain, before you plummet down the long descent to St Leonhard.

All things considered, the Jaufen is fantastic to ride, particularly when you leave the wood 3km before the summit and the view to the Jaufenhaus and the

Stefan Kirchmair was the winner in 2011.

Dekker, who came in third. The 'Ötztaler' demands everything from competitors on the descent as well.

The dreaded Timmelsjoch

St Leonhard in Passeier – famous in particular as the birthplace of the Tyrolean freedom fighter Andreas Hofer – gives you the chance to fill your water bottles once more. The climb to the Timmelsjoch, which begins as soon as you leave the village to the north, is now an absolute hammer on the programme. This climb lasts for 29km and winds its way up over a vertical climb of almost 1800m – values which make you break out in a sweat just reading them! It's the hardest climb of the Ötzi – and right at the end of the marathon too. Many a rider in a promising position has broken down here. Others, on the other hand, start incredible races to catch up here.

In the village you turn right and just follow the signposts. Until you get to Moos (191km) the road climbs relatively gently at 5 per cent. You slowly wind your way up the Passeier valley until the gradient increases to a maximum of 10 per cent when you reach Moos. The hairpin bends also begin here, which bring you to the top of the pass through several tunnels and mixed woodland which gets more and more sparse. After 195km there comes a long, flatter section before the gradient rises again and doesn't let up until you reach Schönau (201km).

Now it's all down to your determination. You're legs are burning, and you just don't want to do it anymore – even the beauty of the South Tyrolean mountains all around doesn't help. Your morale sinks in particular when you pass the treeline after Schönau and you realise that there's still nearly 10km to go to the summit. The road keeps climbing,

top of the pass are unobstructed. The end is fast approaching and seeing it gives you new strength so that you soon reach the Jaufenhaus and then the hairpin bends to the top of the pass (161km). When the Ötzi's being run, many spectators and officials stand here to support the riders. You can only briefly enjoy the next view of the long and energy-sapping descent into the Passeier Valley of the other side of the mountain, before you plummet down the long descent to St Leonhard.

You should take care here: this descent has stretches full of potholes and with the steep slope on the left-hand side it's not for the faint-hearted, especially at the beginning. But after a few hairpin bends you find yourself back in the woods, a situation which makes you relax. The fast ride down to St Leonhard (183km), 750m above sea level, lasts for 22km – so shake yourself and your hands out so that you don't get cramp!

The village is incidentally the home of 2010's second place man, Philip Götsch. And although he knows this course inside out, he had a problem following the breakneck speed of his companions Corradini, who later won, and Bert at up to 12 per cent. It's rougher, narrower and the next two tunnels are – since they're unlit – not exactly safe. The next hairpin bends in particular are hard. The slope falls away steeply without any barriers worth mentioning and you can be glad that you're not going downhill here. The last 2km turn out to be a littlemore human and the approach the top of the pass (209km), at a height of 2509m, is at 4–5 per cent.

Anyone who thinks that they're done now is seriously mistaken: after 4km of breakneck descent – you can reach 80km/hr over the straight section at the end – there's an excruciating vertical climb of 200m up the other side. You're worn out here already, but this short section, which wouldn't be a problem under normal circumstances, robs you of what little strength you have left.

The toll booth at Hochgurgel (217km) finally brings a sigh of relief: from now on you can just bowl down to the finishing line. A few hairpin bends in the woods are followed by a relatively pleasant section through a tunnel, showing that you're almost down. A little hill on the way to Sölden really doesn't have much impact, so that after 238km you finally reach your starting point again and can now call yourself a proud conqueror of the Ötztaler Radmarathon! But unfortunately you only get the much sought-after jersey after the finish of the real Ötzi …

2011 results   <<

1 Stefan Kirchmair (Austria), 7 hours 06' 31"
2 Antonio Corradini (Italy), + 3' 30"
3 Roberto Cunico (Italy), + 1' 42"
4 Bert Dekker (Netherlands), + 3' 01"
5 Alessandro Bertuola Alessandro (Italy), + 0' 06"

Cyclists, check this out!

The so-called Klassic-Ötzi has been organised within the framework of the Ötztaler Radmarathon as an option for history buffs. Anyone wanting to take part has to cover all 238km on a completely classic racing bike. Only the brakes and the saddle are allowed to conform to modern specifications, out of consideration for safety and comfort. Find more information and exact regulations at www.oetztaler-radmarathon.com.

Cycling and sightseeing

One of the most difficult climbs that professionals in the early history of the race had to overcome also began at the start of the Ötzi in Sölden: the climb to the Rettenbachferner glacier. Twice – in 2005 and 2007 – it was on the programme of the now defunct Tour of Germany. You had to climb 1305m over a distance of 12.6km – which says it all. The gradient remains in double figures almost constantly. It was organised as an amateur mountain time trial as part of the Tour of Germany: in 2005 the German Günter Höllige did it in 53 minutes 13 seconds. By comparison, the Spanish winner of the professional race in 2007, David Lopez Garcia, was a good bit faster at 43 minutes 39 seconds. If you want to see how long it takes you to ride it, you can time yourself during the Ötztaler Radtrophy. Find more information at www.oetztaler-radtrophy.com.

Background

Like many cycling events, the Ötztaler Radmarathon evolved from a funny idea. The founder, Helmutmaier, was on an easy tour to the Jaufenpass when he met another rider who told him that he wanted to do the Ötztal circuit all in one go. As a result Maier tried it out himself a little later and managed to do the whole distance. Soon the idea of making it into a cycling marathon was born. A year later, on 22 August 1982 the first Ötztaler set off with 105 participants. The media and athletes soon heard of the event, and the Ötzi became a cult. Nowadays the race is completely booked up almost as soon as online registration opens.

TOUR PROFILE <<

Race date: Early September

Type: Sportive

Start/finish: Buchs, Canton of Zürich (Switzerland)

Distance: 49km (several times round the circuit)

Total vertical climb: 500m

Riding time: 2 hours

URL: www.zueri-metzgete.ch

Route: Unlike the other classics the circuit here is a short one. From the start in Buchs the route goes north to Kaiserstuhl after which the road heads south again. There are two climbs that have to be tackled: the Siglistorfer Höhe and the Regensberg. Caution: ramps of up to 17 per cent await you here!

Fitness: As the route is a short one and the climbs are relatively brief this course is also accessible to beginners. Those taking part in the all-comers' races can choose to do one or two laps of the circuit, amateurs complete three laps. Those using the circuit as a tour have the chance to go on afterwards and cycle south past Zurich to tackle the old World Cup route over the Pfannenstiel – close to 130km in all!

Equipment: A standard set-up with a 25-tooth sprocket should be all you need. If you want to be sure on the Siglistorfer Höhe then fit a 27-tooth sprocket instead. If the weather is fine, don't bother with things like a rain jacket 'just in case' – you'll soon get back to the departure point.

A huge crowd of cyclists at the start of the 'Metzgete'.

Even though the Zurich Championship hasn't been part of the Pro Racing Calendar since 2007, this race still deserves a place in the list of the classics. Indeed, the Züri Metzgete, as the event is popularly known, can look back on 100 years of history. Starting in 1910, it developed over its history into one of the most important one-day classics in the World Cup calendar. The 'Metzgete' part of the name (linked to the German word 'to butcher') is an allusion to the hard conditions the riders often had to face here. Serious pile-ups were not uncommon and the riders' bloody wounds reminded the spectators of a metzgete, or slaughter festival … However this is all a thing of the past because the unpaved roads, which were to blame for the crashes, particularly in the early years of the race, have, as you might expect, been improved since then.

Throughout its history the race became so well established that it figured in both the Cycling World Cup and the UCI ProTour. No wonder then that many well-known people feature in the list of winners: Gino Bartali, Hugo Koblet and Ferdi Kübler in the 1940s and 1950s, Didi Thurau and Francesco Moser in the 1970s, and Johan Museeuw, Davide Rebellin, Michele Bartoli and Paolo Bettini in recent years. The last German winner was Nico Keinath in 2008. In 1987 the classic specialist Rolf Gölz won it and in 1957 Hennes 'If only I hadn't eaten the fish' Junkermann won (his nickname is a reference to a bout of food poisoning just before the 1962 edition of the Tour de France). The unbeaten record holder is the Swiss, Heiri Suter, who won the Metzgete six times between 1919 and 1929.

Once it was a race for professionals; now amateurs take centre stage.

Threatened time and again with extinction

These are all household names, and a brief glance at this list gives no hint of the chequered history of the race: like other traditional events that have dropped out of the calendar, the Züri Metzgete was also faced with collapse on many occasions. But repeatedly the organisers were lucky: again and again celebrities and sponsors were found to resurrect it.

The crunch well and truly came in 2007: as a result of the growing debate on doping after the Fuentes scandal, sponsors bailed out and the budget for running the race could not be guaranteed. This development pushed the organisers in a new direction. And with great success: nowadays this event lives on as a people's cycle race for amateurs and all-comers in the shape of the EKZ Züri Metzgete and the EKZ Volks Metzgete, and so continues to be a huge attraction every season at the beginning of September.

In addition, the route has changed several times in its history: normally this event wound its way through the region of Züricher Unterland, but for a short while at the beginning of the 1990s and with a new name, the 'Swiss Grand Prix', it started in Basel and finished in the Zurich velodrome. From 1999 the site for both the start and the finish was the Utoquai lido; after a warm-up stage, the route went onto the famous circuit with the Pfannenstiel climb (see 'Cycling and Sightseeing', see page 153). The People's Race version, started in 2008, concentrates on the roots of the competition and leads the riders over the Siglistorfer Höhe and the Regensberg.

The start and finish points of the circuit are in Buchs, which lies a good

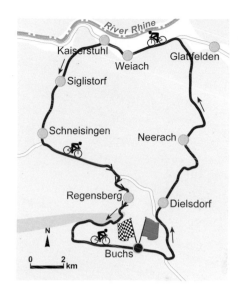

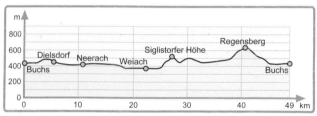

12km north of Lake Zurich in the Furt valley at the foot of the Lägern, a forested ridge which slopes gently upwards north of the town. At 49km the course isn't long, which means that you can enjoy an easy tour on your bike.

On the horizon the high Alpine peaks are glistening, already snow-covered in September. On the left the forested Lägern ridge is visible.

The route leads eastwards along a wide country road to Adlikon. For tourist riders a cycle path offers the chance to escape the traffic. On the horizon the high Alpine peaks are glistening, already snow-covered in September. On the left

The professional peloton makes its way through the countryside round Zurich during the 2004 edition.

the forested Lägern ridge is visible. You'll get to grips with this later when you tackle the Regensberg. In Adlikon (2km), a village typical of the area and dominated by the landscape, you turn left at the traffic lights and head directly north.

The route goes through the forest for a short time and then a little later through the forest again for a longer time and into Dielsdorf (5km). At the first roundabout you turn right, go under the railway and along the road to Riedt (9km), where a wide road takes you through marshes and agricultural land to Neerach. You reach this small village after 11km then simply continue to follow the road. On the left are fields under cultivation, on the right thick forest, until finally after 19km you come to the major junction with Route 7.

There's a lot of traffic here, which is why in the interests of their own safety tourist riders should opt to go along the

quiet country lanes past Zweidlen and Ofen. The route passes through Weiach (22km) and now you can either ride along the original route on the very busy Route 7 or quietly ride alongside the railway line towards Kaiserstuhl. On the right is the Rhine, which marks the border with Germany. Near Kaiserstuhl you turn left to Finsbach (24km) and ride through the village. At the end of the village, near the hotel called the 'Gasthof zum Rossli', the towering forested ridges herald the start of the first killer climb: the climb up to the Siglistorfer Höhe.

The first killer climb

Over the next 2.5km there's a vertical climb of 160m to negotiate. At the start and at the end there are two steep ramps, separated by a flatter middle part. Take care: you can expect a maximum gradient here of 17 per cent. All in all, however, the climb up the mountain is a pleasant ride. The surface is in good condition and the road is wide. In this race the first bit of the ride is usually where the wheat is sorted from the chaff. Unlike those who did the Metzgete here in the early years, today's riders have it easy: in the first half of the last century this climb was still an unmetalled road, with riders often forced to get off and push.

When you've reached the summit after almost 27km, a downhill slope follows, also very steep. Particular care is needed as you come into Siglistorf (28km) where a steep left–right–left set of bends awaits the rider.

As you're leaving Schöfflisdorf you can see the Regensberg looming.

In the centre of Siglistorf the route goes left on a wide country road to Schneisingen (31km). Make sure you don't then miss the left-hand turn to Niederweningen (32km). Passing the station on the left you get to the town sign for Schöfflisdorf after 36km, and as you're leaving you can see the Regensberg looming.

Here you simply follow the road signs, cross the railway lines and start the climb, which with a maximum gradient of 8 per cent is far less steep and rather short too when compared to the Siglistorfer Höhe. A long sweeping left-hand bend marks the end of the mountain before you get to the village of Regensberg. However this is no time to relax: the route goes gently uphill here too. You turn left towards Boppelsen and after about a kilometre of further climbing you get to the mountains classification (40km), which is held in the hikers' car park. From here you have a fantastic view of the village and the surrounding area.

Up and down – Swiss hill country.

The lead group in the Metzgete all-comers classic on the Regensberg.

Michael Boogerd (left) and Samuel Sanchéz battle it out on the 2006 ProTour race.

The descent you're about to embark on with its very bendy middle section is tricky because of a few traffic islands. Keep to the right to avoid any sticky situations. After another left turn after Boppelsen (43km) you go to Otelfingen (44km), a pretty place with nice house fronts. Now it's only another 5km along a wide country road with a cycle path to Buchs, with a last left-hand turn in the town centre.

Bonus round on the World Cup circuit

In the all-comers race this is where the finishing line is and also the beginning of the second lap of the circuit. For the tourist riders who are not tired yet there's a chance to do a second or third lap or to ride the nearby World Cup race

circuit: starting at the Utoquai promenade along the lakeside in nearby Zurich, the route runs south along Lake Zurich until at Herrliberg it starts to climb towards the Pfannenstiel. It goes over this ridge then finally back down to Zurich. At 42km this course is similar in length to the route of the actual race.

If you take on both routes in one day then, together with the ride between the two, it's a total of almost 130km. It's a great tour during which you can really immerse yourself in the history of a classic which has repeatedly managed to meet the changing needs of the times. Which leads you to wish: wouldn't it be great if in the future the professionals came back to battle it out again in the Züri Metzgete?

Sanchéz was the last winner of the professional 'Metzgete'.

2011 results <<

1 Bernhard Oberholzer (Switzerland), 3 hours 38' 39"
2 Dominik Fuchs (Switzerland), same time
3 Primin Lang (Switzerland), + 0' 25"
4 Mirco Sagiorato (Switzerland), same time
5 Christian Heule (Switzerland), same time

Cyclists, check this out!

Not far from the Züri Metzgete course, the Grand Prix of Aargau Canton takes place every year in and around Gippingen. This is currently the most important Swiss one-day race in the professional calendar. Staged for the first time in 1964, this event is of some interest to amateurs as well: the Axpo Volksradrennen takes place as part of the Aargau Grand Prix and is run in the morning just before the main race for the professionals, and over the same route. You can choose between two distances: a short route of six laps with a distance of 64.2km and a total vertical climb of 1092m, or a long one of nine laps with a distance of 96.3km and a total vertical climb of 1638m.

Cycling and sightseeing

From 1999 to 2006, when the Züri Metzgete was part of the Cycling World Cup and later on part of the UCI ProTour as well, one section of the race was the famous climb to the Pfannenstiel. Because the race was ridden then as now on a circular course and because, therefore, the mountain was climbed several times, this was almost always the make or break point in the race. If you're ever in the area, you should ride this hill. You get to the Pfannestiel from Zurich on Route 17 along the eastern side of Lake Zurich and the climb starts in Herrliberg. Over 7.5km you climb nearly 300m, which includes gradients of up to 10 per cent, particularly in the first half.

Background

Zurich is the birthplace of one of the most famous cyclists in Swiss history: Hugo Koblet. In 1950, aged 25, this baker's son was the first non-Italian to win the Giro d'Italia and then a year later he also won the Tour de France. Not only did he bring a certain style to cycling but also in life he was a charmer. But after some early successes, his star faded. In 1952 he got involved with drug-taking, which by his own admission ruined his health. He did manage to come second in the Giro on two other occasions in 1953 and 1954, and to win the Tour de Suisse in 1953 and 1955 – and collected two wins in the Züri Metzgete (1952, 1954) – but he was never able to recapture his earlier form. Six years later he died, aged 39, in a car accident. It was rumoured that he committed suicide. Koblet couldn't cope with giving up cycling.

23 PARIS-TOURS

The 'Autumn Grand Prix'

TOUR PROFILE <<

Race date: Mid-October

Type: Professional race (classic)

Start: Eure-et-Loir, varying communes (France)

Finish: Tours (France)

Distance: ~230km

Total vertical climb: ~450m

Time: 9 hours

URL: www.letour.fr/indexPAT_fr.html

Route: A relatively easy classic because it doesn't have any serious climbs. The only things that can cause problems on this mainly north/south ride are the weather conditions and the long distance. Because the race starts and finishes in different places, it's a good idea to try to get accommodation in Tours beforehand.

Fitness: A good basic level of endurance is essential to ride this tour successfully. Unlike on difficult mountain stretches, here you can get away with being a kilo or two overweight.

Equipment: The lack of hard climbs means you can use the large chainring more often than usual. For the few short slopes that exist, then a 23- or 25-tooth sprocket is fine.

The châteaux along the way are cultural highlights.

Colourful woods, animals grazing on pasture, leaves being blown about by the wind and a peloton struggling against it – these are the things that first spring to mind when you think of the Paris–Tours. This race in north-west central France is also nicknamed the 'Autumn classic'. The reason for this is the late date of the competition. Since its inauguration in 1896 (which incidentally makes it one of the oldest cycle races in the world), the tradition has been that the Paris–Tours doesn't take place until October.

What's more, its long history makes the event a classic and an essential part of the race calendar – even though some people disagree because of its lack of mountains. Here, the 'mountains' are at best hill-sized and so are not very spectacular. The race usually ends in a mass sprint with a fast final burst of speed from the legs to cross the finish line on the famous Avenue de Gramont. This is why Paris–Tours is quite often known as the 'sprinters' classic'.

Flick through the list of winners and you'll see that the race really does deserve this attribute: names like Oscar Freire, Alessandro Petacchi, Nicola Minali, and Erik Zabel grace the list of winners of the last 20 years. With victories on three occasions (1994, 2003, 2005), Zabel rightly belongs among the record-holders, with Gustave Daneels (1934, 1936, 1937), Paul Maye (1941, 1942, 1945) and Guido Reybrouck (1964, 1966, 1968). Sean Kelly (1984), Freddy Martens (1975), and Rik van Looy (1959, 1967) are other well-known names in cycling history who have left their mark on the race.

Merckx's gift

Just one rider's name is missing: Eddy Merckx. This is because Paris–Tours is actually one of the few races the 'Cannibal' was unable to win. However, he did come close in 1968 – he and his team-mate Guido Reybrouck turned into the home-straight far in front of the field, but Merckx held back in the sprint and let his team-mate win as a thank you for all the support and back-up he had given him during the season.

Despite its name, the Paris–Tours race doesn't start in the French capital: in fact in 2011 it started in Voves. Actually this isn't such an unusual thing: the Paris–Roubaix race, for example, also starts in another place, this time in Compiègne. The Paris–Tours event, arranged by the tour organiser ASO, is unusual for a classic in that its route changes frequently: for example, in 2009 the start was in Chartres; in previous years it had been in the Paris suburb of Saint-Arnoult-en-Yvelines. In the old days the race really did begin in Paris, then later on in Versailles. So the route and the distance – ranging between 230 and 342km – have been changed relatively often throughout its history. However, the following description refers to the 2010 course, starting in La Loupe.

The relatively compact town of La Loupe, with only 4000 inhabitants, is small and typical of this region: picture a small château and grounds, a small lake, a station, lots of family homes and many, many trees. You can imagine what a highlight of the year a professional cycle race with the long tradition of the Paris–Tours is for this area (a second highlight is the Apple Festival in November).

With a typically French breakfast in your stomach, you start in the circular town square and leave La Loupe heading towards Champrond-en-Gâtine. The peace and quiet of the area has real benefits for riders: in contrast to most other classic tours, which start in bigger towns, traffic hardly dominates here at all. After 8km you reach Champrond-en-Gâtine and 7km later Les Corvées-les-Yys. The next big place is Illiers-Combray; as you pass the town sign you've covered exactly 26km. This first hour has already given you an impression of the rural tranquility of the area.

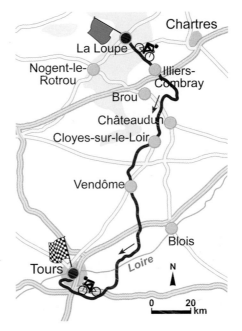

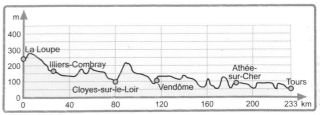

Many meadows and pastures dominate the landscape, and in addition you can often see mares grazing with their foals.

After riding through Illiers-Combray (which incidentally gets its name from, among other things, Marcel Proust's novel *In Search of Lost Time*) you continue on towards Avit-les-Guespières (31km). Here you turn left and reach Saumeray (35km). Many meadows and pastures dominate the landscape, and in addition you can often see mares grazing with their foals.

You ride on past Alluyes (40km) to Bonneval, which is the 46km mark on the schedule. You bear right towards Montharville and at La Brosse you follow the road to Logron (62km). The next two places on the route are Lanneray (69km) and Saint-Hilaire-sur-Yerre (77km). Incidentally, Châteaudun isn't far away, the birthplace of the Feillu brothers, Brice and Romain, who in recent years have attracted some attention in the Tour de France.

For those riding the initial phase of this tour, the only enemy is and always will be the weather. There's a wind, and it hurts. It's usually at this point that a breakaway group forms among the professionals to do battle with nature and then try and extend their lead as much as possible.

Paris–Tours

The peloton crossing the Loire – the Château d'Amboise is straight ahead.

After Cloyes-sur-le-Loir (81km) the road goes gently uphill and takes you through the dark Forêt de Fréteval to La Ville-Aux-Clercs (96km), after which it's a short distance to Rahart, continuing along idyllic little side roads to Saint-Ouen and finally Vendôme. The riders have now got 116km behind them and it's time for a short break here. This small town on the Loir with its impressive Gothic abbey church is the largest place on the tour so far and a good place for a coffee stop.

The wind as the chief enemy

You now cross the river and continue south over flat, wind-swept terrain.

Riding along small rural roads, Saint-Anne, Crucheray and Pray are the next few places you go through. There are still 103km to go to the finish – more than half the distance lies behind the riders now. The big teams of sprinters among the professionals now up the tempo in the peloton in order to whittle away at the breakaway group's lead. There's an art to these tactics and they're usually carefully planned such that you don't catch the breakaway group until the final straight.

In Herbault (139km) the route goes to Santenay (144km) and although there's a little more traffic now this never causes any problem, whatever the time of day.

Those in the breakaway group (like Jacky Durand in 2001, top) look for opportunities in the wind ... and the field must react.

Past Mesland (151km) and Monteaux (154km) you're getting near the river Loire – which, by the way, is not to be confused with much smaller Loir that you crossed at Vendôme – but you don't go over the river yet. Instead, the route now turns right so that you go along the wide riverbank downstream towards Tours.

As far as the professionals are concerned, the real race begins in Amboise.

The long home straight in Tours is one of the classic sprint-finishes in cycle-racing.

It's taken 170km to reach Amboise and this is where you cross the Loire. A small bridge, which also spans the little island called L'Île d'Or, leads you safely over the water. A short break at the large castle here is definitely to be recommended. There are still 63km left before you get to your destination – as far as the professionals are concerned, the real race begins here.

On the way to the finish line there are lots of short inclines, but after the distance you've already travelled these are no worse than unpleasant. You spend a short while in the forest on the way to Athée-sur-Cher, which you pass through after 185km, and turn left to Truyes (194km). There the route leaves the main road and turns to the right onto a minor road to Esvres from where you continue on to Veigné (203km).

The hilly final stretch

Once in Veigné the decisive phase of the race now begins. The Côte de Crochu is where you tackle the first climb, and it deserves the name. Although a vertical climb of 50m over a distance of 800m isn't exactly fierce, the two hairpin bends in the forest are painful enough. The route goes on now to Ballan-Miré (216km) and a little further on the next lot of hills begins: after a total of 221km this is where you reach the Côte de Beau-Soleil. It's just as straightforward as its predecessors, while the next ones, the Côte de l'Epan (224km) and the Côte du Petit Pas d'Anesogar (229km), are even shorter still. Mind you, you're happy to have these three little poison dwarves behind you – the distance you've covered so far means your legs turn to jelly.

The finish isn't far off now – only another 4km of the final stretch are left and you reach the famous Avenue de Grammont in a happy and contented mood. This treelined boulevard is just how you'd imagine an ideal sprint finish: long, flat and wide. This last stretch is 3km long and has in the past seen the end of any hopes that many members of the breakaway group had of staying in front to the finish line. Although the sprinters haven't won every race here (see 'Background', below), they have won most of them. But unlike the professionals, you don't need to put on a faster burst of speed, you can just bowl along in peace.

The Spaniard Oscar Freire wins the 2010 Autumn Grand Prix.

2011 results

1 Greg van Avermaet (Belgium),
 5 hours 21' 43"
2 Marco Marcato (Italy), + 0' 02"
3 Kasper Klostergaard (Denmark), + 0' 15"
4 Ian Stannard (Great Britain), same time

Cyclists, check this out!

Unfortunately at the moment there is no corresponding Paris–Tours race for amateurs. However, anyone who would like to take part in a special competition near this event can go to Lemans, 50km from the course, and take part in the 24-hour race for cyclists there – a quite different kind of racing. Find further information at www.24heuresvelo.fr.

Cycling and sightseeing

On your way from Paris to the start in La Loupe, you can drop into the suburb of Montlhéry: the 1933 Road World Championships were held here. The winner among the professionals was Georges 'The Dandy' Speicher. For the Parisian riders, who had just won the Tour de France, it was almost like a home game. Among the amateurs, Paul Egli from Switzerland came home first. And in 1928, cycling behind a motorised pace-setter on the motor-racing track at Montlhéry, the Belgian racing cyclist, Léon Vanderstuyft, set a new world speed record of 122.771km/hr – a record that stood for decades.

Background

Paris–Tours wasn't always a matter for sprinters and quite often courageous members of the breakaway group could also successfully complete their breakaway. From the recent past particular mention should be made here of Jacky Durand and Richard Virenque. Because of his tireless attacks Jacky Durand in particular made a name for himself among the peloton as the 'King of the Breakaway Groups'. Just look at 1998, when, 23km from the finish line, he broke away from a lead group of riders and went on to snatch victory. Three years later he tried to repeat this triumph: together with Richard Virenque, an equally well-known mountain specialist, he tore away from the others 12km after the start but was overtaken by his French compatriot and had to settle for second place.

TOUR PROFILE <<

Race date: First Sunday in October

Type: Sportive

Start/finish: Gaiole in Chianti (Italy)

Distance: 209km (several short tours are available; *see* 'Fitness', below)

Total vertical climb: 3350m

Time: 9 hours

URL: www.eroica.it

Route: There are good reasons why L'Eroica isn't really a race. One is that the course is often just too beautiful to ride past with your pulse rate at 200 and your gaze fixed firmly on the road ahead. This big course twists and turns round Tuscany for a distance of 209km, crossing over itself twice and taking in all the glories of the Chianti region. First and foremost among these: the 'strade bianche', literally 'white roads', which are unmade and covered in chalky stones. Long climbs are not a feature of the route profile, but the total vertical climb is 3350m. The Poggio di Montalcino is the highest point at 625m.

Fitness: Since there are different distances available (as well as the long and the middle-size tours there is also a 75km one and a 35km one) there's a tour for everyone here. However, the long course calls for a good helping of endurance. The long ride on the gravelly and bumpy 'strade bianche' and the constant ups and downs make so many demands even on experienced cycling professionals – and not only on their legs but also on their hands.

Equipment: The white gravel roads offer special challenges to equipment. Just as in the Paris–Roubaix race you must select wide tyres inflated to a lower pressure. Because you have to ride steep downhill runs on gravel, even cyclo-cross bikes are to be recommended – as long as they are period pieces. You should always bear inmind the tradition of L'Eroica: the older the bike and the clothing, the better. Although tourists who simply wish to ride the route are free to choose whatever outfit they like, if you're going to take part in the classic Eroica, then you must only use historic clothing and equipment: in other words, merino wool jerseys, crocheted gloves, toe-strap pedals, leather shoes. In addition, only bikes made before 1987 may be entered. Down tube gear-change here we come!

Some 40km south of Florence and not far from Siena lies Giaole in the Chianti region. It's actually a rather sleepy village right in the heart of Tuscany, but closer inspection reveals that behind those quiet facades there's a lot going on. The American magazine *Forbes* has rightly put it at the top of its list of 'Europe's most idyllic places to live'. Partly on account of its typical Tuscan characteristics: ancient history, rolling hills, mild climate, vineyards and avenues lined with olive trees. And partly on account of those famous straw basket bottles of the wine that has made the area so famous since the time of the Etruscans. But Giaole in Chianti has something to offer not just to gourmets but also to cyclists: L'Eroica ('the Heroic').

Since it was first held in 1997 the Heroic has developed into a Mecca for all those who have a soft spot for classic cycle races. Unlike normal race events, you are only allowed to use historic equipment in the Heroic. So, steel frames, toe-strap pedals, woollen jerseys and cotton caps are called for when you take your place on the start line of this tour.

Retro is compulsory for L'Eroica – a cult event!

Rescuing the 'strade bianche'

The tour came into being for cultural reasons. Despite being an attraction in the region, the white gravel roads came under threat in the mid-1990s when various local authorities wanted to replace them with tarmacked roads – to the annoyance of the residents of the Chianti region. They saw in the 'strade bianche' a major element of the charm of the area. To show that it's possible to ride on them on delicate and sensitive racing cycles they launched L'Eroica. With great success: up to now, some 3000 participants have taken part in this event and today it's among the major tourist attractions of Giaole and the surrounding area.

Today the route of L'Eroica is indicated by brown road signs so that you needn't worry about which way to go when you start the tour in Gaiole. Although food and drink during the event are no problem thanks to numerous feeding stations, you should nevertheless stock up well on equipment: over 70 of the 209km are over white gravel – so an extra spare inner tube can't hurt. In addition gloves are absolutely essential both to help against vibration and in case of a crash. What's more, you should make an early start. If you do the tour in the autumn, it gets dark early. The real L'Eroica begins at 7 a.m.

With a gradient of well over 15 per cent the road winds uphill. In L'Eroica quite a few participants get off and push.

You leave Gaiole heading south. This tranquil place lies in the relatively steep gorge of a brook and is surrounded by woods. So you don't get to enjoy that typical Tuscan scenery found in coffee-

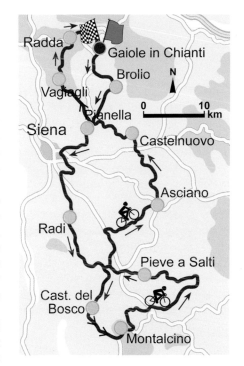

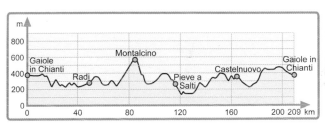

table books. The route goes through Castello di Meleto before turning right after 5km to Brolio. You climb some 250m on the next section winding your way up to Castello (11km). The road snakes uphill through the woods to the Madonna. This is where the first of a total of 15 gravelled sections begins. After a short descent the route goes up to the town along a narrow avenue bordered by cypress trees. The road winds uphill with a gradient of well over 15 per cent. In L'Eroica quite a few participants get off and push.

The next slope is gravelled too. You come down at speed and need to be very careful that the wheel doesn't skid. Wide tyres are clearly essential here. There is so much dust blowing around and you're so busy braking properly that there's no chance of enjoying the surrounding Tuscan picture-book scenery.

The fun lasts a good 2.5km until you come back to the tarmacked main road to Pianella. You pass the huge oak tree at the junction and 20km later reach the town, where you turn left and continue until shortly before San Giovanni when you turn left onto the road to Montechiaro (23km). From here the route goes along a 3km stretch of the 'strade bianche'. It's a slight downhill on loose gravel. At the end you turn left

Even the professionals ride on the 'strade bianche'.

towards Siena and follow the road signs as you ride on through wine country.

An hour on gravel

Quickly passing through some of the suburbs of the university town, you head south again and the woods that have been there from the start are left behind. The third section measures less than a kilometre and starts at kilometre 36. Consisting of a straight slope and an opposing climb, it is a warm-up for the fourth section (41km), which is the first real endurance test for the unpaved road specialists. This bit lasts for a full 13km and leads to Radi (49km) on a road with plenty of bends and many steep ramps. The scenery may still be ever so beautiful and you may be bowling along reasonably well on this stretch, but the gravel slowly sucks the strength out of your legs.

In Radi, which is more like a farmstead, you get the benefit of a tarmacked section before it becomes gravel roads again. On L'Eroica this is where the first feeding station is located. And the organisers have come up with something special: true to its claim that it is a race for enthusiasts, pasta and a glass of Chianti are handed out. Since there are no times or rankings to worry about, you get to meet many nice and interesting people.

A beautiful tarmacked descent gives a fantastic view of the many Tuscan hills.

There then follows a strenuous uphill slope – the first one on the gravel roads, and it goes on and on. It's only a vertical climb of 50m, yet, because of the steep gradient, there's a temptation to ride out of the saddle. This would be a serious mistake because traction on slopes drops by a noticeable 10 per cent. When

When 180 riders hurtle over the gravel in a pack, they trail a cloud of dust behind them.

you get to Murlo (54km) the climb is over. The left-hand turn is for the Etruscan Museum – the inhabitants of this municipality are said to be direct descendants of this ancient people – but you turn right towards Montalcino. Your route down a beautiful tarmacked slope shows a wide green plain opening up in front of you and gives a fantastic view of the many Tuscan hills.

The fifth section of gravel road begins at 60km, just before Piana (64km). You then ride along quite a bendy road towards Bibbiano and at length reach a junction. If you're doing the middle-distance course you go left. If you're doing the long-distance course you turn right and so reach Bibbiano (67km). You leave the small hamlet heading for Montalcino. Fifteen kilometres of gravel start now – the longest and most demanding section of the whole L'Eroica because in addition to many slippery bends this section also has a total vertical climb of just under 500m to be overcome.

The road winds its way uphill over several ramps, flanked with vines to begin with, then further on by avenues of trees, zigzagging in parts (just before you get to Castiglion del Bosco after 74km). Road signs with the figure '15 per cent' say it all: here, too, it's a good idea to stay in the saddle. Riding out of the saddle means a balancing act: pedal too hard and the rear wheel will spin and the sand will throw up a lot of dust.

A break in Montalcino

A small intermediate slope is followed by a short level bit which gives you your first view of Montalcino sitting up there as if on a throne. The climb up to the highest point of L'Eroica lasts just under an hour. The last 4km after Naciarello (78km) are tarmacked road at last and you follow the road signs to the town centre (85km). This mountain community with its stone fortress invites visitors to take a break – with pasta and a glass of wine, of course – and so does

Talking shop before the start. L'Eroica is where old-time cycling fanatics from all over the world meet up.

L'Eroica, which summons you to a refreshment break here.

It's downhill again now. Passing through Valdicava (92km) you reach a wide, 6km-long gravel stretch to Torrenieri, which you reach after a total of 96km. The utmost care is needed on the fast bends – not that anyone's worried you'll slip on the loose surface and land in the vines! After a sharp right-hand bend you come into Torrenieri on tarmacked roads again, and then after a gentle uphill section near Bellaria (101km) the route takes you onto sand again for just under 10km.

The midday sun burns your neck and also makes you sweat from all your pores.

Here again you must take great care on the downhill stretch. There then follows a few hundred metres of tarmac before the road branches off sharply to the left just before San Giovanni and another 8km section begins. The midday sun burns your neck and also makes you sweat from all your pores. In Pieve a Salti (122km) you finally reach tarmacked road again. A steep slope now brings

you into Buonconvento (125km), founded by the Romans, with its museum of sacred art.

No time to really linger, however – you do want to be at the finishing line before dusk. After leaving the village a sharp right-hand turn brings you onto the next bumpy track. On a comparatively very rough surface you approach Piana, which you went through some 3 hours ago, but now the route goes right and past the small village. Near Ponte d'Arabia (129km) you come onto tarmac again – this is your last chance to take it easy on the wide main roads because just before Curriano (135km) the route goes off right onto the next gravel section. And this has got its own share of challenges: for even though the organisers do divide sections 11 and 12 into two parts, with the exception of a 2km stretch of tarmac you've got 25km to do on white gravel.

A Tuscan panorama

Once again the route goes repeatedly uphill and down. Passing through Montauto (137km), you cycle past cypress trees and isolated farms nestling in the hills; you go down a steep slope and up an equally hard climb with a double-figure gradient. The short tarmacked section near the 145km mark seems quite a change after the vast number of gravel tracks. Section 12 also consists of very steep ramps. These take you on an even higher climb from where you can get more impressive views over the romantic Tuscan scenery.

First and foremost, when you're on the hill ridges near the end of the section you get a fantastic feeling. Incidentally, the view isn't the only reason for riding L'Eroica in fine weather in particular: just how much of a mud bath the ride over the 'strade bianche' can develop into was impressively demonstrated in 2010 on the corresponding Tuscan stage of the Giro d'Italia, where you could hardly recognise the riders for all the dirt.

Chianti the prize

In Torre a Castello (159km) you're finally back on a tarmacked road. This brings you via Castelnuovo (166km) to Pianella (176km) – another one of the places you passed at the beginning of the Tour. This is where the next 'strada biancha' starts, which has short stretches of tarmac on and off from just after Pievasciata (182km) to shortly before you get to Vagliagli (188km). Now the ride is nearly finished. And so are you. Riding on sand is much harder work than riding on tarmac.

You follow the signs for another short gravel track to Radda in Chianti. There are 20km left to the finish line and the next section really leaves you gasping for breath. At least the surface is tarmacked this time, and by riding out of the saddle you can relax your badly jolted muscles a bit. By the time you get to Radda (199km), with its very well-preserved 14th-century town walls, you've very nearly finished the course: just one more stretch on gravel past La Villa (200km), for 3km.

After a sharp right-hand bend the route runs downhill, gently at first then more steeply, back to Gaiole – the last 6km on tarmac again. A few downhill hairpin bends and there's the finish line at last (209km). The Tuscan sun is already low as you arrive back at the start, dead tired, but happy – because you've successfully completed what is perhaps one of the most beautiful cycle tours of all.

Note: Since L'Eroica isn't a race or sportive marathon but purely a tourist ride, there's no rankings list for participants in this event – but there is a list of winners! This records all those who have successfully completed this unique event. At the finish line all participants also receive a historic-looking duffel-bag and a bottle of wine – Chianti, naturally! But you must also reward yourself with a similar bottle when you have mastered the 'Heroic' outside of any organised event. For here in the heart of Tuscany, vino rosso simply tastes even better!

Cyclists, check this out!

Even though L'Eroica isn't a race but a tourist cycle ride instead, some organisers are now copying the idea of riding on classic bikes. In 2010, northern Italy developed its own Gran Fondo Race Series for classic enthusiasts. Some 12 events a year can be contested here under retro conditions. Find further information at www.giroditaliadepoca.it.

Cycling and sightseeing

The object of interest in L'Eroica is the race itself. For the entire weekend that this event takes place, old-time cycling fanatics from all over the world meet up at this huge gathering. You could almost mistake this tourist ride for a trade show for classic cycling. For a few days the whole area lives the Eroica lifestyle: every hotel within 30km is filled with cyclists, there are classic racing bikes everywhere, the locals are walking around in traditional dress or woollen jerseys, and in virtually all the cafés in Gaiole or the surrounding area you can see racing cyclists telling each other anecdotes and Eroica stories from the good old days.

Background

On the 10th anniversary of L'Eroica in 2007 a race for professionals was organised, which takes place on an almost equivalent course. Monte Paschi Strade Bianche starts like L'Eroica does in Gaiole in Chianti and runs over a distance of 190km to Siena. Just like the famous tourist cycle ride the route profile of the semi-classic includes 70km on the white gravel roads. In March 2011 Belgian classics king Philippe Gilbert won the race riding for the Omega Pharmo-Lotto team. The best German result in the still brief history of the race was that of Fabian Wegmann, who came in second in 2009. Find further information on this one-day event at www.gazetta.it/Speciali/StradeBianche/it/.

TOUR OF LOMBARDY
The race of the falling leaves

TOUR PROFILE <<

Race date: Mid-October

Type: Professional race (Monument)

Start: Milan (Italy)

Finish: Como (Italy)

Distance: 260km (route described can be shortened to 210km)

Total vertical climb: 3200m

Time: 11 hours

URL: www.gazzetta.it

Route: A breathtaking course. If you get good autumn weather, enjoy every step of the way and soak up the scenery around Lake Como. It's definitely a good idea to omit the first 40km from Milan to Como – first, because of the traffic and, second, to avoid the problem of the different start and finish lines.

Fitness: 260km – this statistic is enough to show that a rider needs to be in exceptionally good shape. Even the shorter route, where the first stretch is simply omitted, is quite long enough at 210km! So prepare yourself well for this ride and get through it properly.

Equipment: The climbs in themselves are not all that difficult but become more and more strenuous the further you go. Most important, the lower part of the ride to the Madonna del Ghisallo has double-figure gradients. A 27-tooth sprocket or a compact chainset are definitely to be recommended.

The Tour of Lombardy is the final race in each cycling season.

The Tour of Lombardy is by tradition the last race of the season. 'La Classica Delle Fogliemorte', the race of the falling leaves, is an extremely romantic name for a classic cycle race. The tour isn't called this for nothing, as there are many people who claim that it's the most beautiful race of all. The reason for this is the breathtaking scenery the route goes through on its way from Milan right around Lake Como and back again to Como. This race combines a Mediterranean climate, lush vegetation and the Alpine world. Held for the first time in 1905, it soon developed into a classic among northern Italian events. However, this wasn't just down to the spectacular route, with its many climbs that are as demanding as they are beautiful, but because of the epic duels fought here by the great athletes of the past.

The reason why the Tour of Lombardy is one of the five Monuments of cycle racing is also clear from a glance at the winners: head and shoulders above the rest stands Fausto Coppi. This incomparable Italian, who dominated the scene in the post-war era, notched up five victories between 1946 and 1954. His fellow countryman Alfredo Binda was successful four times in the 1920s, followed by a whole host of riders with three victories, including Coppi's greatest rival, Gino Bartalli. In more recent times another Italian, Damiano Cunego, has left his mark on the race. He rode to victory three times alongside the shores of Lake Como.

The high point: the climb to the Madonna

The Tour of Lombardy starts in Milan. At least, that has been the most traditional starting point in its history, and also the point of departure selected by the organisers of the 2010 and 2011 season. In fact, over the years the route has undergone many changes. Only the circuit of Lake Como and the famous climb up to the cyclists' Chapel of the Madonna del Ghisallo have always been fixed points in this race. Since 1962 the finish line, though on some occasions in Bergamo and Monza, has usually been in Como.

Because of the long distance involved, it's a good idea to start in Como too. This gets round the problem of different start and finish places – and what's more, breakfast tastes much better on the shores of the lake! Incidentally, only ride in good weather – otherwise this beautiful ride quickly becomes an ordeal. In the 2010 Tour of Lombardy the professionals had to fight against cold and rain throughout the race, and only 34 riders saw it through to the finish line.

At last, you cross the the invisible boundary of Como Province at Copreno. The silhouettes of the Alpine foothills shimmer on the horizon.

While the first (but now suspended) part of the professional race begins in the centre of Milan, the real race starts in the northern suburb of Cormano. The city is quickly left behind as you head north. You cross the invisible boundary of Como Province at Copreno (18km). The silhouettes of the Alpine foothills shimmer on the horizon. Just past Copreno comes the first incline, but one that you – being still full of energy – hardly notice. After Fino Mornasco (27km) riders reach Grandate (30km) where after a short climb up to San Fermo della Battaglia you simply follow the road signs, reaching Como after 37km. This is where the beautiful part of the Tour of Lombardy begins.

Although you've successfully built up your strength as touring cyclists, you need to do as well at the first pass of the day as you did with your food and drink: after 18 flat kilometres on the beautiful western side of the lake there's the first climb of the day up the Intelvi. The town sign for Argegno after 55km marks the start. By this point you should have digested your breakfast properly and braced yourself to engage the small chainring one more time: a vertical climb of 570m really does make the Intelvi a hard nut to crack. With a gradient of 7 or 8 per cent, the route leaves the town round three hairpin bends, from where you can get a fantastic view of Lake Como. Then comes the ride out into the countryside.

Hairpin bends to Osteno

Although you are surrounded by houses at the start, these eventually give way to trees once you're past Dizzasco (59km). The gradient now decreases a little back to 5–6 per cent. After two more kilometres you leave the forest behind again and reach the villages of

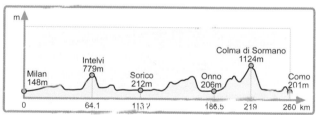

Castiglione d'Intelvi and, straight after that, San Fedele Intelvi. As you come out of San Fedele Intelvi, several hairpin bends mark the end of the climb, which is reached at the turn-off for Porlezza at the 64.1km mark. You turn right and dash down the slope. At first it offers relatively few hairpin bends, but later on there are many narrow ones. So take care and arrive safely in Osteno after a 72km ride!

As a reward the next deep blue lake, the Lago di Lugano, awaits the riders. The route now goes along its eastern shore to Porlezza. In the town centre you

The unmistakeable and fantastic backdrop of Lake Como.

turn right at the major junction onto the Via Ceresio, which, after 89km and after passing by the equally blue Lago Piano on the way, leads back to the shores of Lake Como and the town of Menaggio. But before you get to this tourist centre with its tempting Piazza Garibaldi, it's worth tackling another climb, this time with a vertical climb of 90m at the Croce di Menaggio. Don't worry, you can easily crank up the speed again over the next 50km as the route is completely flat going north along Lake Como.

Cycling along the shore, it's easy to see why celebrities such as George Clooney, Madonna and Brad Pitt have their holiday homes in the area – it's simply beautiful here.

Acquaseria (93km), Calozzo (100km) and Domaso (108km) are the next places, together with two very short tunnels, that you pass through on the way to Sorico (113km). Cycling along the shore, it's easy to see why celebrities such as George Clooney, Madonna and Brad Pitt have their holiday homes in the area – it's simply beautiful here.

Once you get to Sorico, you've finally arrived at the northern tip of Lake Como. A wide bridge spans the River Mera, which links Lake Mezzola a few kilometres away with Lake Como. The route now leads south again to Colico (122km) still on flat terrain as you bowl along by the shore. Only at Bellano after travelling 137km do you leave the water and turn off left: the mountainous part of the Tour of Lombardy now begins.

The splashing waters of the Pionerna

In Bellano, straight after you've crossed the rushing waters of the Pioverna stream, you follow its course and bear left. The railway line is crossed on level ground, then the route heads immediately uphill. Narrow hairpin bends snake up the mountain ridge; there are eight of them in all. After the last one you finally leave the houses behind and reach the Lombardy Forest. The road gently winds up the valley while down below to your left the Pioverna rushes on its way. A tunnel (143km) marks the end of the 5-7 per cent gradient climb. After a mini-slope you cross the Pioverna again, and with a gentle gradient from now on (1-3 per cent) you cycle on down the valley.

That's how it is as far as Pasturo (156km). Even though you are only 500m above sea level, you feel as if you're in the mountains. As you leave Pasturo it actually gets steeper again: the slope has a 5 or 6 per cent gradient waiting for you, and then at last, after a kilometre, reveals the summit of the unremarkable Colle di Basilio situated in the middle of the town of Ballabio. The strenuous last hour is worthwhile: in a flying descent the route goes round several hairpin bends through the town of Malavedo and down to the shores of Lake Como. Now after a total of 175km you reach Lecco, a typical Italian town and an inviting place to rest. And you'll need this too – there's still another 85km to go to the finish line.

The flat terrain that follows is your last chance to take it easy. Near the Isola

Then and now: The Madonna has always been highlight of the race.

169

25 Tour of Lombardy

The Australian Cadel Evans, on the attack.

race is known as a killer climb: with the gradient constantly in double figures, the route goes round hairpin bends at first, then later straight uphill. Near Guello (199km) the road, which leads to the ridge of the 1698m high Monte San Primo, finally becomes a little flatter, and for the next 2km through Civenna you can gather your strength again for the last eight hairpin bends. These herald the final steep stretch and a good 10 per cent gradient.

Once you've reached the Chapel of the Madonna, you should definitely take a break. Even the professionals do – not during the race of course, but it's often the custom to pray here the day before. The many jerseys and trophies hung inside the chapel testify to this. Together with the fantastic view over the northern part of Lake Como and the branch of the lake at Lecco, the all-pervading presence of cycle racing makes this place special.

Viscontea you cross the branch of Lake Como and ride north along its western shore again until you reach Regatola di Bellagio (194km). This is where you start the climb up to one of the most famous mountains in cycle racing: and to the Chapel of the Madonna del Ghisallo. The shrine was dedicated in 1949 by Pope Pius XII to the patroness of cycle racers and in 2006 they opened a cycling museum next to the chapel (*see* 'Cycling and Sightseeing', opposite). So it really is a good place to wind up at.

> *'They dashed along the road as they followed their dream of fame. With the loss of their youth, the Light of God reaches them.'* (Inscription in the Chapel of the Madonna del Ghisallo).

The first 4km are so steep that you immediately find out why this part of the

Final ordeal on the Sormano

Then comes a short 4km descent before the next hammer threatens in the shape of Colma di Sormano. The Sormano begins with a right turn in Maglio (210km). At 7 per cent it isn't really very steep, but it is long: the road snakes round narrow hairpins for a whole 9.5km, climbing up from 495 to 1124m above sea level. For most of the way to Sormano (214.1km) you are surrounded by houses. The second half goes through the forest, and since you've climbed a good 3000m so far and pedalled more than 200km, this half does hurt a fair bit.

Even the beautiful views fail to take your mind off the pain – you can easily imagine how Philippe Gilbert and the rest must have suffered in 2010 as they battled against the pouring rain every inch of the way. You think back to the visit to the Chapel of the Madonna and wish that she would make the ride a bit easier. At last a small clearing marks the end of the climb – you've done it!

At this point anyone who wants to ride along the lakeside promenade and then tumble off their bike exhausted can do so. But they should realise that they haven't done the whole course.

The route rushes downhill past Zelbio. Be careful; the road is steep and dangerous and you shouldn't take any more risks on these last few kilometres! After a few final hairpin bends you come to Nesso (232km) and back to the shores of Lake Como again. You stay close to the lakeside all the way now: two tunnels and a small incline near Blevio (244km) are the only danger points on the way to the finish. At this point anyone who wants to ride along the lakeside promenade and then tumble off their bike exhausted can do so. But they should realise that they haven't done the whole course. No indeed: the clock shows 'only' 252km – twelve short! You complete these by means of a finishing horseshoe-loop section, which once again goes over the 397m high San Fermo della Battaglia. Just engage the small chainring again and ride up 27th of May Street. Once you've crested the summit 3km later, it's finally all over. Now you can relax and enjoy the descent through two small tunnels, round two hairpin bends and down to the lakeside promenade in Como.

2011 results <<

1 Oliver Zaugg (Switzerland), 6 hours 20' 02"
2 Daniel Martin (Ireland), + 0' 08"
3 Joaquin Rodriguez (Spain), same time
...
42 Steve Cummings (Great Britain), + 07' 14"

Cyclists, check this out!

At the moment, the Tour of Lombardy doesn't have its own sportive. There was until recently a spectacular cycle marathon called the 'Gran Fondo Giro di Lombardia', which went along the beautiful roads around Lake Como, but this event hasn't been held since 2009 because of problems with course safety. Whether the sportive will be held again at some point in the future is not yet known. Nevertheless, anyone who wants to be active in Lombardy still has a whole range of other Gran Fondos to choose from.

Cycling and sightseeing

In addition to paying a visit to the Chapel of the Madonna del Ghisallo in Mareglio, it's also worth going next door and having a look at the cycling museum of the same name. Above all, those who like tales of the old racing days will find it of interest. Find more details at www.museodelghisallo.it.

Background

In 2010 the Tour of Lombardy started 10 minutes later than scheduled because of a protest by the riders against Ettore Torri. The head of the Italian Anti-Doping Committee had expressed a general suspicion that every cyclist might be taking drugs. The whole field of riders wanted to send a clear message of protest against these unfounded allegations.

MORE CLASSICS

PARIS-BRUSSELS
The 'Grand Old Lady' of the second rank

TOUR PROFILE

Race date: Mid-September

Type: Professional race (semi-classic)

Start: Soissons (France)

Finish: Brussels (Belgium)

Distance: 219km

Total vertical climb: 1400m

Time: 9 hours

URL: www.paris-bruxelles.be

Until well into the second half of the 20th century, Paris–Brussels was considered to be one of the most important classics in the world of cycling. It was founded in 1893 by the weekly paper *La Bicyclette*, and successive editions recorded in their winners' lists many glorious names such as Octave Lapize, Nicolas Frantz, Rik van Steenbergen, Rik van Looy, Felice Gimondi and Eddy Merckx. In later years such famous athletes as Roger de Vlaeminck, Franco Ballerini, Frank Vandenbroucke and Robbie McEwen stamped their mark on the race.

This race between capital cities was not held between 1967 and 1972, and so, gradually declining in importance, it got pushed down into the second rank of an ever-growing cycling calendar. One reason for this was certainly the long distance, which when it started was more than 400km and until 1987 was still 300km.

Today riders have to cope with a mere 220km, and so they start not in the French capital, as they used to, but in Soissons, 85km to the north. From there the route goes north over a total of 10 'hellings'. It passes some distance to the east of St Quentin (73km), crosses the Belgian frontier at Goegnies-Chaussee (135km) and then a few kilometres west of Charleroi (154km) heads for Brussels over minor roads.

Although the present route is peppered with many small, nasty climbs and undulating stretches, it does suit lovers of road racing. In recent races, the sprint specialists among the professionals have exclusively had the

Francisco Ventoso wins the 2010 Paris–Brussels race.

edge, so not since Nick Nuyens' victory in 2004 has a cyclist broken away from the group and won.

Anyone considering doing this course must be prepared for this region's strong headwinds and crosswinds, which can make a relatively flat course really hard going. Wind or rain jackets are essential. Otherwise this tour poses no problems.

RUND UM DIE HAINLEITE
The oldest continuing classic in Germany

TOUR PROFILE

Race date: Mid-June

Type: Professional race (semi-classic)

Start/finish: Erfurt (Germany)

Distance: 185km

Total vertical climb: 1800m

Time: 8 hours

URL: www.radklassiker-hainleite.de

The 'Rund um die Hainleite' is the name given to Germany's oldest continuing cycle race: the race has been held in the area around Erfurt since 1907. This means that it's actually 11 years younger than the 'Rund um Berlin', but since the capital's race has not been run on a regular basis for the past 10 years, the Hainleite has taken this status. Famous winners of Germany's most popular race include Olaf Ludwig, Uwe Ampler, Mario Kummer, Bert Grabsch and Jens Voigt.

When it started, the race was run over an impressive 350km. Today – with the race no longer attracting professional riders but having become part of the 'Thüringen-Rundfahrt' for under-23 riders instead - the distance is no more than 200km.

Jan Ullrich (centre) led repeatedly in the Hainleite race.

From Erfurt the route goes north in a clockwise circle via Sondershausen (53km) and then after 75km the riders face the highest climb of the day up the Kyffhäuser. After this the route heads south via Sömmerda (115km) and back to the regional capital of Thüringen, where the riders must do six laps round a demanding finishing circuit.

GP OUEST-FRANCE
Cycling festival in western France

TOUR PROFILE

Race date: End of August

Type: Professional race/sportive

Start/finish: Plouay (France)

Distance: 19km circuit/248km racing distance

Total vertical climb: 250m/3250m

Time: 1 hour/10 hours

URL: http://www.uciprotour.com/templates/UCI/UCI5/layout.asp?MenuId=MTUzMDA&LangId=1

The 'Grand Prix Ouest-France' was first held in 1931. It developed over the years into an event of increasing importance in the cycling calendar, as shown by the victories of famous riders such as Gilbert Duclos-Lasalle, Sean Kelly, Andrei Tchmil, Frank Vandenbroucke and Michele Bartoli. Since its inclusion into the UCI ProTour calendar, the event ranks among the most important one-day races in the world. Nowadays the Grand Prix in Plouay in northern Brittany – incidentally already the venue back in 2000 for the Road World Championships – is a real festival of cycling where, alongside the professional race, they also hold a women's and a juniors' World Cup race, as well as an all-comers' event.

What is especially interesting for spectators is the fact that the GP Ouest-France is held on a circular route. So you can comfortably follow the racing live unlike other classic races where you have to change your viewing position. Altogether the professional riders must do 13 laps of the circuit which contains three very short climbs. However, these are technically easy and never more than 7 per cent. So, despite the climbs, sprinters too have their chance in this event (at the

The field during the GP Plouay.

appropriate moment in the course of the race). In 2010, for example, the young Australian rising star Matthew Goss beat the American sprinter Tyler Farrar. It was one of the very few foreign victories so far – in fact, in the 80-year history of the race the French have come in first 61 times.

BORDEAUX–PARIS
The almost forgotten 'Derby'

TOUR PROFILE

Race date: Mid-June

Type: Marathon sportive/brevet

Start: Bordeaux (France)

Finish: Paris (France)

Distance: 624km

Total vertical climb: 3500m

Time: 30 hours

URL: www.bordeaux-paris-cyclos.com

This race is legendary but unfortunately lives on nowadays only as a marathon sportive and a brevet. First held in 1891, Bordeaux–Paris is among the oldest cycle races and even before the beginning of the 20th century it was the most prestigious race in the calendar, as the winners' list for the 'Derby', the nickname for the 'BP', shows: the Frenchman Eugène Christophe, the two Swiss Heiri Suter and Ferdy Kübler, as well as the Frenchman Louison Bobet, the British rider Tom Simpson and the five-times winner of the Tour de France Jacques Anquetil – every one of them has managed to secure first place.

In the 1960s, however, the race slowly lost its status as a major classic. The main reason for this was the long racing distance of over 600km. It's true that the riders could partly rely on help from pacesetters, but this long-distance race needed specific training, and fewer and fewer professionals wanted to do this. The year 1988 was the last time professionals rode the Bordeaux–Paris race.

The man who has won the most times to date is the Belgian Herman van Springel, who has triumphed a full seven times. The only German victory here – and in the Paris–Roubaix, too – belongs to Josef Fischer, who was first across the finish line in 1900.

PARIS-BREST-PARIS
The epitome of the long-distance classic

TOUR PROFILE

Race date: Mid-August (every four years)

Type: *Randonnées*

Start/finish: Saint-Quentin-en-Yvelines (France)

Distance: 1225km

Total vertical climb: 10,000m

Time: 80 hours

URL: www.paris-brest-paris.org

Some races are just extreme, many because of the total vertical climb, others because of the speed – and still others because of the racing distance. The Paris–Brest–Paris randonnée is just such an extreme. Anyone who thinks the 600km of the Trondheim–Oslo and the Bordeaux–Paris events are a long way will need to take a deep breath before they read the route description of this classic: those who take part in the 'PBP' have to do more than 1225km – and all in one go!

Like Bordeaux–Paris, this race also first took place in 1891 and so is one of the oldest cycle races. Its origins go back to the journalist Pierre Giffard, who

wanted to use this large-scale event not only to show how high-performance the human body can be but also to demonstrate the potential of cycling technology, at that time in its infancy.

The first winner, the Frenchman Charles Terront, needed more than 71 hours to cover this crazy distance – an unbelievable time in the saddle. Even though the time of the ride decreased over the years – in 1951 another Frenchman, Maurice Diot, clocked up a mere 39 hours – it wasn't long before the number of professionals interested in taking part decreased. Just as was the case with the Bordeaux–Paris race, the distance was just too long. The tradition of the 'PBP' still lived on but in the form of a randonnée, where it's not so much about winning as about actually reaching the finish in the Paris suburb of Saint-Quentin-en-Yvelines.

The route from the capital to Brest on the Atlantic coast in Brittany in north-western France and back again is not an easy one. Anyone who takes part faces a total vertical climb of some 10,000m made up of over 350 small climbs. This event takes place every four years. It's an extreme challenge – and everyone who has completed it is an extremist!

LA FAUSTO COPPI
In memory of the 'Campionissimo'

TOUR PROFILE

Race date: Beginning of July

Type: Marathon sportive

Start/finish: Cuneo (Italy)

Distance: 198km

Total vertical climb: 4500m

Time: 8 hours

URL: www.faustocoppi.net

The histories of the Ötztaler Radmarathon, the Maratona dles Dolomites and the Nove Colli show how a cycle marathon can become something

Fausto Coppi is a legend in the history of cycling.

of a classic. La Fausto Coppi, too, belongs in this marathon classics club.

The northern Italian town of Cuneo is both the pivot and central point of this race, which is named after the great 'Campionissimo' Fausto Coppi. Thousands of cycling fans take part.

The route runs through the northern Italian province of Piedmont; here riders climb some 4500m over 198km – a real mountain race that plays to the strengths of the climbers and was exactly to the taste of the former Italian cycling ace. In addition, a short route known as the Medio Fondo is offered: it runs for 120km and riders must tackle a vertical climb of 2500m.

ALPEN BREVET
One for the climbing specialists!

TOUR PROFILE

Race date: Mid-August

Type: Marathon sportive

Start/finish: Meiringen (Switzerland)

Distance: 276km

Total vertical climb: 7031m

Time: 12 hours

URL: www.alpenbrevet.ch

Switzerland is the land of mountains, and so it's not surprising that races there go over high Alpine passes, as the often mountainous nature of the famous Tour de Suisse shows.

Also, the Swiss sportives are just the thing for climbing freaks. 'The Alpine Experience' is what the participants call the 'Alpen-Challenge', a marathon whose statistics overshadow the Ötztaler Radmarathon: on this long-distance race, called the Platinum Tour,

riders cover some 276km and face a total vertical climb of over 7000m – a real battle.

Five passes are crossed: Grimsel, Nufenen, Lukmanier, Oberalp and Susten. These also feature regularly in the Tour de Suisse. For anyone not wanting to spend so much time in the saddle, there are also Gold and Silver Tours. However, with a distance of 172km and a total vertical climb of 5294m, the former still offers a real challenge, as indeed does the 'little' one, where participants face 131km and a total vertical climb of 3875m.

VÄTTERNRUNDAN
Round Sweden's second-biggest lake

TOUR PROFILE

Race date: Mid-June

Type: Fun ride (timed but no official ranking)

Start/finish: Motala (Sweden)

Distance: 300km

Total vertical climb: 1300m

Time: 12 hours

URL: www.cyklavaettern.com

Gentle waves lap against the shore of the deep blue Lake Vättern as, early one morning in the middle of June, an enormous crowd of 20,000 cyclists get ready on the waterfront in Motala to ride round the second-biggest lake in Sweden. It's the start of the Vätternrundan, the biggest cycling event in northern Europe. Using the formula 'total participants x length of course', you could even go so far as to say that this is the biggest cycling event in the world!

Sunrise on the Vätternrundan.

This tourist cycle ride is 300km long – a challenge, but the route to be conquered is mostly flat. An important factor here: for safety's sake, no one ever rides alone. Riders go round Lake Vättern in a clockwise direction. From Motala on the northern shore, the route leads to Hästholmen (43km) and Gränna (81km), and after 109km reaches Jönköping on the southern shore of the lake. Heading north again, the route takes in Fagerhult (140km), Hjo (178km), Karlsborg (210km) and Boviken (232km). After 262km the route finally arrives in Hammarsundet at the northern tip of the lake – now comes the final stretch. Medevi (282km) is the last stop before riders cross the finish line on the Promenade after a total of 300km. This course has no big climbs. Riders travel the whole way alongside the water and at an altitude of 100–200m.

INDEXES

Index of places

General index

Indexes